SHAKER FOLK ART AND INDUSTRIES

BOOKS BY MARIAN KLAMKIN

FLOWER ARRANGING FOR PERIOD DECORATION

FLOWER ARRANGEMENTS THAT LAST

THE COLLECTOR'S BOOK OF ART NOUVEAU

THE COLLECTOR'S BOOK OF BOTTLES

THE COLLECTOR'S BOOK OF BOXES

THE COLLECTOR'S BOOK OF WEDGWOOD

HANDS TO WORK: SHAKER FOLK ART AND INDUSTRIES

SHAKER FOLK ART AND INDUSTRIES

MARIAN KLAMKIN

Illustrated with photographs by Charles Klamkin

DODD, MEAD & COMPANY
New York

CREDITS FOR PHOTOGRAPHS

Belfit: Mr. and Mrs. Robert Belfit
Hancock: Shaker Village, Hancock, Massachusetts
Mattatuck: Mattatuck Museum, Waterbury, Connecticut
Old Chatham: The Shaker Museum, Old Chatham, New York
From *Frank Leslie's Popular Monthly, December 1885:*
Illustrations 2, 3, 4, 7, 8, 9, 56, 76
From *Harper's New Monthly Magazine,* July 1857: Illustrations 5, 6
From *Shaker Almanac,* New York 1886: Illustration 12

First published as a Dodd, Mead Quality Paperback in 1984

Published by Dodd, Mead & Company, Inc.
79 Madison Avenue, New York, N.Y. 10016
Distributed in Canada by
McClelland and Stewart Limited, Toronto
Manufactured in the United States of America

First Edition

Library of Congress Cataloging in Publication Data

Klamkin, Marian.
Shaker folk art and industries.
Previously published as: Hands to work.
Bibliography: p.
Includes index.
1. Decorative arts, Shaker. I. Title.
[NK805.K57 1984] 745'.088288 84-10342
ISBN 0-396-08434-6 (pbk.)

ACKNOWLEDGMENTS

I am deeply grateful for the help and cooperation as well as knowledgeable information given me by Hazel and Robert Belfit, who have a deep affection for, and understanding of, the Shakers and their crafts.

The cooperation and courtesy shown both me and my husband, Charles, at The Shaker Museum, Old Chatham, New York, by Mr. Robert F. W. Meader, director, Mr. Warden McL. Williams, president, and Mrs. Claire Wheeler, librarian, are most appreciated. Special thanks goes to the help we received from Mrs. Madalene LaTulippe. Without the kind permission of Mr. John S. Williams, Sr., chairman of the Board and chief executive officer at The Shaker Museum, this work would have been most difficult. I am also grateful for permission to photograph at Hancock Shaker Village.

Special thanks are also due Mrs. Caroline Stark, Mrs. Joyce Reid, and Mrs. Marian Sumner for their help in finding source material.

CONTENTS

SHAKER FOLK ART AND INDUSTRIES

CHAPTER

1

THE RISE OF THE SHAKER SECT IN AMERICA

Believers in Christ's Second Appearing, who are united in one body, possess one united and consecrated interest, and therefore, must, in all things, and under all circumstances, be influenced, led, and governed, by one spirit, which is the spirit of God, and be subject to one general law, which is the law of Christ, in this day of his Second Appearing. Millenial Laws, 1821. Revised, 1845.

The first settlement of The United Society of Believers in Christ's Second Appearing, or the Shakers, was established in Niskayuna, near Albany, New York, in 1776. Therefore, the beginnings of the American Shakers as an organized religious sect and a communal society coincide chronologically with the establishment of the United States of America as a free and independent nation. The original Shaker settlers were eight Believers who followed their spiritual leader, Mother Ann Lee, from England to settle in a new world where they hoped to be free to practice their religion and to proselytize new members.

The small band of Shakers, and particularly Mother

Ann, had not had an easy time worshipping according to their beliefs in their home in Manchester, England, but persecution seems to have been a secondary cause for them to have come to America. Mother Ann was convinced that God had a chosen people in America and she could see the expansion of her group in the new land.

Ann Lees (shortened to Lee after she settled in America) was an uneducated girl from a poor blacksmith's family in Manchester. She joined the Shaker church at the age of twenty-two and struggled during nine years of fervent prayer for her soul to be delivered from sin. Several members of the Shaker sect had believed that Christ would soon appear to them through the instrument of a woman, and their form of worship manifested itself in violent shaking, trembling, shouting, and singing. For this "profanement of the Sabbath," Ann Lee had been arrested and thrown into a Manchester jail. It was during this confinement that she experienced her "grand vision," and she believed that the spirit of Christ spoke through her thereafter. Following this experience, she became the spiritual leader of the small group of "Shaking Quakers" that had been formed by James and Jane Wardley, and two years later Mother Ann led her group of eight Believers to America.

Ann Lee had suffered a great deal in her personal life before she was overcome with her "vision." An unhappy marriage, difficult deliveries, and the infant deaths of her four children probably had a lot to do with her embracing the Shaker religion so wholeheartedly that she became its spiritual leader and "Mother." Mother Ann believed that sex was truly the root of all evil, as indeed it must have been for her, and that it was the cause of all other vices in the world. She was able to convince her followers that a life of celibacy and hard work was the only way to total redemption.

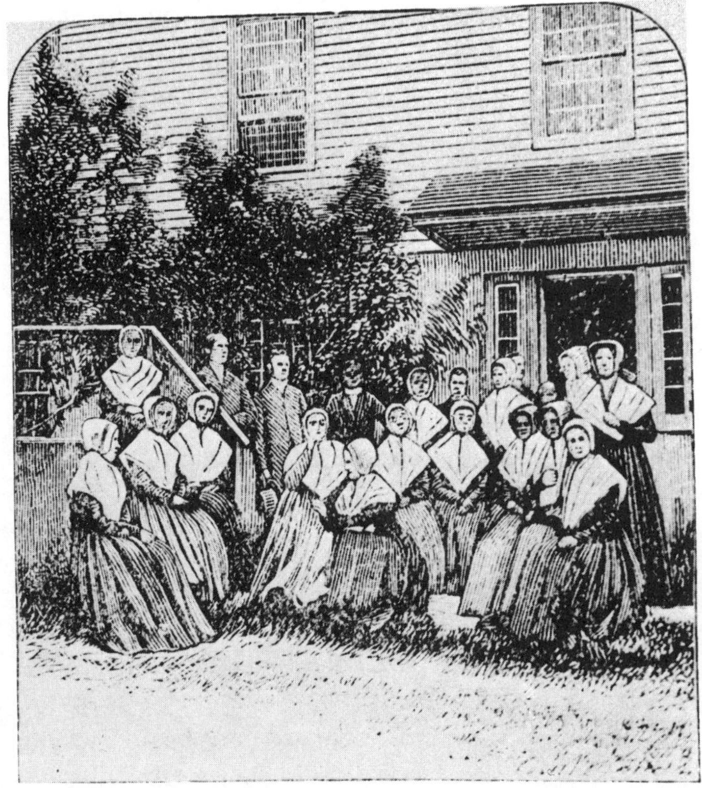

Engraving of group of Shakers from Mt. Lebanon, New York. From Shaker Almanac, 1879. MATTATUCK.

The Shakers arrived in New York City in August 1774, after a difficult and lengthy sea voyage. They had sailed through a violent storm during which Mother Ann never wavered in her belief that all would be well. It is said that the prayers of the Believers caused a great wave to push loose planks back into place at the moment, during a violent storm, when it was feared the ship was about to sink.

The Shakers found employment wherever they could, since all but one of them had no money. The group that came to America included Mother Ann; John Hocknell, an elderly member who paid for the voyage; Ann's brother William, who was a blacksmith and former horseman in the royal bodyguard; Ann's niece Nancy;

James Whittaker, a weaver; and Abraham Stanley, Ann's husband, who soon was to leave his celibate wife and run off with a less pious woman.

The small group scattered and worked and saved for two years while they made plans for the future. John Hocknell purchased land in Niskayuna and the group set about clearing it and building a log cabin. William and James found work in their trades in Albany. The first few years were difficult, since the group was poor and the land was a wilderness. However, by 1779 the Shakers had built a frame house to replace the log cabin, but the new building burned to the ground shortly after it was completed. Hard work and faithful worship occupied the days of this dedicated handful of Believers.

If abstinence from "weaknesses of the flesh" was one way to salvation, hard labor, according to Mother Ann, was the other. "Do your work as though you had a thousand years to live, and as if you were to die tomorrow," and "Put your hands to work, and your hearts to God" were sayings of Ann Lee that were quoted often throughout Shaker history. Shaker days were occupied with very hard work that found release in the shaking and trembling that had become the Shaker way of worship and communication with God.

If Mother Ann had been disappointed in those early years at the lack of interest by outsiders in joining the band of Shakers, she did not become discouraged. By 1780 her group had begun to grow, and many converts came into the sect. That year Mother Ann toured through Massachusetts, Connecticut, and New York to add to her already growing flock. New settlements were soon formed in Harvard, Shirley, and Hancock, Massachusetts; Enfield, Connecticut; and New Lebanon, New York. However, by the time these communities were fully settled and organized, and others at Tyringham, Massachusetts; Alfred and Sabbathday Lake, Maine; and

Canterbury, New Hampshire, were fully established, Mother Ann Lee had died.

During Ann Lee's travels she encountered a great many indignities, and this harassment had weakened her considerably. In this early post-Revolutionary period in American history, earlier settlers became suspicious of Americans of British origins, and a female religious mystic lately arrived from the mother country was fair game for many citizens who did what they saw as their duty in the name of freedom. In some communities Ann Lee was tied to a wagon and dragged through the streets. She died on September 8, 1784.

The rapid growth of Shakerdom following Mother Ann's death can be attributed to James Whittaker, one of the original eight from England and a religious zealot. His strong faith was not shared entirely by several others of the original group, who were disillusioned by the death of their leader. They had hoped that their abstinence from "weaknesses of the flesh" and their sacrifice and hard work would bring them immortality on earth, and when Ann Lee died, these few left the order in grave disappointment. If Mother was mortal, then certainly they were, also.

Father James Whittaker became spiritual leader of the Shakers following Ann Lee's death and he continued preaching her doctrines. He organized many of the scattered Believers into groups. He, too, worked beyond his endurance to promote the faith and lived only two years longer than Ann Lee. When Father James died in 1787, it fell to Joseph Meacham, a Shaker convert from Enfield, Connecticut, to lead the Shakers to successful organization.

Father Joseph appointed Lucy Wright, a young married woman from Pittsfield, Massachusetts, who had converted to the Shaker sect under the leadership of Mother Ann, to be leader of the women in the group.

RIGHT: *Brethren and sisters were allowed to get together for singing meeting.* SKETCH BY JOSEPH BECKER.

BELOW: *Brethrens' retiring room. Note double-flue stove. Hangings on bed wall are blue and white check homespun.*

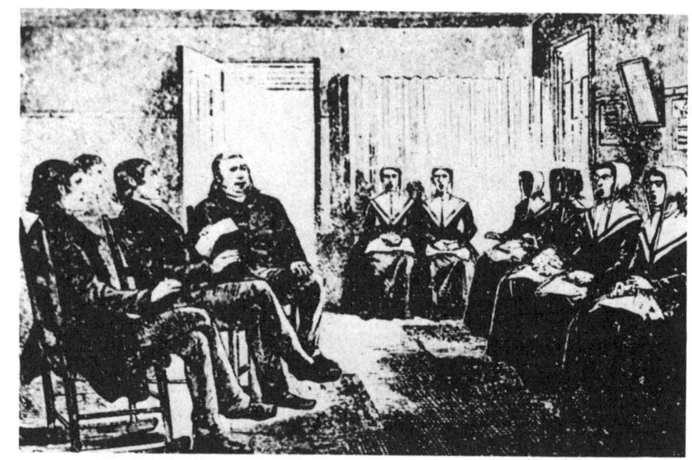

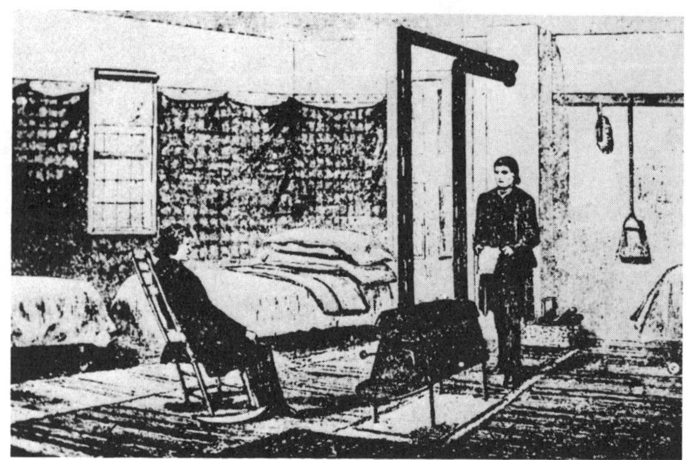

At this point women were given equal rights with the men, a fact that continued throughout Shaker history. Father Joseph and Mother Lucy believed that if the sexes were to be separated, each deserved its own leadership. Meacham brought further organization to the church in 1788. He organized the community structure designating different groups to carry on the various types of work thought necessary for survival.

By 1789 the Shakers, following the same occupations

that they had pursued before their conversions, had established some of the many industries at New Lebanon (changed to Mount Lebanon in 1861) and other communities that became the economic basis of all Shaker settlements throughout the nineteenth century. In that year leather and leather products were produced, clothing was made from Shaker textiles, furniture was manufactured in the brethrens' shops, and blacksmiths' and cobblers' shops were built. Woodenware, tinware, cooper's ware, and garden and farm tools were made. Trees and crops were planted, and soon the garden seed industry was established. This was to become a major source of income for the Shakers and remained so for many years.

It was Joseph Meacham who brought growth and order to the Shaker sect. He wrote the first list of covenants in New Lebanon in 1795, giving the Shakers "one Joint Interest and Union" and declaring that all members "might have equal right and privilege, according to their calling and needs." Meacham and Mother Lucy settled at New Lebanon, which became the mother church and the model society for all others to follow. It was at New Lebanon that the first "society-order" was set up. There were usually three groups, called "families," in a society. New Lebanon, at its peak, had eight families. A family

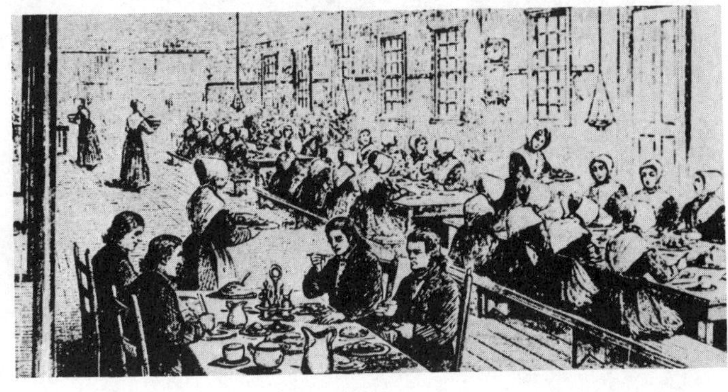

Dining room of North Family, Niskayuna. Men and women sat at separate tables and did not speak during meals.

was made up of men and women who lived in separate parts of a building with separate staircases and doors for either sex. Each family was governed by a set of elders and eldresses, deacons and deaconesses, and trustees, male and female, who handled all business of the family and to whom all other members of the sect were answerable.

A family consisted of from thirty to ninety members who shared a common dining hall, where the men and women sat at separate tables. The families were named either by the order in which they had been established in a certain Shaker community, such as the First Family, Second Family, etc., or by geographical location such as North Family, South Family, Hill Family, etc.

The positions in the hierarchy of the Shaker communities were appointed by the central ministry of the church, who chose people according to their talents and ability. All goods and properties were jointly owned and everyone was expected to work. Only the trustees were allowed to have dealings with outsiders, and they were responsible for the extensive buying and selling necessary to the maintenance of the Shaker communes.

Following Father Meacham's death in 1796, the Shaker movement spread westward, with communities being

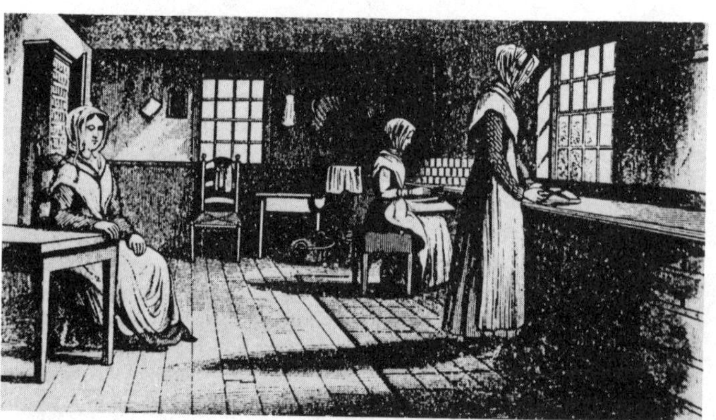

Shaker sisters' shop. DRAWING BY BENJAMIN LOSSING.

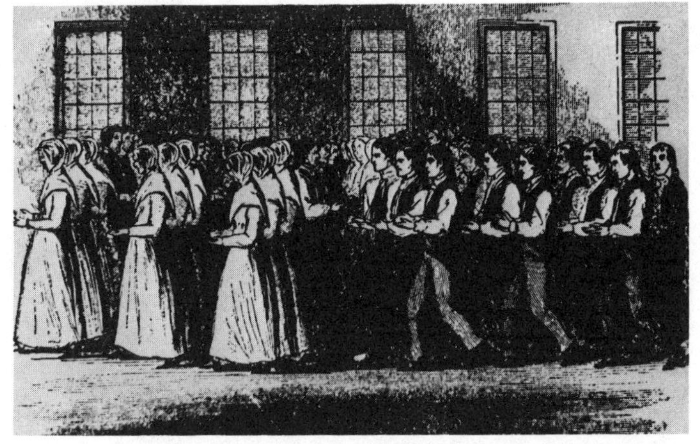

Square Order Shuffle. Shakers rehearsed and planned dances. In this dance, palms are held to receive "gifts from God." DRAWING BY BENJAMIN LOSSING.

established in West Union, Indiana, in 1810; South Union, Kentucky, in 1811; Watervliet, Ohio, (near Dayton) in 1813; Pleasant Hill, Kentucky, in 1814; Whitewater, Ohio, in 1824; and North Union (now Shaker Heights), Ohio, in 1826. Another New York community, Groveland, was established in 1826 as well.

At the peak of its growth, shortly before the Civil War, the Shaker sect numbered six thousand Believers. A gradual decline in the second half of the nineteenth century brought the membership down to one thousand by the turn of the century. Today, there are only a few Shakers living, all women, who occupy the original Shaker villages of Canterbury, New Hampshire, and Sabbathday Lake, Maine.

While the Shakers and their history have received a large amount of attention recently, most of the emphasis has been placed on their communal way of life, their architecture, furniture, and religious practices. The United Society of Believers in Christ's Second Appearing was basically an "order of trades." The work to which they put their hands was vital to their survival and became an important part of their daily lives and religion. The choice of trades in which each family of Shakers worked was dependent upon the talents of its members. Since most of the early Shakers were farmers, the first products of Shaker societies were those that could be produced from the land. In their earliest days, crops and fruit trees were planted and livestock was purchased, bred, and raised. In their efforts to lead lives that were completely separate from the world's people, it was necessary from the outset that the Shakers produce all goods for their own use. They also found it necessary to earn money for the purchase of more land as they grew in number.

A variety of businesses was started; the earliest derived from the agrarian enterprises in which the Shakers became engaged. Shaker seeds were well known for their quality from the earliest times. The sale of herbs and herbal medicines became a second means of support for the early Shakers. Hundreds of other products of their farms and shops soon were sold to outsiders by the trustees. Although the Shakers' first obligation was to clothe

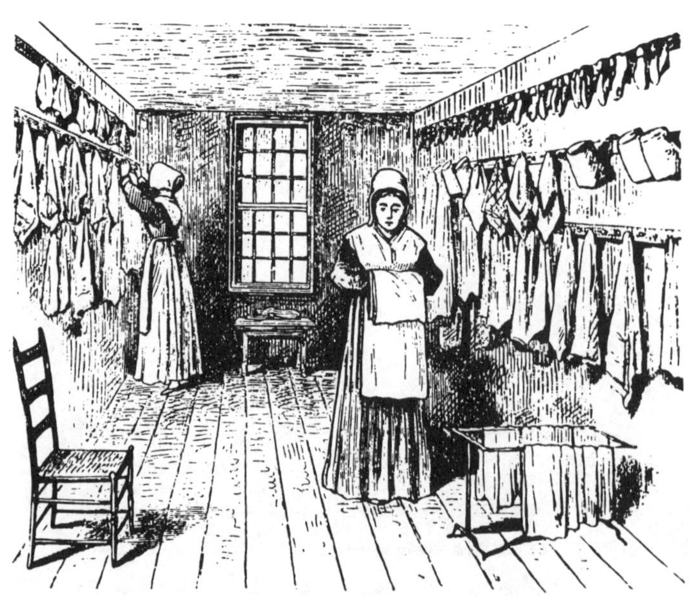

Girls' clothes room of Church Family, Niskayuna.

and feed one another and to help the growing number of Shaker families begin their own communities, purchase land, and erect their buildings, the early Shakers found that by following Mother Ann's philosophy of hard work and sincere worship they could produce much more than they needed themselves, and they engaged in a great variety of trades with the outside world.

Although they were separated from the outside world, the Shakers developed a highly structured economic policy and carefully developed industrial and economic practices that were far in advance of the times. From the outset they had a reputation for being scrupulously honest in their business practices, and because their industries were so closely integrated with their religious beliefs, they took enormous care that all products were of the highest possible quality. Each family was an independent economic unit that depended upon the sale of its products to outsiders for sustenance.

A great variety of Shaker products was made for sale to the world, and many examples of these products exist today as part of the American heritage. Each Shaker worked according to his talents and the needs of the community, and all felt that their work was God's work. Simple functional products of the highest quality were made with little thought being given to competition for these goods from outside manufacturers.

Along with Shaker products, there were many almanacs, diaries, journals, and other records, printed or handwritten. Labels for some of the early products such as seeds, herbs, and prepared foods were printed by the Shakers themselves, on Shaker-designed-and-built label presses. Invoices and bills exist that give us some idea of how Shaker business with the world's people was transacted. The Shakers were an honest group who did business only for cash and owed no one.

The story of the Shaker communal religious sect in

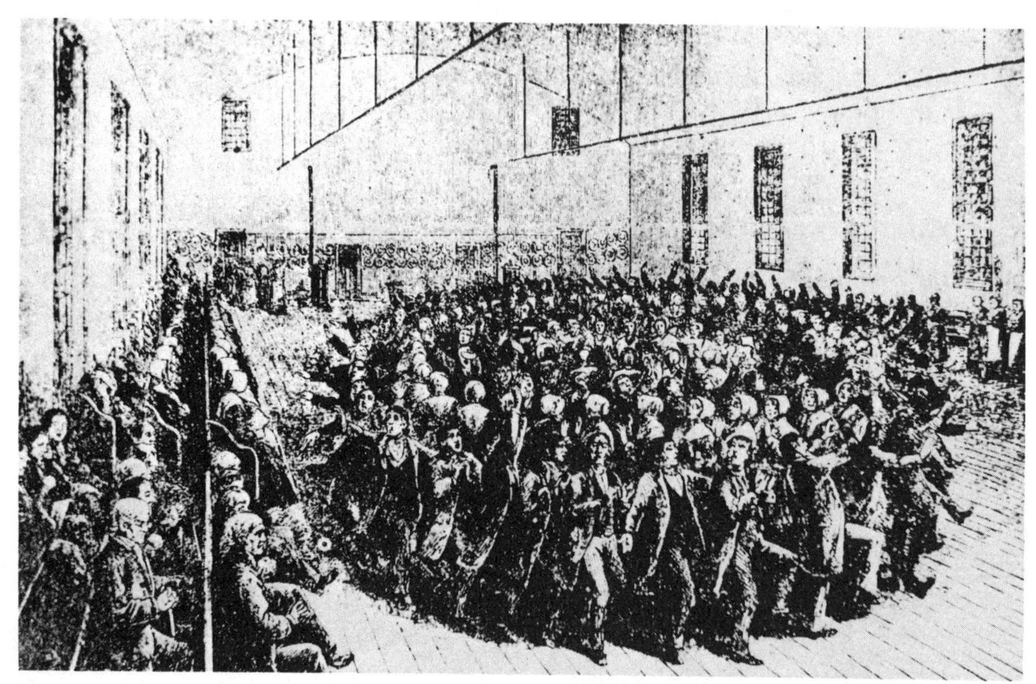

America will have come full circle in the two hundred years of its history. Separated voluntarily from outside influences for many years of its existence, the Shaker sect produced, through hard work dictated by its fervent religious beliefs, some of the most beautiful and functional objects for household use that have ever been made. While some products were made exclusively for their own use, many others were developed and produced for sale to the world's people. A study of the Shaker legacy of fine examples of tinsmithing, woodworking, weaving, spinning, sewing, basketry, clockmaking, and many other handcrafted articles tells us a great deal about quality of fine craftsmanship of Shaker goods.

The Ring Dance. Visitors to the Shakers were allowed to watch dances, which were planned and rehearsed.

CHAPTER 2

THE COMMUNITY INDUSTRIES OF THE SHAKERS

Those who go out on business for the Deacons or Trustees, have no more right to buy, sell, barter or trade in any way, than any other member in the family, save by the authority of those who send them.

Those called as Deacons or Trustees, shall stand as stewards in the house of God, and their dwelling place should be at the outer court.

It is the duty of the Deacons and Deaconesses, or Trustees, to see to the domestic concerns of the family in which they reside, and to perform all business transaction, either with the world, or with believers in other families or societies. All trade and traffic, buying and selling, changing and swapping, must be done by them or by their immediate knowledge and consent.

Believers must not run into debt to the world. Millenial Laws, 1821. Revised, 1845.

The Shakers believed that, to survive, their separate way of life had to be unified into one body of common interests. According to Edward Deming Andrews, in his book *The People Called Shakers,* " 'Consecrated labor' was the foundation of the New Jerusalem." As opposed to other communes of the eighteenth century, the Shakers were not dropouts or escapists, but practical-minded Yankees who developed a successful economic system that was vital to the success of the Shaker sect. According to Andrews, "Hand labor ... was good for both the individual soul and the collective welfare, mortifying lust, teaching humility, creating order and convenience, supplying a surplus for charity, supporting the structure of fraternity, protecting it against the world, and strengthening it for increasing service."

If one understands that labor, to the Shakers, was a sacred commitment, one can better understand the high quality of their workmanship and the easy acceptance of their products among their customers. The Shaker objective was to "improve our time and talents in this Life, in that manner in which we might be most useful." Within the order, responsibility for each type of work in which the Shakers engaged themselves was given to those best qualified.

Each family carried on its industrial activities independently, their trustees buying and selling goods. The

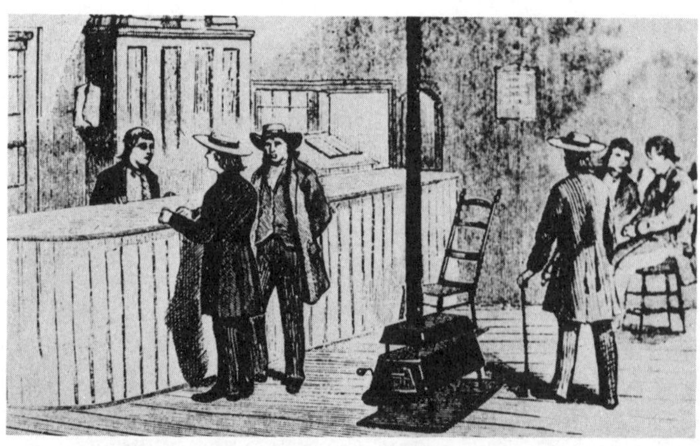

Trustee's office and store at Niskayuna.

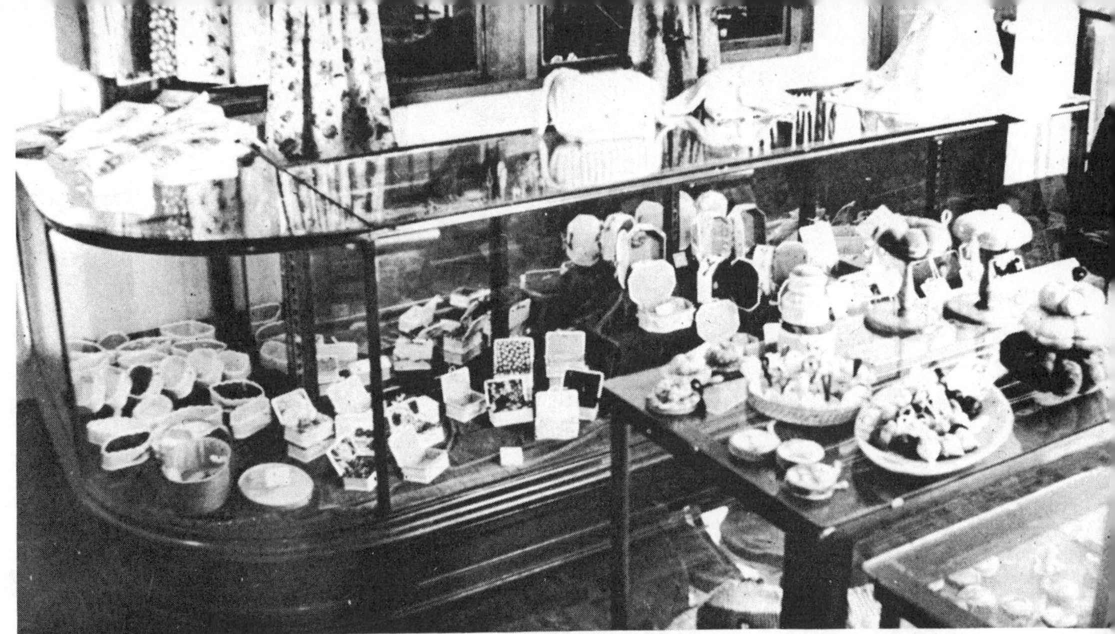

business office was the family store or trustees' office, which served as a clearinghouse or depot for incoming products. Each family was responsible for its own business transactions, but in cases of emergency or need, other families would help out.

The serene atmosphere of Shaker communities was commented upon often by late eighteenth- and early nineteenth-century writers. No one was hurried in his work and temperate labor was carried on in the unpressured communities. Each worked according to his abilities, and no one was overworked. Conscience dictated what must be done, and an English visitor, Hepworth Dixon, found everyone at New Lebanon moving "in an easy kind of rhythm." Horace Greeley described the Shakers' "constant, but never excessive toil."

Meacham said, "We have a right to improve the inventions of man, so far as is useful and necessary, but not to vain glory, or anything superfluous ... We are not called to labor to excell, or be like the world: but to excell them in order, union and peace, and in good works—works that are truly virtuous and useful to man,

Copy of contemporary photograph of Shaker sisters' shop (c. 1900). Sewing boxes and accessories were a large part of inventory. Note child's cloak on counter and Shaker-dressed doll in case at far right. OLD CHATHAM.

in this life." Superfluous decoration was not used on Shaker products and only objects thought to be helpful and useful to mankind were made and sold. The Shakers' reputation for quality merchandise soon led their products to be in demand in the marketplace.

Because each family was a community of industries, work was carried on in an organized manner. Each person was assigned special tasks at certain times. Each person's duties were varied enough to keep members from becoming bored. Thus a Shaker sister might in one day wash windows, work in the kitchen, mend clothes, and attend the sick. When crops ripened, concerted group efforts accomplished a quick harvest. A Shaker brother could record in his journal in September 1838 that on one day he "help cut onion seed; and began a blue jacket for Hiram Rude." On another day, "I finish said jacket, & do various chores." Although a tailor by trade, this Shaker, Benjamin Gates, also printed seed bills, dug potatoes, picked apples, distilled spirits, gathered roots and barks, cut carpet rags, bound books, worked in the gardens, trimmed the trees, and did many other tasks.

With everyone pitching in to accomplish all work necessary to keep the Shaker communes running smoothly, a lot could be accomplished in a day. Since temporal labor and worship were the only two activities of the Shakers, there were a great many hours in which to work, and many industries were established at New Lebanon before the nineteenth century. The brethren and sisters developed separate activities of their own, helping each other where necessary. The sisters had their own workshops on one side of the dwelling and took care of all the domestic tasks such as washing, ironing, weaving, spinning, sewing, and knitting. The earliest business activities of the women were the making of diaper materials, textiles of other kinds, baskets, men's palm-leaf hats, women's bonnets, mops, brushes, paper boxes, table mats,

NOTICE.

IN consequence of the increasing amount of company to which we are at all times subject, it becomes necessary to adopt the following

RULES FOR VISITORS.

FIRST. We wish it to be understood that we do not keep a Public House, and wish to have our Rules attended to as much as any one would the rules of their own private dwelling.

SECOND. Those who call to see their Friends or Relatives, are to visit them at the Office, and not to go elsewhere, except by permission of those in care at the office.

THIRD. Those who live near and can call at their own convenience are not expected to stay more than a few hours; but such as live at a great distance, or cannot come often, and have near relatives here, can stay from one to four days, according to circumstances. This we consider sufficient time, as a general rule.

FOURTH. All Visitors are requested to rise to take Breakfast at half past Six in the Summer, and half past Seven in the Winter.

FIFTH. At the Table we wish all to be as free as at home, but we dislike the wasteful habit of leaving food on the plate. No vice is with us the less ridiculous for being in fashion.

SIXTH. Married Persons tarrying with us over night, are respectfully notified that each sex occupy separate sleeping apartments while they remain. This rule will not be departed from under any circumstances.

SEVENTH. Strangers calling for meals or lodging are expected to pay if accommodated.

UNITED SOCIETY.

Shaker visitors were welcomed, but were requested to conform to Shaker schedule and way of life.
OLD CHATHAM.

fans, workboxes and workstands, seed bags, gloves, etc. When the herb and seed industries were developed, the women helped in the gathering and preparation of the herbs and roots, sorting and packaging seeds, and making the many medicines that were sold. They all helped with the preparation and packaging of the various kitchen products that were always sold by the Shakers. In addition, of course, they preserved those goods needed in the kitchen for the Shakers' own use.

Sluggards were never tolerated in Shaker communes, and although the charitable Shakers would never turn anyone from their doors who was in need of food or

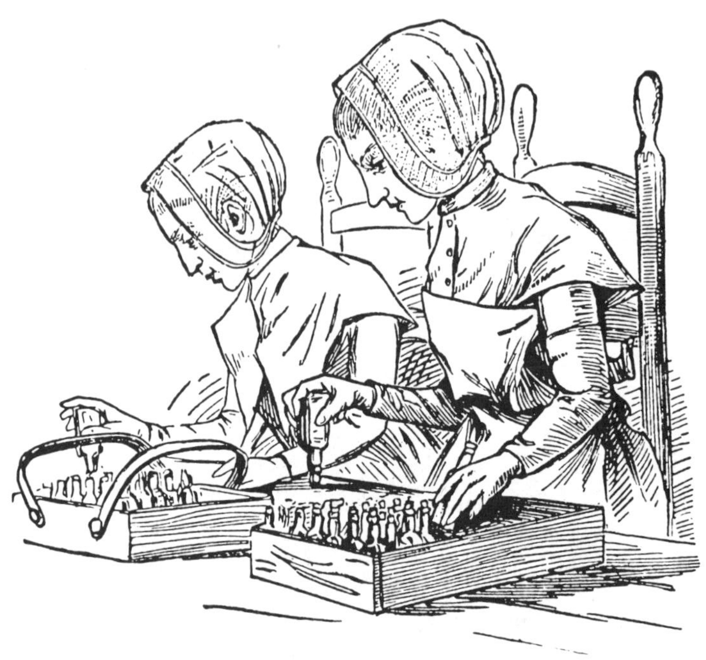

Shaker sisters corking bottles of herbal medicines.

a bed, those who did not work were made to feel uncomfortable and they did not stay long. Extra clothing was kept to be given away to those in need, and food could always be found for the hungry.

Because each family was a separate unit and controlled its own business and property, some families prospered more than others. Established families helped new families get started. Often furniture was made to help fill the necessary functions of a newly established Shaker family. Trade was carried on among the Shakers as well, and there are many objects found today with alleged provenance from a particular Shaker community that can be proved to have been made elsewhere. Brethren who were knowledgeable in a certain industry would travel to other communes to teach methods of manufacture of products that might otherwise have been unknown.

If the Shakers evidenced a lack of compulsion in their

labor, they also lacked competitiveness. They seemed to be competitive neither with outside manufacturers of goods similar to theirs nor with each other. While the "world's people", as outsiders were referred to by the Believers, involved in manufacturing, had to concern themselves with labor, material, and distribution costs, the Shakers felt no pressure of time, and most raw materials were home grown. Far from being unrealistic or impractical in their business dealings, the Shakers were hardheaded Yankee traders who could be counted on to put only superior products in the marketplace.

CHAPTER 3

SHAKER-MADE PRODUCTS

The Deacons and Deaconesses or Trustees are required by the orders of the gospels, to give to the Elders from time to time a correct account of all matters of importance that have come within their knowledge, concerning the temporal business of the family, and of things that have given out.

It is the duty of the Deacons and Deaconesses, to see that suitable furniture for rooms and suitable food for the family are provided, (as far as lies in their power,) and to see that the food is cooked with good economy.

Brethren and sisters have no liberty to make for themselves or for others, accommodations, or conveniences without the union and consent of the Deacons and Deaconesses, each sex in their own order. Millenial Laws, 1821. Revised, 1845.

Although Shaker furniture, pure and simple in design and beautifully handcrafted, has long been the subject of much discussion in the world of American applied arts, there are hundreds of other Shaker-grown or Shaker-manufactured products that have enjoyed much less attention. Beautiful textiles, hand woven long after the rest of our citizenry was using machine-woven products, were produced by the Shakers from their homegrown flax, wool, and silk. Honest and functional tinware and ironware, handmade leather goods, rugs, baskets, boxes made from many materials, warm and attractive cloaks, sweaters, mittens, and many other articles are legacies of the Shakers' dedicated hands and hearts.

The quality of Shaker labor is evident, not only in

TOP: *Group of small items made to sell in sisters' shops. Left to right: polished walnut shell pin-cushion; green felt needlecase, hand embroidered; chamois penwiper. Pincushion and needlecase from Hancock, Massachusetts. Penwiper is from Mount Lebanon, New York.* OLD CHATHAM.

BOTTOM: *Bone and ivory buttons, knobs, rings, and other small objects were made by the Church Family of New Lebanon before 1825.* OLD CHATHAM.

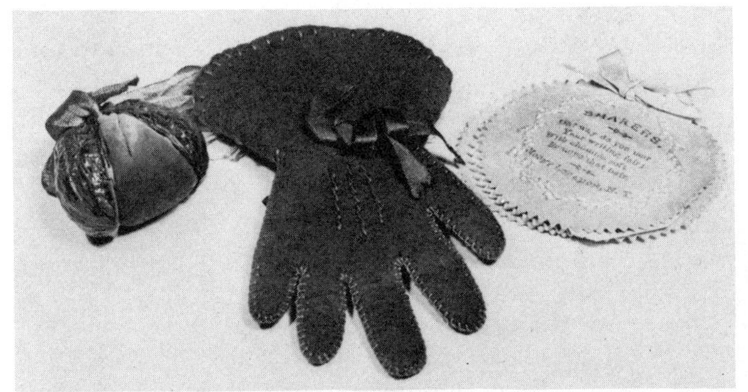

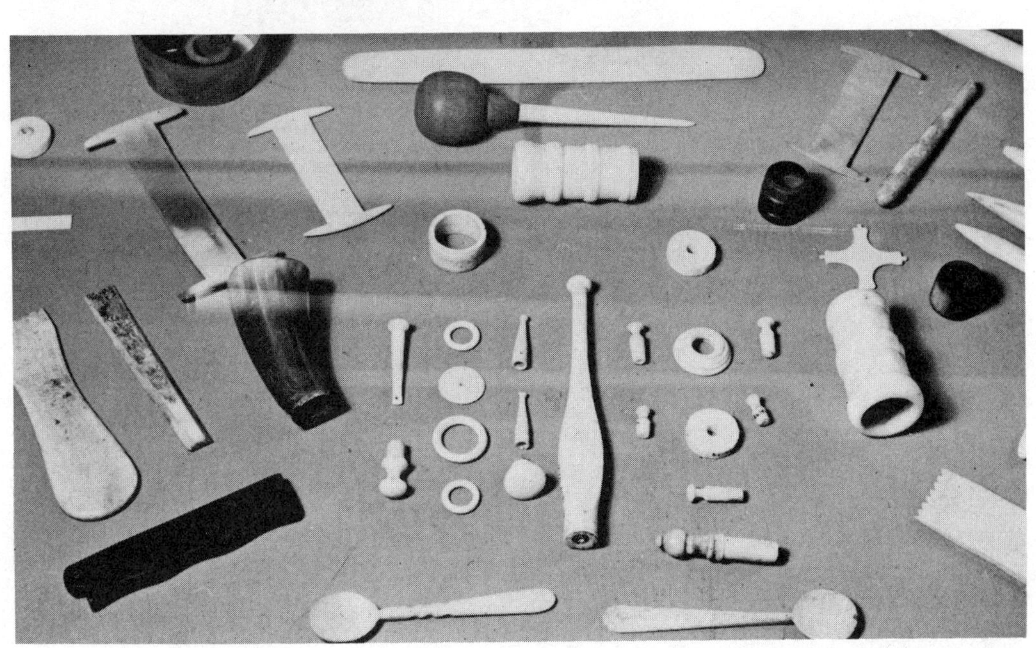

the early communal furniture made for their own use, but in the variety of household items made for sale to the world. Although removed from the various decorative influences of the nineteenth century, some indications of changes in patterns and styles can be found in goods made for sale following the Civil War.

Early Shakers concerned themselves only with the quality of their own goods, for which they became known in the areas where they traded. In the latter half of the nineteenth century, as their membership dwindled and competition for many of their products became stiffer, the Shakers were forced to change with the times to some extent. They resorted to promotion and advertising and they ran some of their more lucrative businesses in much the same way as the competition did. Not believing in patents, they were forced to patent many of their more innovative products.

Dr. Corbett's Sarsaparilla.

Manufactured at East Canterbury, N. H.

This Syrup is composed of the most active and accredited ingredients of the vegetable kingdom, as recognized by the ablest Dispensatories of the day. It has proved to be most valuable in the following diseases ; Indigestion, Sourness of the Stomach; Functional disorders of the Liver, and all Scrofulous Disorders arising from impurities of the blood.

Dose. **For an adult, a teaspoonful, four or five times a day, which may be increased to a table spoonful, as best suits the patient.**

To guard against counterfeits, observe the signature of the inventor on each label and on the wrapper.

Ask your Druggist for it or send your order to Arthur Bruce, East Canterbury, Mer. Co., N. H.

"Dr. Corbett's Sarsaparilla" was advertised as a cure for "Scrofulous disorders arising from impurities of the blood," a nineteenth-century euphemism for syphilis. OLD CHATHAM.

Dr. Corbett's Cherry Pectoral.

Manufactured by the Shakers.

This preparation of Wild Cherry is highly recommended by the medical faculty. It is valuable for Colds, Coughs, Hoarseness, Bronchitis, and Pain in the Side and Chest. It has been used by the Society for forty years and has been thoroughly proved by thousands.

Dose. For an adult, one teaspoonful four or five times a day, more or less, as the case may require.

Send all orders to A. Bruce, East Canterbury, N. H.

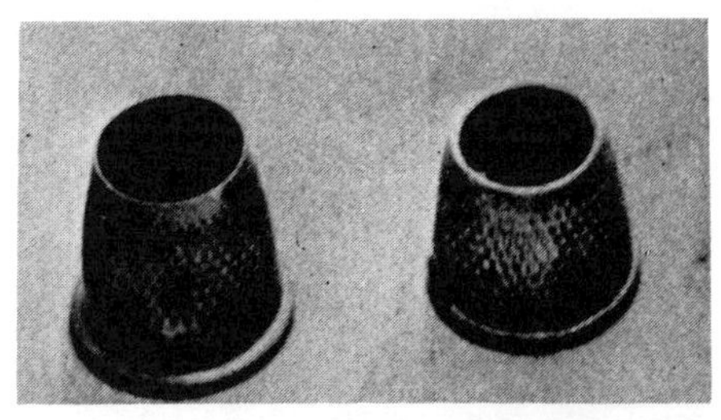

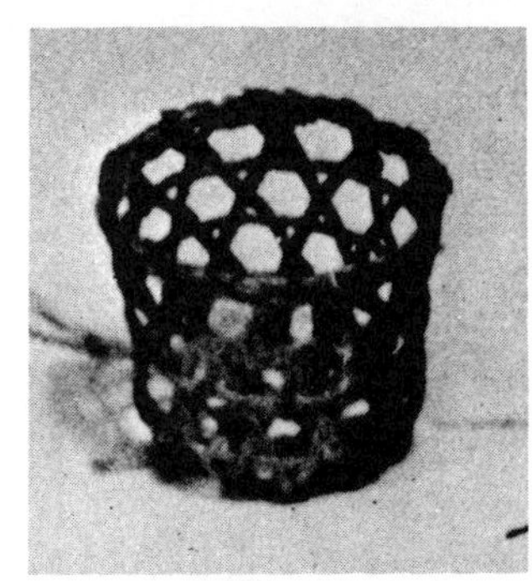

By the end of the nineteenth century the advertising of Shaker goods was an established fact. Since they now lacked the manpower to produce the enormous amount of goods that had kept them going through their years of rapid growth, more expedient methods of making and selling goods became necessary. The vast landholdings, necessary when the population was at its peak, became a burden and expense for the relatively few Shakers who were left in charge by 1900.

Many products of the Shaker shops, kitchens, and gardens were no longer manufactured, and other areas of trade became more successful. Outside help was needed in many of the communities just to carry on the basic work, to keep the settlements in repair, and to help plant and harvest the crops. In 1889 the first Shaker community to close was North Union, Ohio. By 1920, ten of the formerly thriving communes had closed, with the remaining Shakers moving to other communities. The disbanding of the Shaker communities occurred gradual-

TOP LEFT: *Advertisement for "Dr. Corbett's Cherry Pectoral," a popular Shaker medicine.* OLD CHATHAM.

TOP RIGHT: *Tailor's thimbles made and used by Shakers.* OLD CHATHAM.

BOTTOM: *Even smallest items were made with precision and care. This is a woven straw thimble case.* OLD CHATHAM.

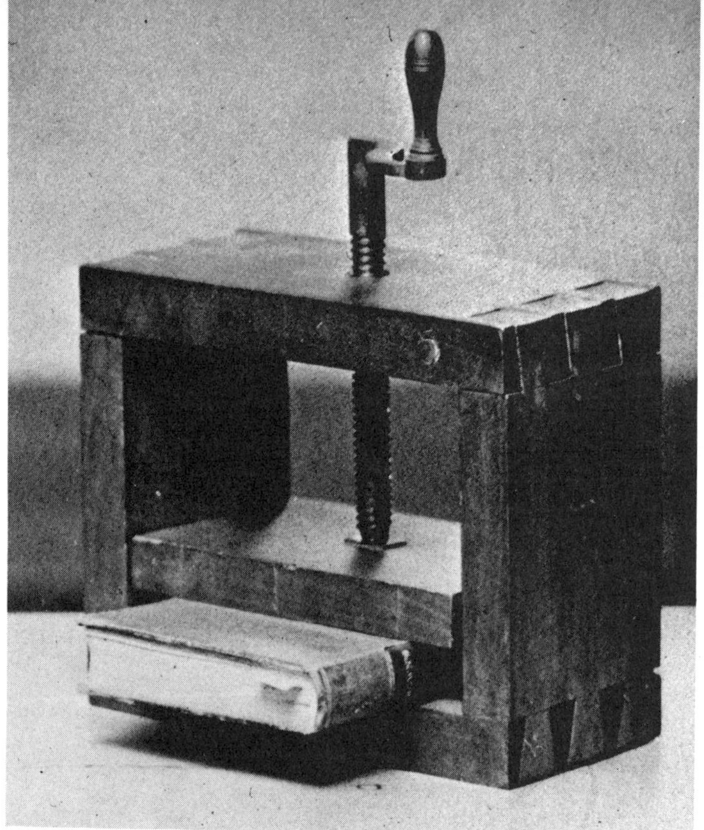

Bookbinding was engaged in by many of the Shaker families. This small binding press is made with usual Shaker precision. HANCOCK.

ly, with the members of each commune selling their holdings, often at disadvantageous prices. In the remaining communities some trades were still carried on, while others were abandoned. The box and the chair industries, both lucrative in their time, were the last to go.

In the growing and manufacturing of their many products, the Shakers were not averse to using time-and effort-saving devices if they felt that doing so would not impede the quality of the product. There are a great many inventions and innovations credited to the Shakers for which the world may well be indebted. A proper record of the Shakers' development of tools, machinery, and household products may never be complete, since many of these innovations and inventions were not recorded or patented. Some of the known Shaker accomplishments in these areas are: the rotary or revolving harrow; a turbine waterwheel; a threshing machine; an innovative and functional sash balance; machinery for compressing herbs; a silk-reeling machine, and many types of spinning and weaving devices; an improved commercial washing machine; a self-acting cheese press; a circular saw, said to have been invented by a Shaker sister who adapted her spinning wheel for the purpose; metal pins; the one-horse wagon; a sidehill plow; a pipe machine; a pea sheller; a butterworker; an automatic apple parer; an improved wood-burning stove; a revolving oven; a turbine waterwheel and screw propeller; a

Advertisement for one of many Shaker inventions. OLD CHATHAM.

Shaker Sash Balance,

PATENTED BY S. J. RUSSELL, JULY 16, 1872, IMPROVED AND PERFECTED WITH CORD-HOLDER ATTACHMENT, FEB'Y 1, 1875.

A long felt want now fully supplied.

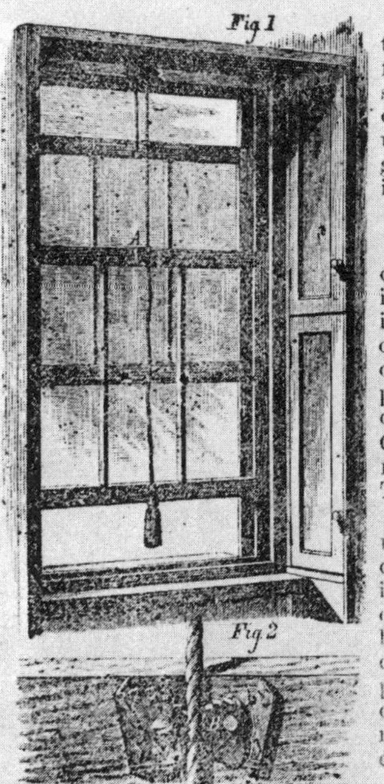

For years many our leading mechanics and others interested in the subject have been endeavoring to perfect a device to superceede the cumbrous and expensive sash-weights for the easy adjustment of windows, cheap, durable, easy in operation, and combining economy with utility. We are now fully prepared to supply this great want, having perfected a Sash Balance, combining the three great requisites, to-wit:

SIMPLICITY, ECONOMY, and DURABILITY.

We furthermore claim, and can fully establish, that our device is so utterly simple in its workings, in the impossibility of its getting out of order, the advantage it possesses over the unsightly catches and locks in an ornamental point of view, setting aside the cheapness of our Balance, that no intelligent housekeeper will fail to possess it as soon as its advantages are thoroughly understood.

OUR SASH BALANCE HAS THE UNQUALIFIED APPROVAL OF ALL BUILDERS, HOUSE CARPENTERS, ETC.

To further simplify the matter, we claim for the SHAKER BALANCE the following undoubted advantages over all other devices: 1st. The readiness with which it can be attached to any window, large or small, without the slightest cost. 2nd. The ease with which it can be operated. 3rd. Its great durability. 4th. The window is more securely locked in any position. 5th. Its perfect ventilation. 6th. It obviates the necessity of curtains or other hangings, as it is of itself highly ornamental. 7th. The advantage in a pecuniary fight over every other device of the kind ever offered to the public.

THE SAVING IN COST IS IMMENSE.

INSTRUCTIONS FOR OPERATING THE BALANCE.

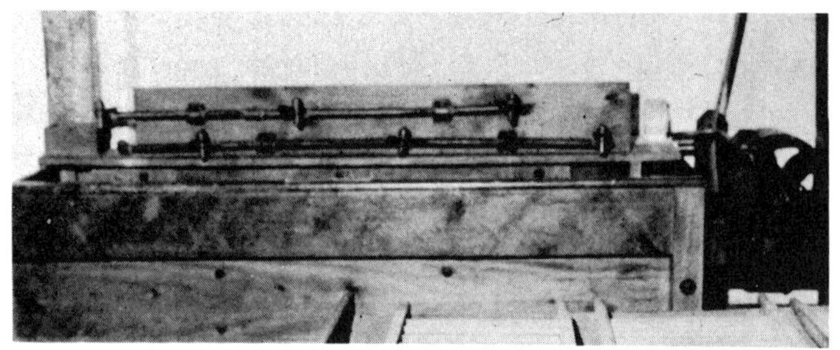

This Shaker washing machine was used for institutional purposes and received a bronze medal at the Philadelphia Centennial. Many were made for sale. OLD CHATHAM.

machine for matching boards and cutting and planing; an improved press for printing labels; machinery for splint-making, basket-working and-cutting; and an improved kiln for drying sweet corn.

The first metal pen nib, which replaced feather quills, and the flat broom were important Shaker inventions. Hundreds of other products in general use throughout the nineteenth century were changed or improved in many ways by the Shakers. In over a hundred years of production and labor, the Shakers not only provided for their own needs, but contributed greatly to the industrial and agricultural development of America.

The variety of occupations that were carried on in each Shaker community depended on need and the talents of the members. The manufacture of food products such as dried sweet corn, dried apples, and prepared applesauce, cheese, sausage, and butter; the spinning and dyeing of yarn and the weaving of cloth; the making of palm-leaf and straw bonnets and other clothing; the manufacture of fur and wool hats for men; the manufacture of leather goods such as whips and whiplashes, shoes and boots; the making, packaging, and labeling of a variety of medicines; the manufacture of boxes, chairs, cooper's ware, spinning wheels, and wool cards; the weaving of baskets; and the manufacture of pipes and bricks and ironware were just some of the better-known occupations of the Shakers.

In order to understand how the Shaker industries were carried on, it is necessary to understand something of the social and economic systems which governed all communities. As new members entered the order, all worldly goods became the property of the sect. Every new member had, also, to be free of debt before he was allowed to enter into Shaker life. As organized by Father Joseph Meacham, each member of the sect was equal, with each community further broken down into "families." Each "family" was independent in its economic pursuits, although often more than one family would work together on projects if this was advantageous to the entire community. The highest interest was, of course, the church. Separation from the world was felt to be an absolute necessity to further these interests.

Everyone worked in Shaker communes, since the Millenial Laws stipulated that "Drones, sluggards, thieves and liars, or deceivers, [did] not belong among the people of God." Although work was a necessity and important to the Shaker way of life, no one was pushed beyond his endurance, and each worked according to his own

LEFT: *This adjustable, portable reading stand made by Shakers is possibly a one-of-a-kind object.* OLD CHATHAM.

RIGHT: *Knitting needle scabbards hand sewn by Shaker sisters.* OLD CHATHAM.

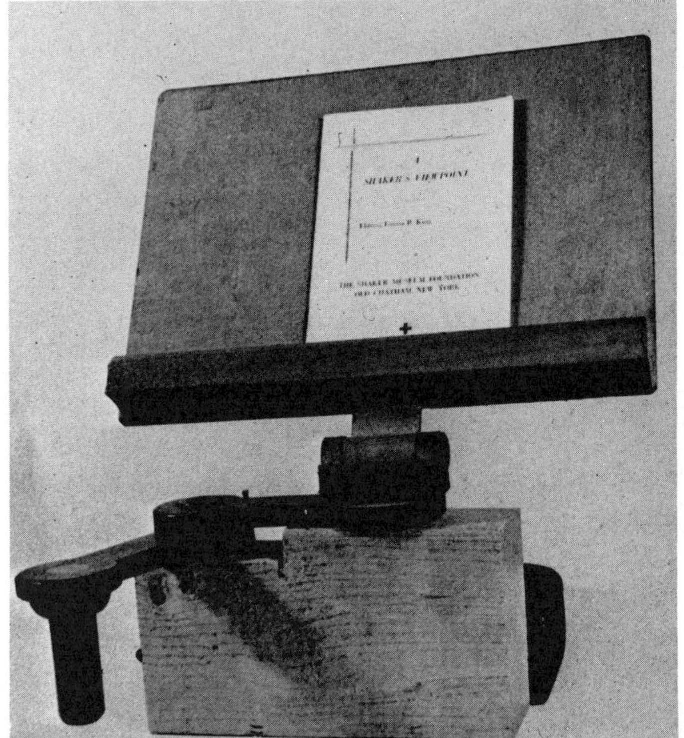

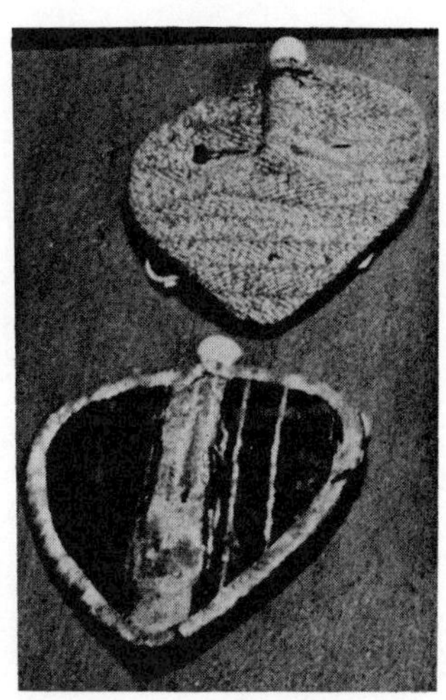

talents. A rotation of duties made it possible for many to become proficient at more than one trade.

While some of the Shaker industries can be divided into two groups, that of goods made for their own use and that provided for sale to support the group, there is often difficulty in discovering which goods or services were not offered to outsiders as well as to the Shaker communities. The division is arbitrary when discussing certain industries. For instance, bonnets were made for the Shaker sisters' use primarily, until there became a demand for the same style of bonnet on the open market. Shaker cloaks became extremely fashionable in the late nineteenth-century non-Shaker society, and therefore they were profitable as an industry. The same cloaks were also made and worn by the Shaker sisters.

There was no distinction in the quality of the goods the Shakers made for themselves and those that they made for sale. Those laws governing the quality and design of products were as applicable to the commercial products as they were to the domestic products. Although self-sustaining, the Shakers were not averse to purchasing outside wares when they could find quality products at prices lower than the cost of their own, homemade items.

Each family was in charge of its own accounts, which were kept by the appointed trustees, or deacons. The trustees also took charge of all business affairs. Other duties of the deacons or deaconesses were "to see to the domestic concerns of the family in which they reside." They were in charge of "all trade and traffic, buying and selling, changing and swapping."

Since each family within a Shaker community was a distinct economic unity, we find many advertisements, seed, herb, and medicine labels that record that the product was made or distributed by the North Family, the South Family, the Church Family, etc., of a particular Shaker community. Some families acted as distributors of certain Shaker products that they had purchased from another family.

There seems to have been little or no competition among the various Shaker families that were involved in similar enterprises. When certain of the families could not provide enough of the raw materials for their thriving seed, herbal, or foodstuffs businesses, neighboring farmers sold their raw materials to the Shakers, provided, of course, that the quality suited the perfectionist members of the sect. Shaker standards for quality did not seem to be sacrificed at any time in their industrial and commercial history.

A study of the many products made by the Shakers for sale to the world must also include information about their methods of selling, distribution, and advertising. Not only the products themselves, but the many tools made by the Shakers that were necessary to produce them are also a fascinating part of the folk art and industries of the sect.

In their recognition of equality of the sexes, their strict dedication to the spirit of community living, their hundreds of innovations designed to lighten the burden of their work, and their fervent belief that they must toil to obtain the state of grace that was their ultimate goal, the Shakers have become a subject of interest and fascination to many students of American history and Yankee ingenuity. If it is true that we can come to know a people by studying the objects that were a part of their lives, this is even more true of the Shakers to whom work with their hands was a way of life and a part of their religion. They truly believed, as they had been told by their founder, "If you improve in one talent, God will give you more."

CHAPTER 4

THE GARDEN SEED INDUSTRY

Believers may not spend their time cultivating fruits and plants, not adapted to the climate in which they live. Millenial Laws, 1821, Revised 1845.

Believers involved in cultivation of plants would, in any case, hardly have time to cultivate exotic plants. Very early in the history of the Shakers, the garden seed industry became an important economic mainstay for most of the families. It is probable that the raising of garden seeds to sell began as early as 1789 at Watervliet, New York, and New Lebanon and was the longest lasting and probably the most lucrative of all Shaker industries. Before 1800 seeds were cultivated to sell at Hancock, Massachusetts, and Enfield, New Hampshire, as well as the two communities already mentioned, and gradually the seed industry became an important source of income for all the Shaker communities. As with most Shaker industries, the garden seed business gradually declined in most families after 1840, although it continued to thrive in the New (Mount) Lebanon community until

SQUASH.
Winter Hubbard.

SHAKERS' SEED.

Soak the seed 12 hours, plant (from the 10th to the end of May) in good soil, in hills well filled with rotten manure, 6 feet apart each way, cover the seed an inch, thin to 3 or 4 plants in a hill, and sprinkle with ashes. 8

N. F., New Lebanon, N. Y.

Winter Hubbard.
SQUASH.

TOMATO,

General Grant

SHAKERS' SEED.

Sow in a hot-bed by the first of April, transplant in rows 3 feet apart each way, and hill them up well.

E. F. MT. LEBANON, N. Y.

General Grant.

TOMATO,

Mix in a Shovel-full of well-decomposed manure in each hill, 4 feet apart each way, leaving 4 plants to the hill.

10 cts.

Mount Lebanon, N. Y.

JAPAN

MUSK MELON,

VERY EARLY & SWEET.

Mix in a Shovel-full of well-decomposed manure in each hill, 4 feet apart each way, leaving 4 plants to the hill.

10 cts.

Mount Lebanon, N. Y.

Early Frame.

SHAKERS' SEED.

Soak the seed 12 hours; plant (in May) in good soil, in hills filled with rotten manure, 4 feet apart each way, cover the seed an inch, thin to 3 or 4 plants in a hill, and sprinkle ashes.

N. F., New Lebanon, N. Y.

Early Frame.

SHAKERS'

BELL PEPPER.

—:—

Soak the seed 12 hours in warm water; sow in hot-bed by the 1st of April: transplant into warm soil, in rows 2 feet apart each way.

N. F. New Lebanon, N. Y.

SHAKERS'

Lupinus Affinis.

Blue, white and purple, from California; half-hardy annual. Height, ½ foot.

S. F., NEW LEBANON, N. Y.

the end of the century.

At the beginning of the garden seed industry, seeds were purchased from outside sources and packaged along with Shaker-grown seeds as their own products. However,

Shaker printed labels for garden seeds. OLD CHATHAM.

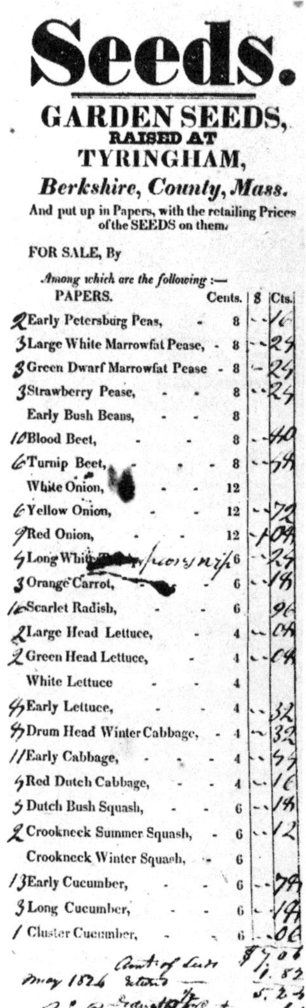

Seeds.

GARDEN SEEDS,
RAISED AT
TYRINGHAM,
Berkshire, County, Mass.
And put up in Papers, with the retailing Prices of the SEEDS on them.

FOR SALE, By

Among which are the following:—

	PAPERS.	Cents.	$	Cts.
2	Early Petersburg Peas,	8		16
3	Large White Marrowfat Pease,	8		24
3	Green Dwarf Marrowfat Pease	8		24
3	Strawberry Pease,	8		24
	Early Bush Beans,	8		
10	Blood Beet,	8		40
6	Turnip Beet,	8		54
	White Onion,	12		
6	Yellow Onion,	12		72
9	Red Onion,	12	1	08
4	Long White [illegible]	6		24
3	Orange Carrot,	6		18
16	Scarlet Radish,	6		96
2	Large Head Lettuce,	4		08
2	Green Head Lettuce,	4		08
	White Lettuce	4		
8	Early Lettuce,	4		32
8	Drum Head Winter Cabbage,	4		32
11	Early Cabbage,	4		44
4	Red Dutch Cabbage,	4		16
3	Dutch Bush Squash,	6		18
2	Crookneck Summer Squash,	6		12
	Crookneck Winter Squash,	6		
13	Early Cucumber,	6		78
3	Long Cucumber,	6		18
1	Cluster Cucumber,	6		06

Every Shaker community was involved in lucrative seed business. This account sheet is from the relatively small settlement in Tyringham, Massachusetts. OLD CHATHAM.

by 1819 deacons, gardeners, and trustees from Hancock, New Lebanon, and Watervliet signed a manifesto claiming:

> We, the undersigned, having for sometime past felt a concern, lest there should come loss upon the joint interest, and dishonor upon the gospel, by purchasing seeds of the world, and mixing them with ours for sale; and having duly considered the matter, we are confident that it is best to leave off the practise, and we do hereby convenant and agree that we will not, hereafter, put up, or sell, any seeds to the world which are not raised among believers (excepting melon seeds).

At first, Watervliet and New Lebanon were the leading seed producers. In 1811 Watervliet sold three hundred dollars' worth of seeds, and as early as 1800 sales at New Lebanon totaled over a thousand dollars. In the early part of the century the price for Shaker seeds was about a dollar a pound.

Since the business of growing and packaging garden seeds became such an important source of income in what were basically agrarian communes, it was not long before all the Shaker communities engaged in the business. Territories overlapped and eventually had to be divided so that each community had what amounted to its own area where the trustees could peddle their seeds, and there was little encroachment on another's market. This problem seems to have been settled amicably in New York State as early as 1822 when a Watervliet Shaker wrote to a brother at Hancock that although there seemed to have been some overlap in the territories that were covered, everyone involved sold all the seeds he had. The Watervliet Believer described his area at the time as being "confined to less than one fifth part of the state we live in." He also complained in a rather un-Shaker like manner, "Excepting we sell as many seeds in Albany and Troy as we can, and our Lebanon Brethren

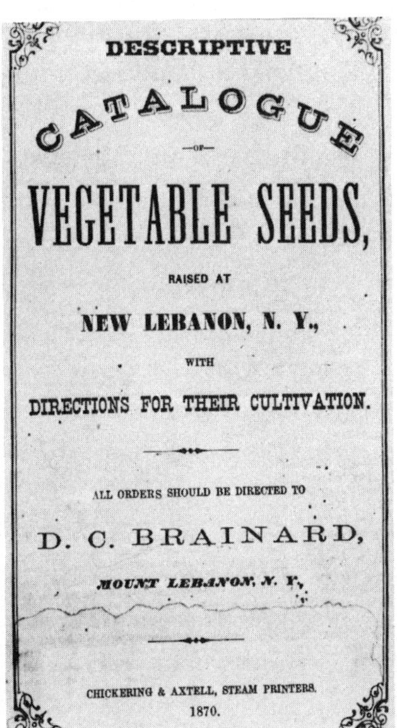

DESCRIPTIVE

CATALOGUE

—OF—

VEGETABLE SEEDS,

RAISED AT

NEW LEBANON, N. Y.,

WITH

DIRECTIONS FOR THEIR CULTIVATION.

ALL ORDERS SHOULD BE DIRECTED TO

D. C. BRAINARD,

MOUNT LEBANON, N. Y.,

CHICKERING & AXTELL, STEAM PRINTERS.

1870.

SPECIAL DESCRIPTION OF

VARIOUS KINDS OF VEGETABLES,

WITH NOTICE OF NEW VARIETIES.

Beans.

Yellow Six Weeks.—This is the earliest Snap or String Bean. The Red Valentine, Refugee, and Newington Wonder, though from one to two weeks later than the Six Weeks Bean, are really the best for string, being very tender and succulent, and continue longest in season.

German Wax Pole.—This is one of the best Beans for snap. When nearly ripe the pods are of a waxen color, semi-transparent and very tender.

Indian Chief Bush Bean.—This Bean resembles the German Wax Bean in all respects, except that it is a bush instead of a pole bean.

Beet.

Extra Early Turnip, or Bassano.—This is the earliest Beet, but as the flesh boils white, is but little used after the Blood Turnip becomes sufficiently grown.

Long Blood.—This is an excellent late kind, and keeps well through winter.

The cultivation of this vegetable, not only for table use but also for feeding stock, has not received the attention which it deserves.

Cabbage.

The earliest kind is the Early York variety. The Early Wakefield is also one of the earliest kinds, and in some localities is a great favorite. As the above-named varieties produce but small heads, we would not recommend their culture to any great extent.

Early Wi[illegible]nin[illegible]stadt.—For a second early Cabbage this is decidedly the best, being sure to produce a good head. It is not only an excellent early Cabbage, but will also keep well through the winter. Head cone-shaped, compact and very fine.

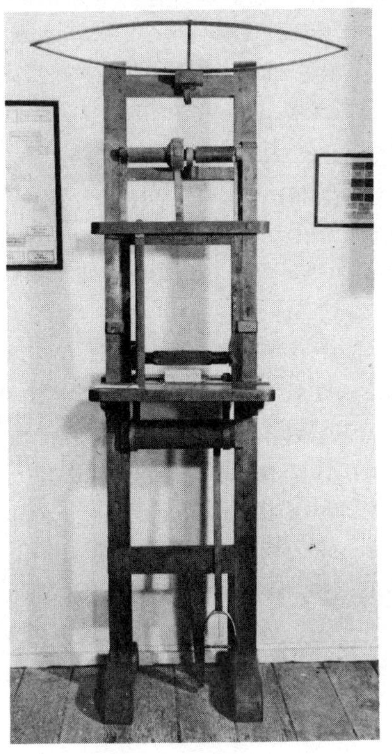

ABOVE: *Cover and first page of catalogue for Shaker Vegetable seeds.* OLD CHATHAM.

LEFT: *Label press, designed and built by Shakers for printing labels for garden seed and herbal medicine businesses.* OLD CHATHAM.

do so too at both of these places, we also sell a few at New York and some at Brooklyn and our Lebanon Brethren do likewise."

At its peak the garden seed industry was obviously a great enterprise for the Shakers, and in the five year period, 1836 to 1840, 930,400 seed bags were printed at New Lebanon alone. As competition grew, however, the seed business gradually became less profitable. A decline in the business took place during the Civil War, but most communities recovered from this and continued in the garden seed industry until the end of the century. After 1870, however, the industry began to decline very gradually, and it became a less important source of income for most Shaker farms. The one Shaker community that never recovered financially from the war was Enfield, Connecticut. Its territory included many Southern states.

For the seedsmen responsible for selecting, growing, cultivating, and harvesting the seed crops, the winter months gave no respite from the arduous work involved. The seeds had to be sorted and cleaned during the fall and winter. Thousands of bags were cut and pasted. Printing the bags or labels was also a time-consuming task. Packaging, at first done entirely by hand, was an arduous part of the business. The Shakers are probably the first American seedsmen to put up their seeds in individual bags.

Because of the number of families engaged in the garden seed industry, great varieties of seeds, including variations of many common vegetables were grown. Shaker seeds became known throughout the country for their quality. In the early days of the industry there was no need for promotion nor advertising, save for the modestly printed colored labels. Competition in the decades following the Civil War, however, made the Shakers aware of methods being used by others to promote their

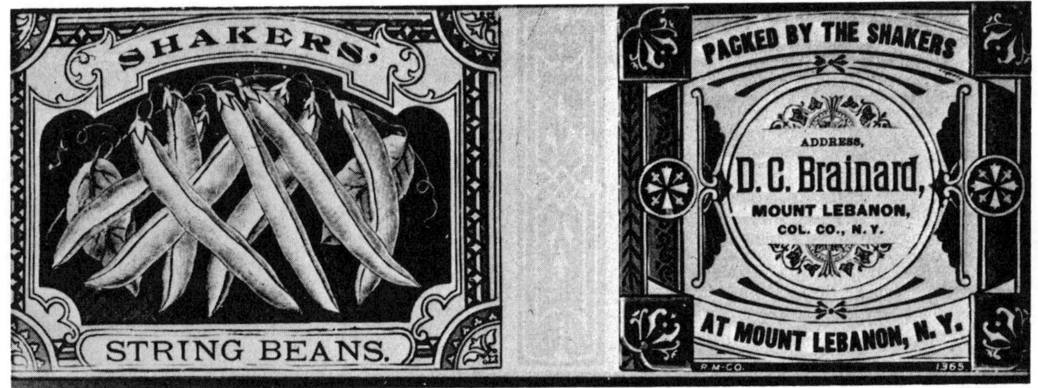

products, and "worldly" methods of advertising were adopted. Brightly printed seed boxes and labels were ordered from outside printers, and posters and banners were sent to dealers to promote Shaker seeds.

As early as 1836 the New Lebanon Shakers saw the value of printed matter in helping to promote their seed industry. The first *Gardener's Manual* was printed in that year. It contained "Plain and Practical Directions for the Cultivation and Management of Some of the Most Useful Culinary Vegetables." The *Manual* contained a list of the various kinds of garden seeds raised in the United Society at New Lebanon and a "few general remarks on the management of a kitchen garden." Charles F. Crosman was the author or editor of this leaflet, which was sold to dealers for three or four cents. The dealers, in turn, charged their customers six cents for the informative booklet, listing twenty-seven different vegetables, from asparagus to turnip. Many of the vegetable seeds were variations developed and grown by the Shakers alone.

Another manual, more complete in its instructions for planning and planting a kitchen garden, was issued in 1843. It contained twelve chapters ranging from "Directions for the selection of a garden spot and implements"

Following the Civil War, labels were printed in bright colors by outside printers. OLD CHATHAM.

to "Preservation of vegetables in winter," and "Recipes for Cookery" and "Pickling." In 1870 a *Descriptive Catalogue of Vegetable Seeds, Raised at New Lebanon, N. Y."* gave the varieties of seeds available, with directions for their cultivation.

Packaging, alone, became a major time-consuming task for both Shaker men and women. Shaker labels were printed on Shaker-made and-invented label presses. Since the labels contained directions for planting, someone had to write them. The paper bags were cut and glued by the Shakers, also. In January, 1847 a journal kept by the head gardeners at New (Mount) Lebanon had an entry that tells us "Samuel W. says he has printed 30 thousand [bags] in one day when the press worked well, and run steady." This same journal also tells us that on the twenty-ninth of the same month "Gideon has put up 6000 papers of Cucumber seeds this week." By February 3, "Samuel W." had finished printing "The common small baggs." He had printed altogether 200,000 of them. While the sisters were generally responsible for cutting and pasting the "small baggs," obviously the work of printing them fell to the brethren.

A large percentage of the Shakers' vast landholdings was used for the growing of seeds, and much of the Shaker labor went into the tedious work of planting, growing, harvesting, culling, and packaging the seeds. All available hands were put to work where and when they were needed, since the garden seed industry provided many of the families with a substantial portion of their income. It is difficult to comprehend that many other industries were carried on simultaneously with the garden seed industry and that buildings were built and furniture and clothing were made at the same time.

The closely related herbal medicine business, also important economically to the Shakers, was another year-round project that required a lot of attention and labor.

It is no wonder that inventions and innovations in farm machinery, printing presses, and other equipment that would lighten the burden of those Shakers involved in these two agrarian occupations were of major importance, although patenting these inventions was neglected. A machine for filling seed bags, invented at Watervliet, saved countless hours. A threshing machine and fertilizing machine are credited to the creative Shakers. A rotary or revolving harrow was the invention of Daniel W. Baird

TOP: *Stack of seed boxes from Mount Lebanon. Sieve on top is Shaker product, also.* OLD CHATHAM.

BOTTOM: *Advertising banner for Shaker garden seeds.* BELFIT.

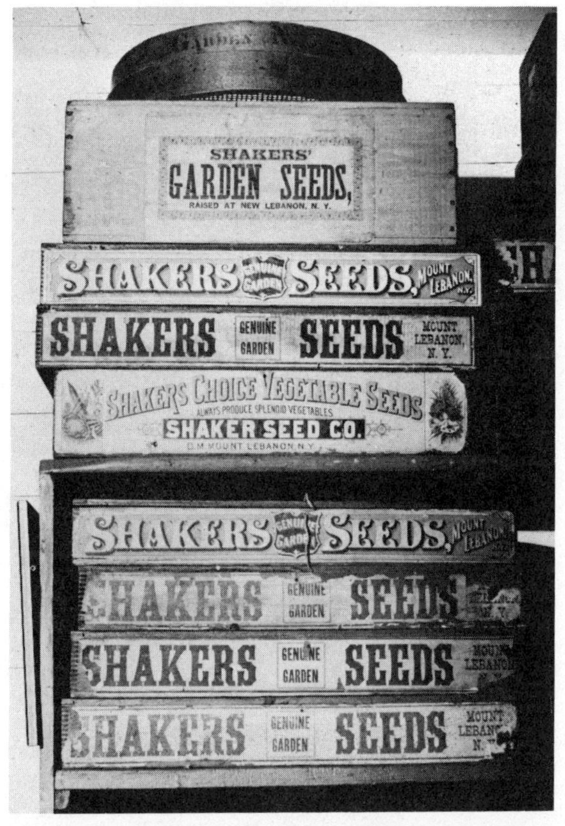

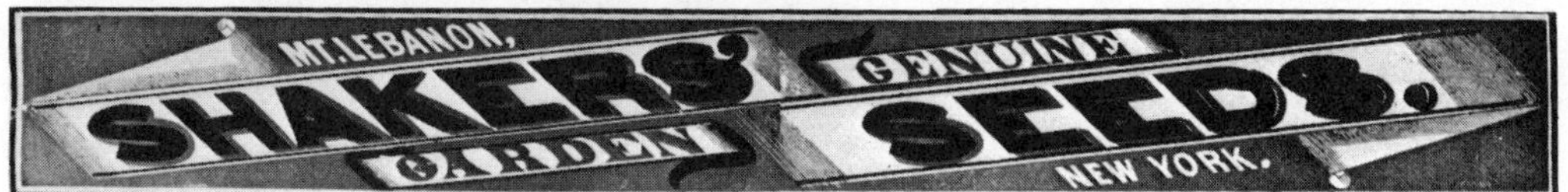

of North Union, Ohio. Many other laborsaving devices were Shaker inventions that were aids in using their time and energy more productively.

The decline of the garden seed industry as an important means of income for the Shakers came about slowly and for the same reasons that other Shaker farm industries declined. As there were less and less members and families consolidated, land was sold. By 1900 there were only a thousand Shakers, and by 1930 that number had decreased by eight hundred; the majority of the remaining two hundred Shakers were women. The task of keeping up their own kitchen gardens to supply food for their tables was a problem, and other types of farming were gradually abandoned. For all practical purposes, the garden seed industry was abandoned by the Shakers before the turn of the century.

CHAPTER 5

SHAKER HERBS AND MEDICINES

Those appointed as physicians or nurses, should give to the Elders from time to time, a full account of their proceedings with the family in regard to the administration of medicine. Millenial Laws, 1821, Revised 1845.

In their belief that they should be separate from the world and independent and self-sufficient, the Shakers appointed certain members of each family to look after the health of its members. As stated in the Millenial Laws, "The order of God forbids that Believers should employ Doctors of the world, except in some extreme cases, or the case of a sick child, whose parents are among the world, and desire such aid; and in such cases, the Ministry or Elders should decide whether it be proper or not."

Trained doctors were not easily found in any case in the late eighteenth century, especially in the isolated rural areas that the Shakers had chosen as settlements. Anyone could call himself "Doctor", and those remedies available on the world's market were, for the most part,

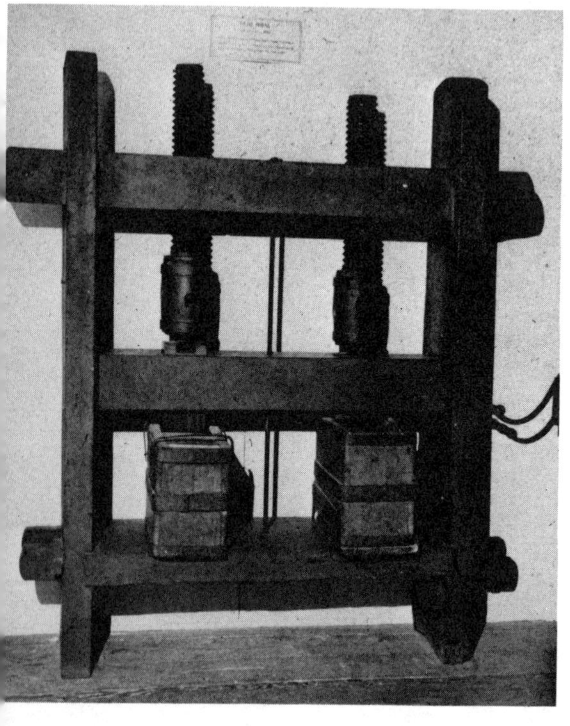

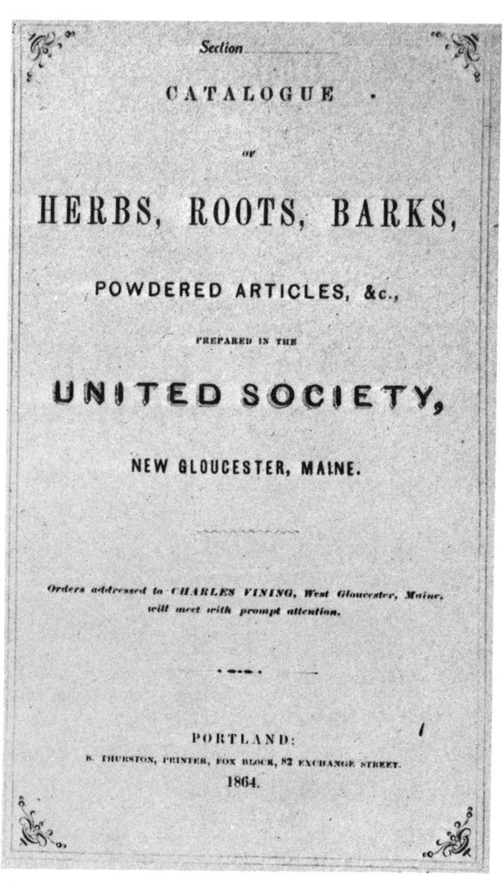

Section

CATALOGUE

OF

HERBS, ROOTS, BARKS,

POWDERED ARTICLES, &c.,

PREPARED IN THE

UNITED SOCIETY,

NEW GLOUCESTER, MAINE.

Orders addressed to CHARLES VINING, West Gloucester, Maine, will meet with prompt attention.

PORTLAND:

B. THURSTON, PRINTER, FOX BLOCK, 82 EXCHANGE STREET.

1864.

LEFT: *Double press for compressing herbs and roots into compact blocks.* OLD CHATHAM.

RIGHT: *Cover of catalogue listing herbs, roots, and barks sold by Maine Shakers.* OLD CHATHAM.

homemade concoctions with unidentified ingredients. There is little doubt that the Shakers were better off caring for their own sick and administering their own homemade medicines. It was a short step from making herbal medicines for their own use to making and marketing their cures as a business.

Since the Shaker communities were originally set up as agrarian societies, they searched for ways to utilize nature's products as a means of earning money to support themselves. The ability of the Shakers to see the possibilities for economic opportunity in the herbal medicine business was typical of their enterprise in utilizing many

HOLLYHOCK FLOWERS,
Althæa rosea.
D. M. & Co.,
WATERVLIET, N. Y.

Feverfew.
D. M. & Co.
Watervliet, N. Y.

HYSSOP.
Hyssopus officinalis.
D. M. & Co.
WATERVLIET, N. Y.

FLEABANE.
Erigeron canadense.
D. M. & Co.
WATERVLIET, N. Y.

Goldenrod.
Solidago odora
D. M. & Co.
Watervliet N. Y.

LOBELIA
Inflata.
D. M. & Co.
Watervliet, N. Y.

Slippery Elm
(Ground.)
Ulmus fulva
D. M. & Co.
Watervliet, N Y

SWEET MARJORUM.
Origanum marjorana.
D. M. & Co.
WATERVLIET, N. Y.

Pennyroyal.
D. M. & Co.
Watervliet, N. Y.

FOXGLOVE,
Digitalis purpurea.
D. M. & Co.
Watervliet, N. Y.

EXTRACT MANDRAKE.
PODOPHYLLUM PELTATUM.

PARSLEY ROOT.
Apium Petroselinum,
D. M. & Co.,
WATERVLIET, N. Y.

HOREHOUND.
Marrubium vulgare.
D. M. & Co.
Watervliet, N. Y.

Black Henbane,
Hyoscyamus niger.
D. M. & Co.,
WATERVLIET, N. Y.

BLOOD ROOT.
Sanguinaria canadensis.
D. M. & Co.
WATERVLIET, N. Y.

Group of Shaker printed labels for herbal medicine business. Flowers were grown only for this purpose and were raised in rows, like vegetables. OLD CHATHAM.

Cabinet for filing labels and stacks of packaged herbs. OLD CHATHAM.

of the natural products on their own land. In keeping with their beliefs that everything they produced must be useful and that the decorative was sinful and a waste, they grew only what could be utilized by them or sold to support their communities.

Flower gardens were purely utilitarian and flowers that could be utilized in the manufacture of medicines or other salable and useful products were grown with no thought to their beauty. Flower gardens were laid out in rows like vegetables and were considered to be crops. Flowers were used in the manufacture of dye for textiles as well as for medicinal products. One of the earliest Shaker products made from flowers was rose water. This product was being sold in the New Lebanon community as early as 1809.

The Shakers became known for their medicines and tonics very early in the nineteenth century. Tree bark and leaves were utilized along with Shaker-grown herbs, flowers, and other plants. Records show that little trade in herbal medicines took place among the Shakers until 1820. By 1830 the Shaker herbal medicine business was well established and by the middle of the century in most Shaker communities was run on a semi-automated

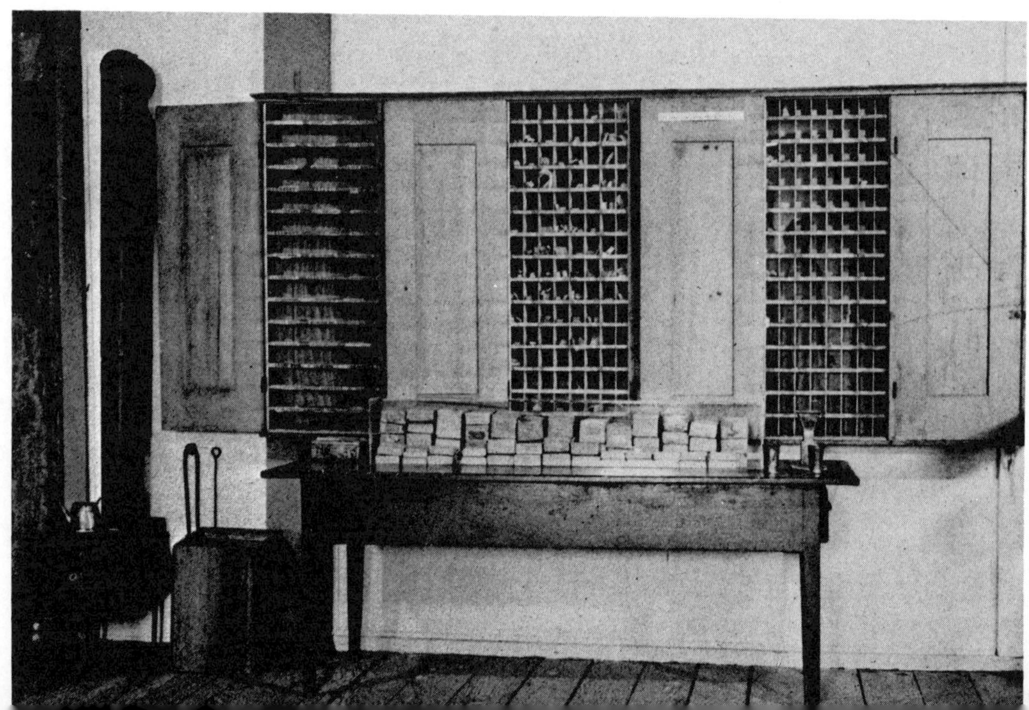

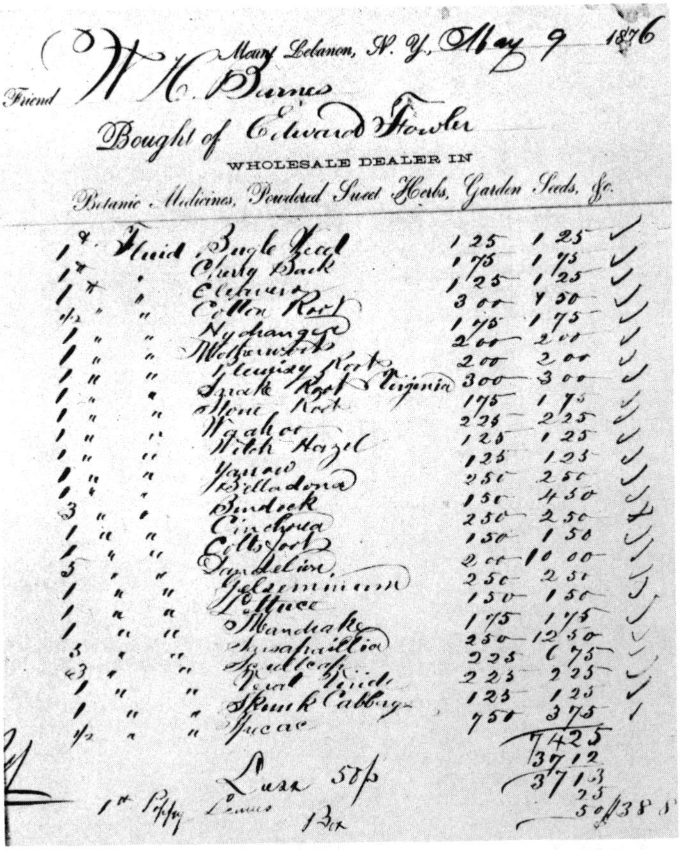

Invoice for Shaker "Botanic Medicines" dated 1876. OLD CHATHAM.

basis. The drying and preparation, as well as the gathering of the plants, were the business of the women. Sales lists of mid-century show the Shakers to have had a rather extensive knowledge of both the wild-growing and cultivated herbs and other plants of their area.

By 1828 the Shakers of New Lebanon and other communities were shipping rather large quantities of products such as Flour of Elm, Pressed Elder Flowers, Oak Jerusalem, Spikenard, Ground Ivy, and Wormwood to dealers in pharmaceutical supplies. The refinement and packaging of raw products became a lucrative part of the herbal business. Large orders of herbs were also

Since the Shakers could not grow or gather all herbs and roots needed in their successful medicinal herb business, they advertised for additional supplies. OLD CHATHAM.

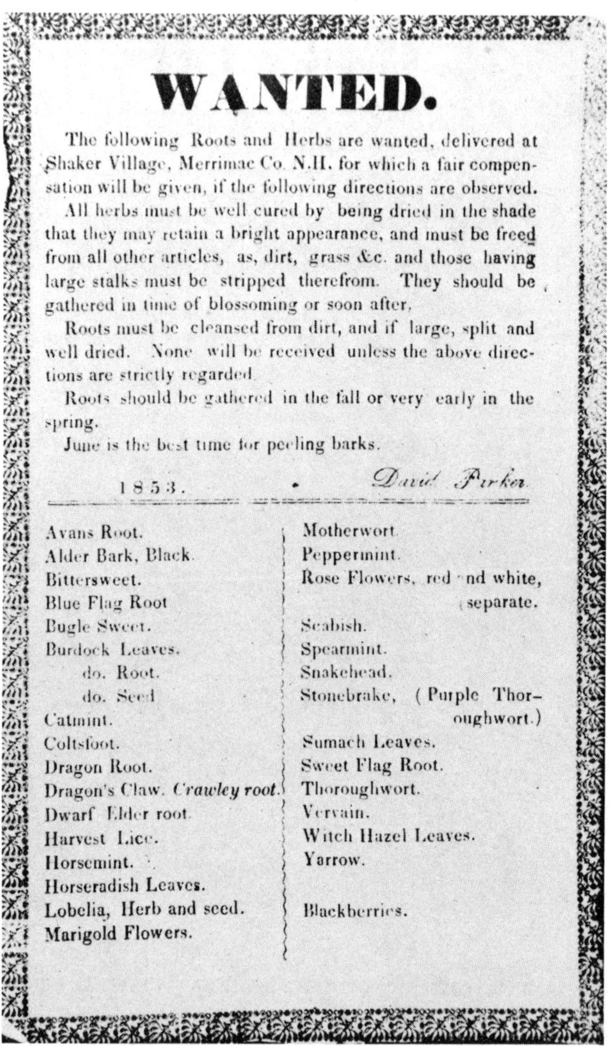

WANTED.

The following Roots and Herbs are wanted, delivered at Shaker Village, Merrimac Co. N.H. for which a fair compensation will be given, if the following directions are observed.

All herbs must be well cured by being dried in the shade that they may retain a bright appearance, and must be freed from all other articles, as, dirt, grass &c. and those having large stalks must be stripped therefrom. They should be gathered in time of blossoming or soon after.

Roots must be cleansed from dirt, and if large, split and well dried. None will be received unless the above directions are strictly regarded.

Roots should be gathered in the fall or very early in the spring.

June is the best time for peeling barks.

1853. David Parker.

Avans Root.
Alder Bark, Black.
Bittersweet.
Blue Flag Root
Bugle Sweet.
Burdock Leaves.
do. Root.
do. Seed
Catmint.
Coltsfoot.
Dragon Root.
Dragon's Claw. *Crawley root.*
Dwarf Elder root.
Harvest Lice.
Horsemint.
Horseradish Leaves.
Lobelia, Herb and seed.
Marigold Flowers.

Motherwort.
Peppermint.
Rose Flowers, red and white, separate.
Scabish.
Spearmint.
Snakehead.
Stonebrake, (Purple Thoroughwort.)
Sumach Leaves.
Sweet Flag Root.
Thoroughwort.
Vervain.
Witch Hazel Leaves.
Yarrow.

Blackberries.

shipped abroad, notably to one Charles Whitlaw, botanist, in London.

While wild herbs constituted the early business in this category of Shaker commerce, by 1836 herbs were being cultivated in Shaker gardens to satisfy the demand from the Shakers' customers for these products. Unable to produce all that were needed, the Shakers also purchased quantities of herbs from outside sources. There were many herbs that could not be grown in the New York and New England climate. However, plants not indigenous to these areas appeared in Shaker catalogs as early as 1832. In 1850 a physics garden at New Lebanon covered fifty acres of land. Hyoscyamus, belladonna, taratacum, aconite, poppy, lettuce, sage, summer savory, marjoram, dock, burdock, valerian, and horehound are some of the plants that were grown. Other indigenous wild plants, leaf, and bark were collected and still others purchased from various sources in America and abroad.

A direct offshoot of the packaging and selling of herbs and roots was the development of the extract and medicine business which brought many Shaker families a large proportion of their income for many years. During the second half of the nineteenth century anyone could manufacture medicine, using any ingredients, and there were a great many products being promoted in America that did more harm than good to a healthy person and could be extremely damaging (although soothing) to the sick. The Shakers had a reputation for cleanliness and honesty that made their herbal medicines extremely successful.

The medicine manufacturing and packaging became a lucrative industry for the Shakers and certain members earned worldwide reputations for their special concoctions. Contrary to other business enterprises where individual Shakers were not given credit for a product they had developed, many Shaker herbalists gained immortality with the development of a "soothing syrup" or an asthma cure. The addition of the Shaker name helped sell the product and there is little doubt that, among the thousands of terrible concoctions made by less conscientious, self-styled "doctors" and "chemists" of the period, the Shaker medicines were superior.

A page from a Shaker Brethren's journal dated September 1862 explains how Shaker medicines were prepared:

3rd Wed. Alonzo goes to Hudson with Andrew after Savin.

5th Fri. To make 76 lbs Savin Ointment. Thus, Weigh out 33 lbs. lard and 18 lbs. green Savin leaves and fine twigs chopped. Cook them together until the leaves begin to crisp; strain out the leaves and add 3¾ lbs. of rosin, the regular proportion, and 7 lbs. of beeswax, being one pound more than the regular proportion, and one cake of spermatic and strain in pots to cool. This, added to what we had on hand, makes 108 lbs. Savin ointment. The sisters distill wormwood while I am absent. Emanuel painting and assisting Robert all this week.

6th Sat. Finish distilling Wormwood Oil, having done a kettle full every day but 1 since the 12th of Aug. 12 lbs. oil. Alonzo putting up extracts.

8th Mon. Grind about 130 or 40 lbs. Inspicated Circuta down cellar and put up 110 lbs. in a 10 gallon keg for Lee Sissons & Co.

A study of the ingredients used in the manufacture of "Savin Ointment" might be of interest. Savin, or

A Collection of Medicinal Receipts for the use of Physicians compiled by Sarah A. Standish

Bitters for jaundice —
Take Balmony, Barberry & Poplar bark equal parts. Pulverize —
One ounce of the powders to a pint of hot water & half a pint of spirits
Dose half a wine glass -
for hot bitters add a teaspoonful of No 2.

Wheatons Bitters
White Wood bark of the root - one table spoonful, Bloodroot one teaspoonfull
Mandrake one teaspoonfull
Cinnamon & Cloves as much as you like to one Quart of spirits
shake it often — take a spoonful one hour before meals.

Undated "receipts" for Shaker Bitters. As with all nineteenth-century bitters, the main ingredient was alcohol. OLD CHATHAM.

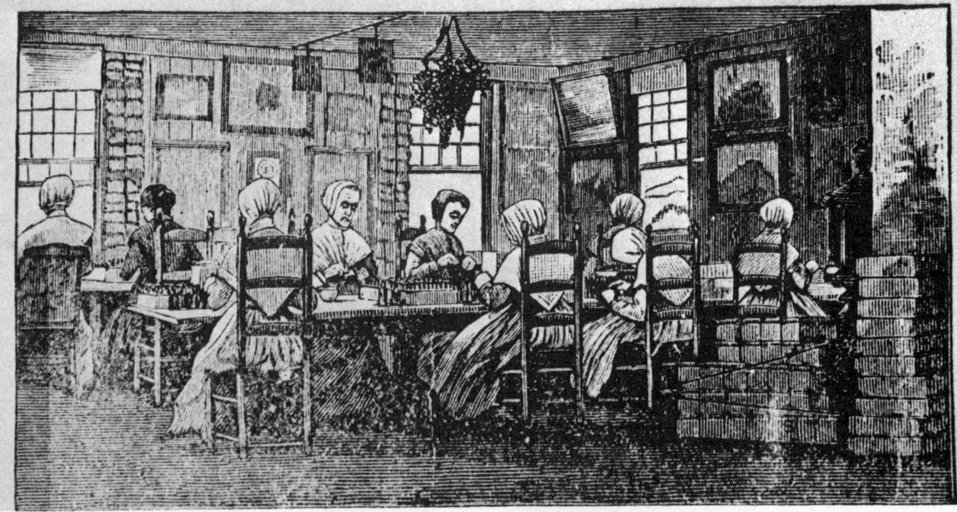

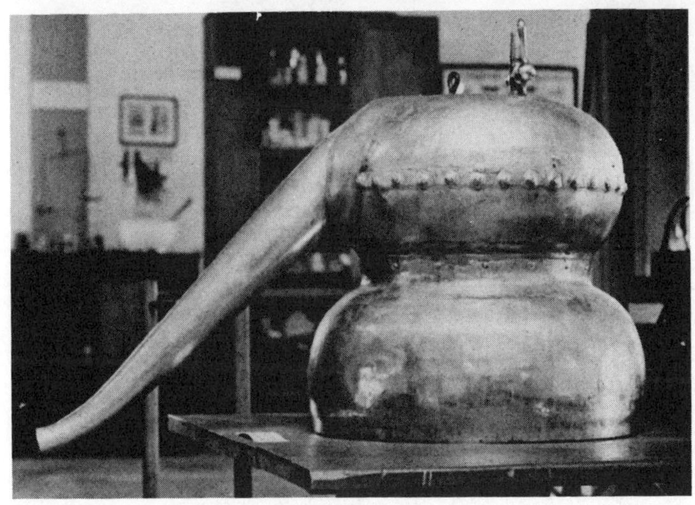

Sabine, is a member of the Juniper family and is indigenous to North America. As an external medication it was known as a cure for gout. An extract of the same plant, if taken internally, was also known to have been an abortifacient. The "spermatic" mentioned by the

TOP: *Engraving from 1884 Shaker* Almanac. MATTATUCK.

BOTTOM: *Shaker-made copper still head for the manufacture of witch hazel.* OLD CHATHAM.

30 THE MYSTERY EXPLAINED.

THE SHAKERS

Have had an experience of *fifty years* in growing and preparing Roots, Barks and Herbs.

Everything made by the Shakers is good beyond a doubt. Their character stands very high.

Everything that the Shakers make sells readily, and always gives satisfaction.

When the Shakers put their name on an article you can rely upon it.

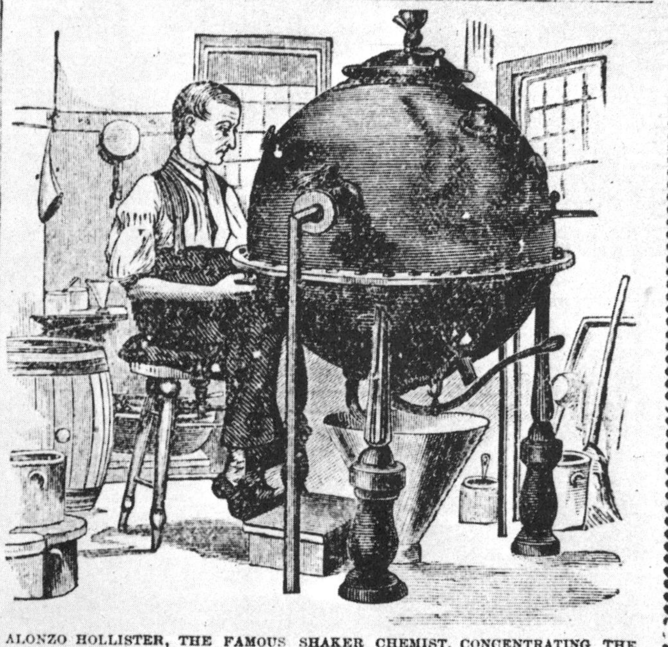

ALONZO HOLLISTER, THE FAMOUS SHAKER CHEMIST, CONCENTRATING THE SHAKER EXTRACT OF ROOTS, OR SEIGEL'S SYRUP, IN VACUUM PAN, MOUNT LEBANON, N. Y.

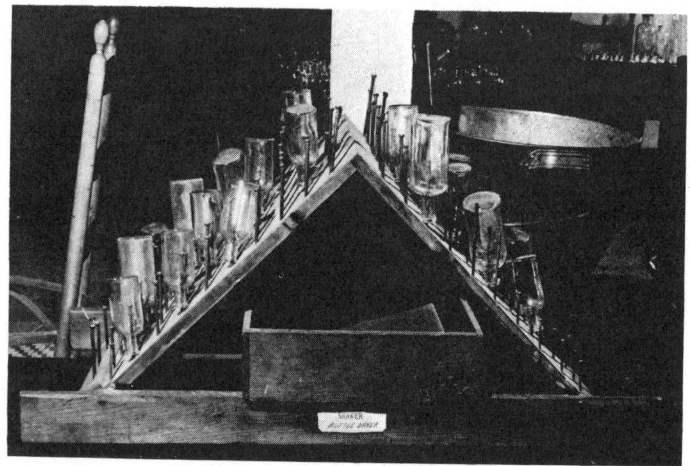

TOP: *Copy of engraving from Shaker* Almanac. OLD CHATHAM.

BOTTOM: *Functional drying rack for bottles was made by inserting long nails in boards.* OLD CHATHAM.

Shaker brethren is really spermaceti, a white waxy solid which separates from the oil of the sperm whale and was used in making candles and ointments. The lard, rosin, and beeswax were also vehicles to hold the savin extract.

The Shaker sisters were, meanwhile, engaged in the manufacture of a more interesting product. Wormwood, which had to have been imported from Europe since it does not grow in North America, is the woody herb from which a bitter and very potent "medicine" was made. It is to be hoped that the sisters did not feel it necessary to taste their product too often. What the sisters

TOP: *Shaker carrying rack for bottles of medicine.* OLD CHATHAM.

BOTTOM: *Box of corked bottles used in medicinal trade by Shakers. The Shakers did not make their own bottles.* OLD CHATHAM.

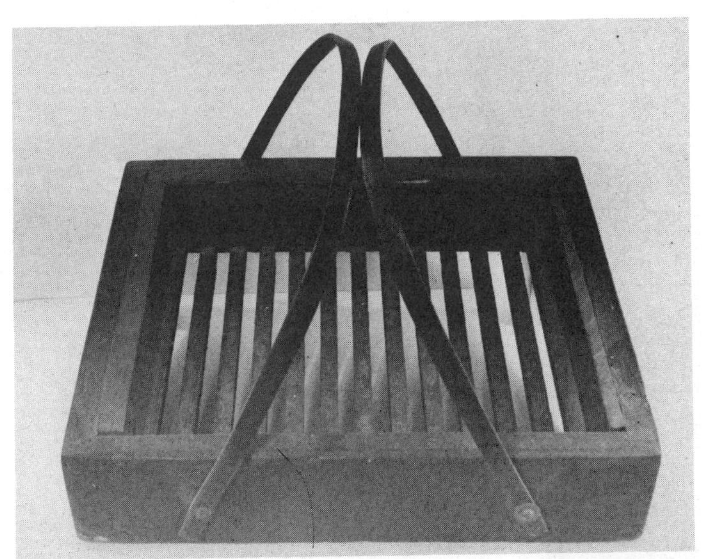

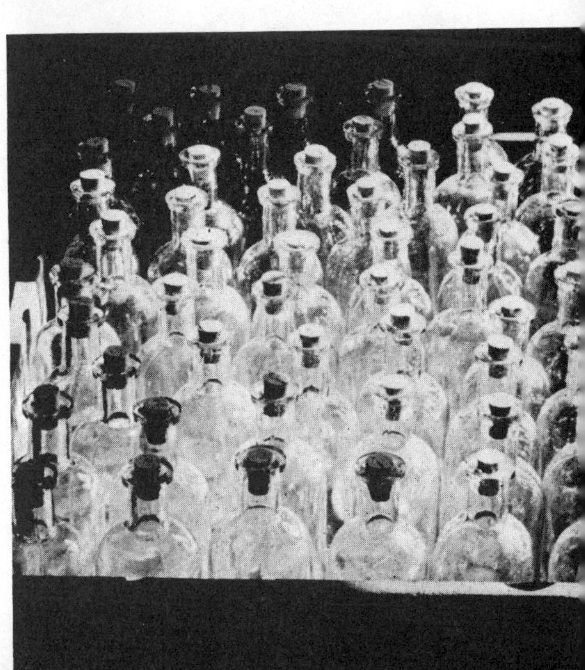

Shaker stencils for marking shipping boxes for herbal medicine business. OLD CHATHAM.

OPPOSITE: *Advertisement for popular Shaker product.* OLD CHATHAM.

were distilling and our Shaker writer finished preparing was absinthe.

One can only speculate on the use to which Lee Sissons & Co. put the 110 pounds of "Inspicated Cicuta." That is a very large amount of deadly poisonous hemlock.

Throughout most of the nineteenth century, medicine was made up mainly of extracts of natural herbs, flowers and roots, often mixed with a base of alcohol. There was little else available to give relief to the sick. The Shakers seemed to have an excellent knowledge of the curative powers of herbs and other materials from nature. Many of their products became extremely important during the Civil War, when all effective painkillers were in short supply. Opium, made from Shaker-grown poppies, sold at "a large price" during the war. New (Mount) Lebanon, Watervliet, Harvard, Canterbury, Enfield

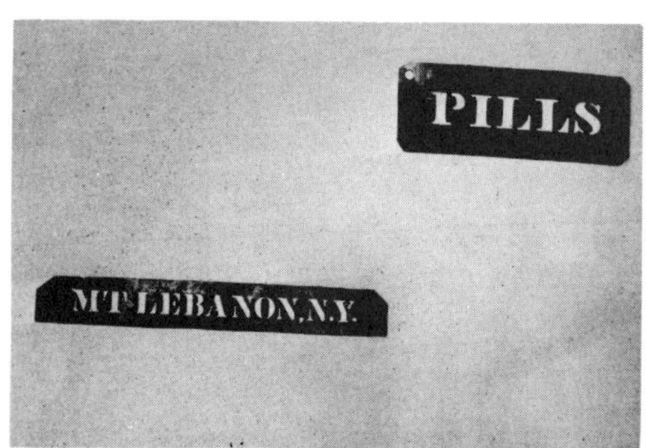

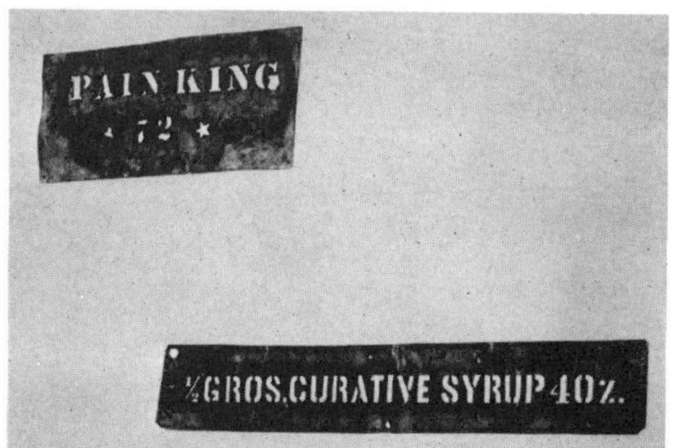

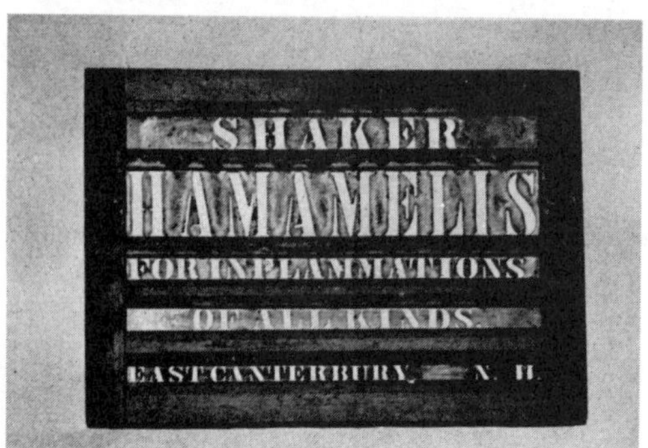

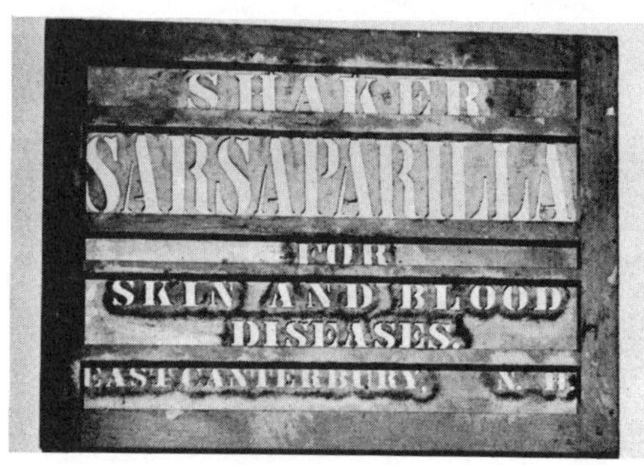

SHAKER PREPARATION.

THE GENIUS OF BEAUTY!

Toilet Prize & Sufferer's Panacea,

OR

IMPERIAL ROSE BALM.

UNEQUALED FOR

CLEANSING THE TEETH,

Healing Sore or Spongy Gums, or the Apthous Sore Mouth of Children, and cleansing Foul Ulcers; curing Pimples, Tetters, Ringworms, Salt Rheum; Softening, Whitening and Healing Sore Face; cure for Chapped Hands or Face; cures Burns, Scalds and Bruised Skin; cure for Freckles, Sunburn, &c. A beautiful and useful article as a Toilet Soap. An excellent Shaving Fluid. Gentlemen should use it to shave with and rub on the face immediately after. This article is excellent for Cleansing Kid Gloves, or Toilet wares.

This Balm is a beautiful Perfume, and is warranted free from all those injurious acids and acidulated powders often sold for whitening and cleansing the teeth, which often positively ruin them, using in their stead the most cleansing and healing curatives. We think its equal is not before the public.

There are in this Balm ten of the Best Curatives for Skin Diseases, Ulcers, &c., &c., and nothing injurious.

DIRECTIONS.

To Cleanse the Teeth—Put three or four drops on a soft tooth brush, and brush the mouth and gums.

For Shaving—Put a few drops on a soft lather brush and rub over the face, then slightly dip the brush in hot water and rub as with common lather of shaving soap.

As a Wash for the Face—Put a small tea spoonful in as much water, and rub on with a soft sponge, lather brush, towel, or with the hand, as suits best.

For Sore Mouth—Mix a tea spoonful with its bulk of water, and hold in the mouth as long as consistent, thoroughly rinsing the mouth.

To Clean Clothing—Put a few drops on the garment where greased or soiled, and rub thoroughly.

For Chapped Hands—Apply the Balm clear, a few drops.

For Scalds or Burns—Use the Balm clear, a few drops.

For Chapped or Sore Face—Put a few drops in as much water, and rub over the face.

Prepared only by the SHAKER SOCIETY,
New Lebanon, Columbia Co., N. Y.,

And sold by Druggists and Fancy Goods Dealers. Persons wishing to Purchase for sale, address

THOMAS ESTES or RUFUS CROSSMAN,
New Lebanon, Columbia Co., N. Y.

TOP: *Embossed blown-in-mold bottle for "Shaker Syrup." Syrup was made by the North Family of Canterbury, New Hampshire, Shakers. Aqua glass. Height, 8 inches.* BELFIT.

BOTTOM: *Shaker witch hazel sold in great quantities.* OLD CHATHAM.

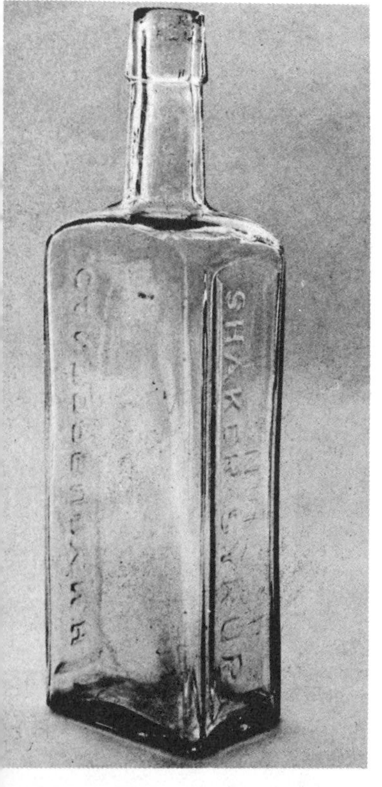

(New Hampshire) and New Gloucester were the Shaker communities that all carried on lucrative herbal medicine businesses throughout the nineteenth century.

In the latter half of the nineteenth century Shaker medicines became well known throughout this country and abroad, with England becoming a major market for certain products. During a period when anyone could make and sell remedies and when there were no controls as to cleanliness during preparation or as to what ingredients or proportions went into a product, there were thousands of "cures" on the market that were produced under less than sanitary conditions. The Shakers, with their reputation for honesty and cleanliness, manufactured and packaged medicines that were cleaner, safer, and more standardized than the products of their competitors.

By mid-century, when the herbal medicine business became a major source of income for the Shaker communities that were involved in it, buildings were constructed on their property for the purpose of drying and preparing the huge quantities of herbs, roots, and other natural material that the Shakers marketed or used in the manufacture of their own brands of cures. Storing and drying were but two of the functions of the herbal barns. Extracts were prepared and syrup and pills were made. A section of each building was given over to the cleaning and

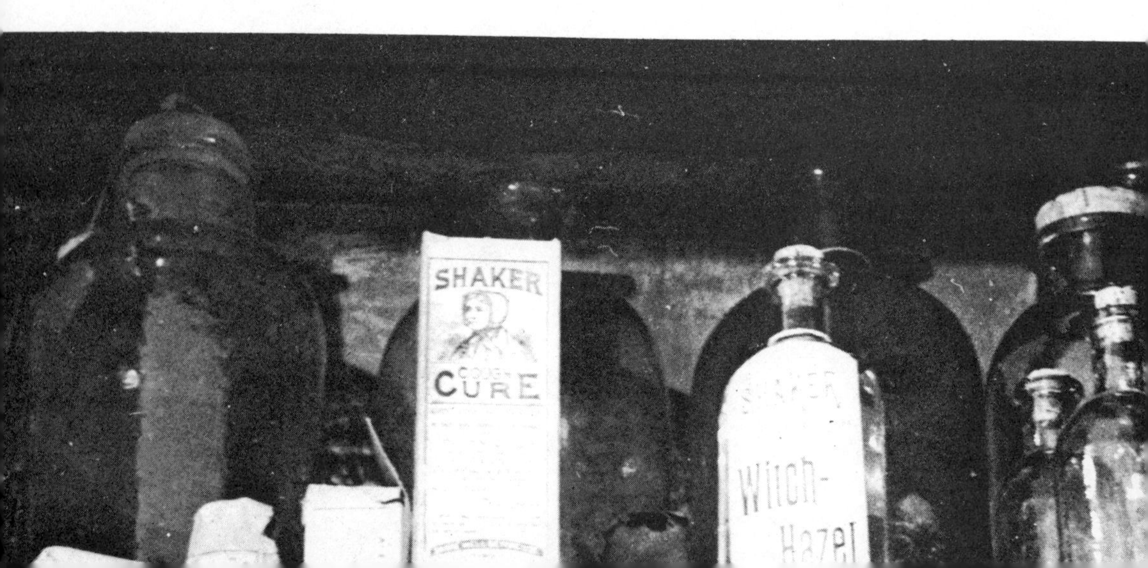

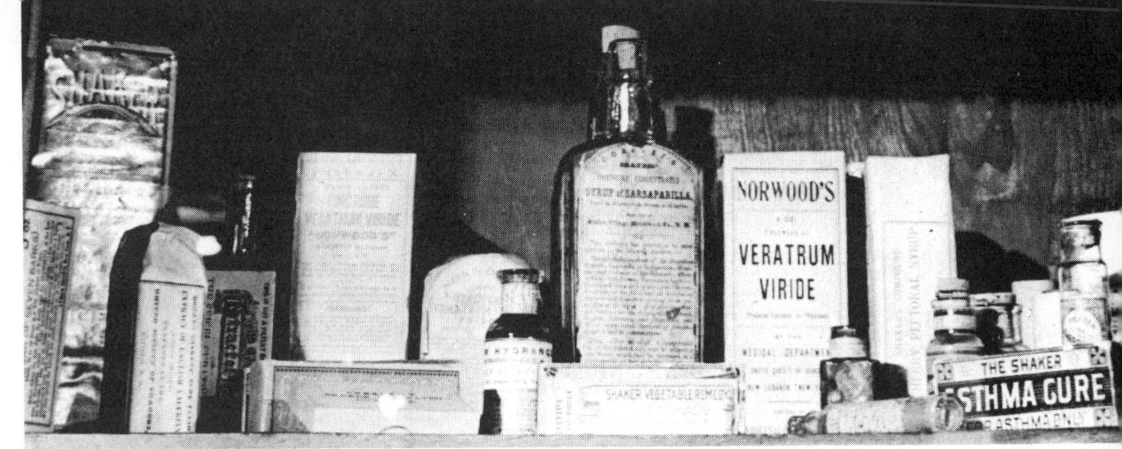

steaming of the plants and another section was used for sorting, packaging, and the printing of labels. Many of the herbs were compressed into blocks for storage or shipping. Roots were pulverized and various ointments were made.

While many of the Shaker communities strove to be as self-sufficient as possible, there was no rule dictating that certain products that were inexpedient for the Shakers to manufacture could not be purchased from outside sources. Since they did not engage in glassblowing, bottles and other ceramic and glass vessels needed in the preparation and packaging of medicines were purchased elsewhere. In 1856 the Boston and Sandwich Glass Company supplied several dozen half-gallon, three-pint, and quart blown jugs and bottles. Other bottles and jars were purchased from such manufacturers as Dexter and Nellegar, Albany; Schieffelin Bros. & Co., New York; and A.B. Sands from New York. The firm of Mc Kesson and Robbins of New York also supplied covered jars in the same year to the New Lebanon Shakers. Pottery jars were made in Bennington, Vermont for some of the Shaker products.

Self-sealing preserve jars were purchased from Nathan Clark, Jr., of New York City. The date of this revolutionary type of preserve jar should be of interest to today's

Group of medicines with labels and cartons. "Mother Siegel's Laxative Syrup" and "Veratrum Viride" were important products for Shakers. OLD CHATHAM.

FLUID EXTRACT.

COLCHICUM SEED.

Colchicum Autumnale.

TINCTURE. Fluid Extract, Two ounces; Diluted Alcohol. Six ounces

DOSE—Ten to thirty drops.

SYRUP. Fluid Extract, Two ounces; Syrup, Fourteen ounces

DOSE—One quarter to one dram.

WINE. Fluid Extract, Six ounces; Sherry Wine, Two pints

DOSE—One quarter to half dram.

MIXTURE. Wine of Colchicum, One ounce; Fluid Extract Opium, Half dram; Syrup, Two ounces

DOSE—One and a half to three drams.

FLUID EXTRACT.

LOBELIA.

Lobelia Inflata.

TINCTURE. Fluid Extract, Two ounces; Diluted Alcohol, One Pint

DOSE—One to Three Drams.

INFUSION. Fluid Extract, Two ounces; Water, Two pints

DOSE—One ounce every half hour till vomiting ensues

SYRUP. Fluid Extract, One ounce; Syrup, Five ounces

DOSE—Two drams.

FLUID EXTRACT.

MOTHERWORT.

Leonorus Cardiaca.

INFUSION. Fluid Extract, One ounce; Hot Water, One pint

DOSE—One to two ounces.

Shaker printed labels for medicinal extracts. OLD CHATHAM.

bottle collectors, since 1856 is early for the manufacture of any jars with "self-sealing" lids.

Early in the history of Shaker herbal and medicine business, a printing device for labels was constructed and used at various communities. Labels were hand printed by the thousands on various colored papers. As the herbal medicine business became widespread, labels were printed or electrotyped outside the communities. Thousands of labels were ordered each year, and existing Shaker accounts indicate how popular their herbal products were. In 1862 an order for twenty thousand printed labels was sent to Lewis and Goodwin of Albany. Paper and twill bags were purchased for the packaging of herbs. Similar bags were used in the seed business as well. In the year 1870 the sisters of the Second Order at Mount Lebanon cut more than a million labels for use in their herbal and extract trade.

While one million labels might seem like an enormous and possibly exaggerated amount, the Shaker *Almanac* for 1884 makes the claim that "the Shakers have sent to London alone 15,000,000 bottles of their EXTRACT OF ROOTS, to cure dyspepsia." The famous extract was not the only curative medicine exported by the Shakers. Obviously, a great many labels were needed.

Parties who wish the Agency for the sale of our goods will please fill up this form and return to us.

SHIPPING DIRECTIONS.

Order for Shaker Extract and Pills to be sent on Commission, to be paid for when sold. I agree to distribute all Pamphlets and to make prompt settlements for what Medicines I sell—your portion of the money received for the Medicine to be held sacred for you; all Medicines not sold I agree to hold subject to your order without any charge. I also agree to pay the freight on arrival of the goods, the same to be deducted from your share of the money.

Write full name, ...

Post Office, ...

County, ...

State, ...

Name of Rail Road Station nearest my place,

....

Occupation, ...

No. of English Pamphlets required, ...

No. of German Pamphlets required, ...

(Please fill out the Blanks for Pamphlets and affix your card in print.)

THE SHAKER EXTRACT OF ROOTS,

Or SEIGEL'S CURATIVE SYRUP.

PRICE LIST.

Retail Price, ... 60 cts. per bottle.
1 Dozen, ... $4.80

SHAKER FAMILY PILLS.

Retail Price, ... 25 cts. per box
1 Dozen, ... $2.00

SHAKER SOOTHING PLASTERS.

Retail Price, ... 25 cts. each
1 Dozen, ... $2.00

Copy of order blank for Shaker medicinal and health products.
OLD CHATHAM.

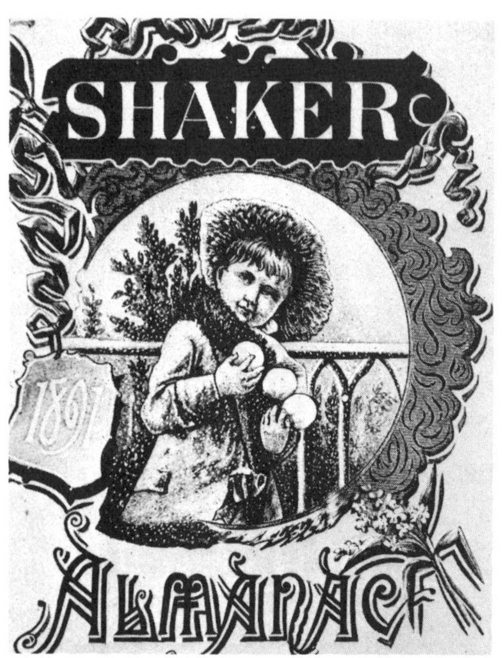

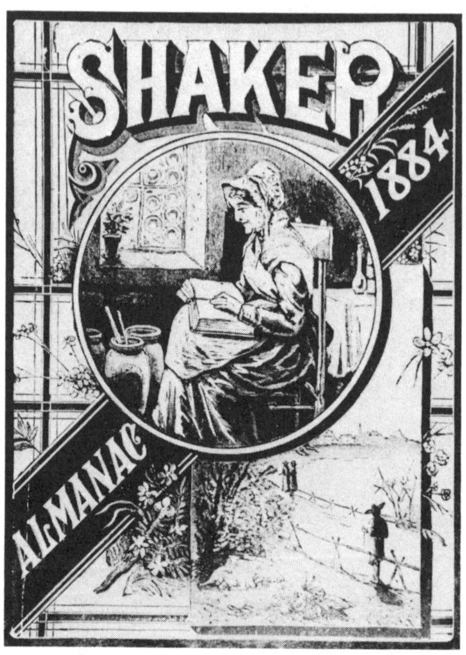

In order to advertise their medicinal products, the Shakers issued catalogs and almanacs. Stories of "Wonderful and Accidental Discoveries" concerning formulae for Shaker medicines appeared often. "Never-failing Shaker Extract of Roots", said to "release one from the shackles of disease," was advertised in a Shaker almanac of 1884. In a section called "The Shakers of Lebanon, New York," it was claimed: No one in America doubts for a moment any statement the Shakers may make. Every article they manufacture can be relied on as genuine. Every bottle of the Syrup contains the active medicinal virtues of more than one pound of Roots, Barks and Herbs in a very concentrated form. The bottles *contain more doses* than any other medicine in the market at the same price.

The Shakers have had an experience of *Fifty Years* in growing and preparing Roots, Barks, and Herbs.

Everything made by the Shakers is good beyond a doubt. Their character stands above reproach.

Everything that the Shakers make sells readily and always gives satisfaction.

In latter part of nineteenth century, almanacs were printed to advertise Shaker medicines. OLD CHATHAM.

Page from 1884 Shaker Almanac. MATTATUCK.

HOW TO READ CHARACTER

In presenting to the public our new Shaker Family Almanac for 1884, we desire to call attention to the subject of Character Reading from the formation and expression of the various features. The subject is one fraught with interest to every person—and the illustrations shown in the following pages have been carefully prepared and their correctness as indications of character may be depended on.

The Story of a Wonderful & Accidental Discovery,

As herein related, and to which your attention is directed, will be found one of the most interesting accounts of an important discovery that has ever been published—as has been proved by the fact that thousands of suffering people who have used the medicine are now in the enjoyment of perfect health—released from the shackles of disease by the never-failing Shaker Extract of Roots, or Mother Seigel's Curative Syrup.

Our New Shaker Family Almanac

We confidently recommend as the most reliable and trustworthy publication of its kind before the public. No care or expense has been spared in its preparation, and the astronomical calculations are the result of many months' untiring labor, both for us and the scientific men whose services we engaged for this purpose. Most of the so-called Almanacs are simply a rehash of the previous years' figures, and are utterly valueless. The Shaker Family Almanac forms a striking contrast when compared with publications of such a class.

The Shakers of Mount Lebanon, N. Y.

No one in America doubts for a moment any statement the Shakers may make. Every article they manufacture can be relied upon as genuine.

Every bottle of the Syrup contains the active medicinal virtues of more than one pound of Roots, Barks and Herbs in a very concentrated form. The bottles *contain more doses* than any other medicine in the market at the same price.

The Shakers have had an experience of *Fifty Years* in growing and preparing Roots, Barks and Herbs.

Everything made by the Shakers is good beyond a doubt. Their character stands above reproach.

Everything that the Shakers make sells readily, and always gives satisfaction.

When the Shakers put their name on an article you can rely upon it.

Should any one doubt about the medicine being made by the Shakers, they may address Benjamin Gates, Trustee of Shaker Community, Mt. Lebanon, N.Y.

PALPITATION OF THE HEART.

Flat Shoal, Surry Co., N. C.

Mr. A. J. White, 54 Warren St., New York.

Dear Sir:—I have used your Shaker Extract of Roots and consider it the best medicine I ever used. I have been afflicted with palpitation of the heart and other diseases for some time, and it has entirely cured me. Yours truly, D. A. TERRELL.

AN ILLUSTRATION of stinginess is cited by an Arkansaw editor, who knows a man who talks through his nose in order to save the wear and tear on his false teeth.

DYSPEPSIA.

Ervington, Va., Jan. 13, 1883.

Gentlemen:—I have used two bottles of Shaker Extract of Roots as prescribed, and have received greater

SICK HEADACHE.

Laurel Creek, Clay Co., Ky., March 10, 1883.

To Mr. A. J. White, 54 Warren St., New York.

Dear Sir:—Two bottles of your medicine cured my wife of sick headache, and has proved a magic in this county. Yours resp'y, D. V. NORN.

Almanacs printed many "unsolicited testimonials" extolling Shaker medicinal products. MATTATUCK.

When the Shakers put their name on an article you can rely upon it.

Should anyone doubt about the medicine being made by the Shakers, they may address Benjamin Gates, Trustee of Shaker Community, Mt. Lebanon, N. Y.

This article, lacking only a "money back if not satisfied" guarantee, illustrates that by the latter part of the century the Shakers had succumbed to more worldly methods of promoting their products. In keeping with the many other commercial almanacs of the period, this Shaker almanac also carried many letters of testimony to the effectiveness of Shaker Extract. Typical is the following, entitled "Liver and Kidney Diseases":

Mr. A. J. White, 54 Warren St., Batavia, N. Y. Dear Sir: I have been troubled for eight years with liver and kidney disease and have tried many patent and doctor's medicines, but they only relieved me for a short time. Finally I tried your Shaker Extract and to my astonishment it is really curing me, and I want to recommend it to all my afflicted neighbors and all the rest of mankind. Yours respectfully, B. C. Sawyer.

Attesting to the fact that Shaker medicines were as well known in England as they were in the United States by 1889, this same almanac includes three lengthy letters from satisfied customers in England, claiming that the Shaker Extract had cured such diverse chronic afflictions as "pains in the head," "indigestion," a "twelve-year cough," "diseases of the bowels," as well as "pains" and "fits." One letter claimed that the famous Extract had snatched the writer's husband "from the jaws of death."

Shaker Extract of Roots sold for sixty cents in 1889. Other popular products such as "Shaker Family Pills" for twenty-five cents and "Pain King" for fifty cents were

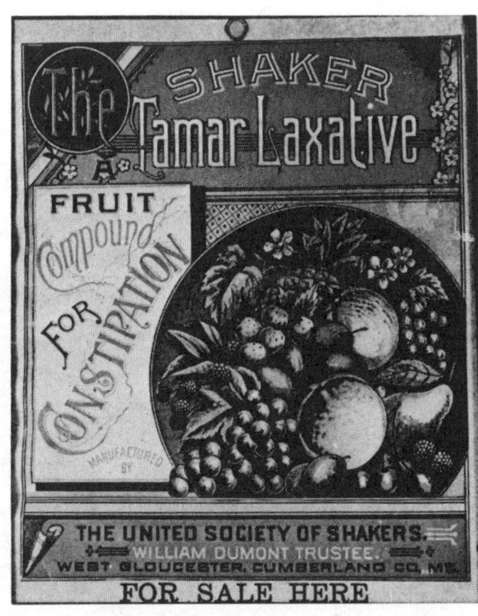

LEFT: *Advertising poster for laxative product made by Shakers.* OLD CHATHAM.

RE-IMPROVED ROCKING TRUSSES.

Single, Double, and Umbilical Trusses; adapted to all ages and sexes; for the relief and permanent cure of Hernia, or Rupture; invented, manufactured, applied and sold in the United Society of Shakers, in Canterbury, New Hampshire.

☞ All Orders to be addressed to THOMAS CORBETT, Shaker Village. Merrimack Co., N. H.

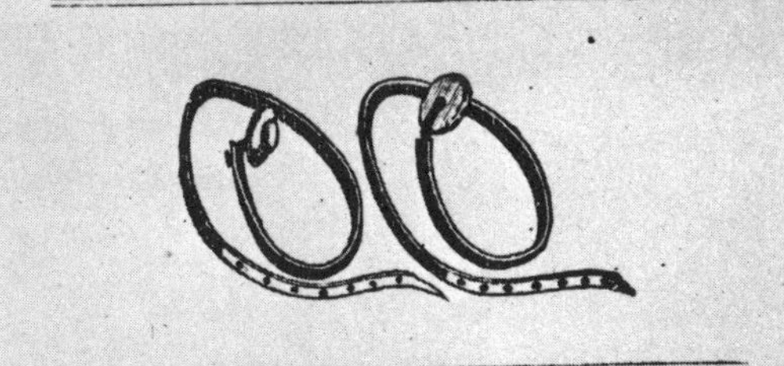

For more than thirty years past the Society have manufactured trusses of various construction for the cure of that painful disease, Hernia; and at different periods since that time have made such alterations and improvements as experience dictated, and the opinions of skilful and eminent surgeons suggested.

The Rocking Truss was invented about twenty years since, and improved about twelve years since; by which many radical cures have been effected, and great relief afforded in all cases where it

RIGHT: *Advertisement for another Shaker health aid.* OLD CHATHAM.

also advertised in this almanac. One popular product, "Mother Siegel's Curative Syrup", was sold in quantity during this period. It was manufactured by the Shakers of Mount Lebanon "who have had experience in growing herbs and extracting from them their best medicinal properties."

Toward the end of the century, even though the herbal medicine business was flourishing, the Shaker sect was not. By the end of the century there were only a thousand Shakers who could carry on the thriving industries of the various communities. The less popular products were abandoned and the relatively few Shakers struggled to keep the more profitable products on the market. One of their most popular products, Veratrum Viride, made by the Shakers at Mount Lebanon, was still being made and marketed in 1933. Not only the Shakers, but the many hundreds of other manufacturers of medicines in America had to abandon the manufacture of most of their products at the beginning of this century. The Pure Food and Drug Act of 1906 made the manufacture of many of the "miracle" cures too difficult. The percentage of alcohol and other addictive ingredients had to be clearly stated on labels. Since a great many medicines of the period were almost all alcohol, products had to be adjusted or abandoned. Shaker medicines were no exception, and it is probably just as well that other industries were used as a method of support for many of the Shaker communities in this century.

CHAPTER

6

SHAKER FOOD PRODUCTS

All not engaged in duty in the kitchens, are forbidden to throng them at mealtime, or at any time, unnecessarily, or to hold unnecessary conversation in them at any time. Millenial Laws, 1821. Revised, 1845.

Shaker kitchens, built for easy care and efficiency, were obviously busy places where no interruptions could be tolerated. The Shakers were good cooks and were fortunate in that all equipment they could wish for to aid in preparing food was made for them in the brethrens' shops. Besides the preparation of meals for each family, vegetables, fruits, and berries in season and other foods were preserved for the winter months to furnish Shaker tables with a variety of plain and wholesome fare.

The sisters of most families also prepared a great many food products to sell in their shops and eventually to outside sources for distribution and re-sale. Two food products for which the Shakers became well known began as kitchen industries and soon became important sources of income for the New York and New England Shakers.

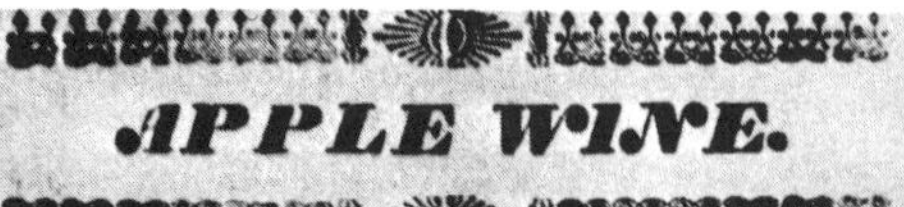
APPLE WINE.

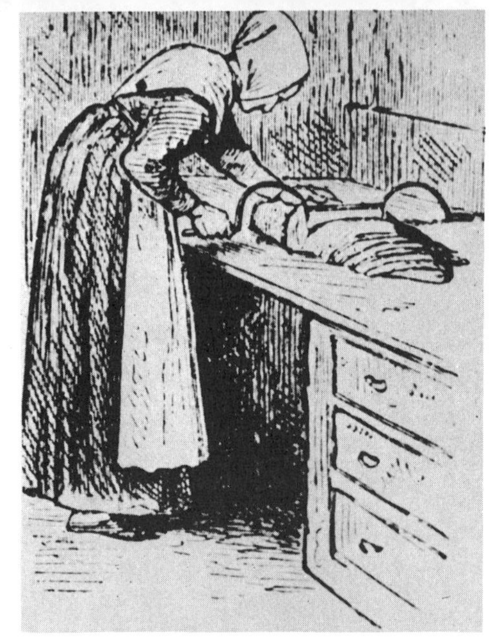

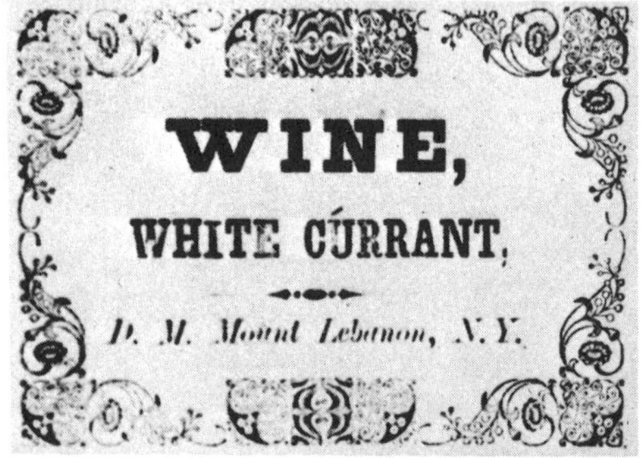
WINE,
WHITE CURRANT,
D. M. Mount Lebanon, N.Y.

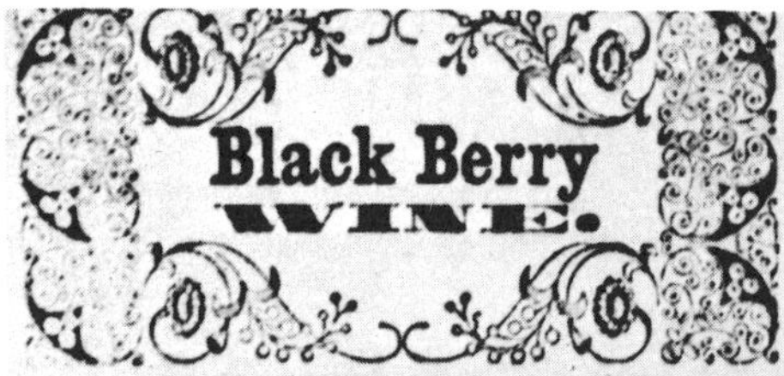
Black Berry
WINE.

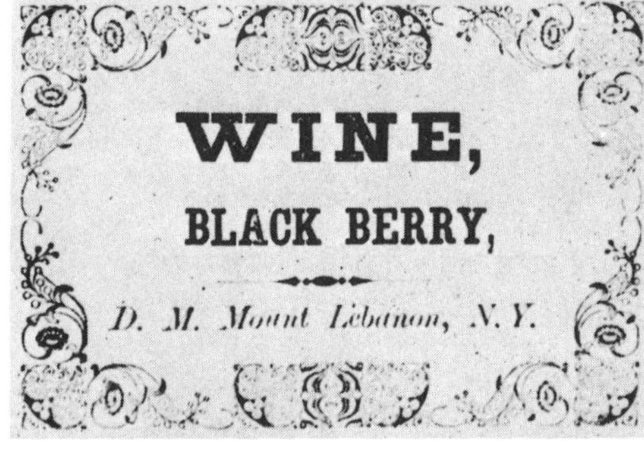
WINE,
BLACK BERRY,
D. M. Mount Lebanon, N.Y.

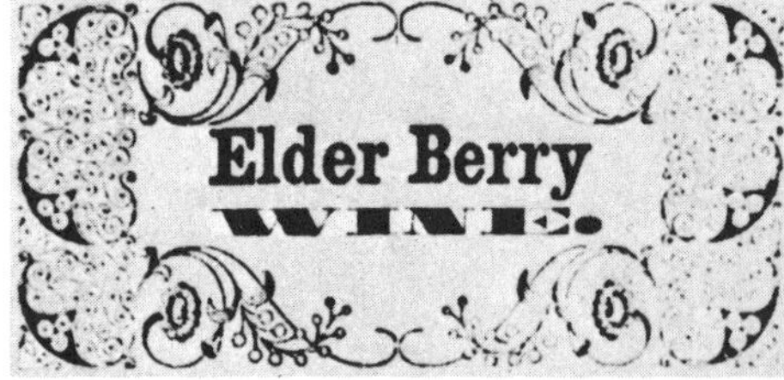
Elder Berry
WINE.

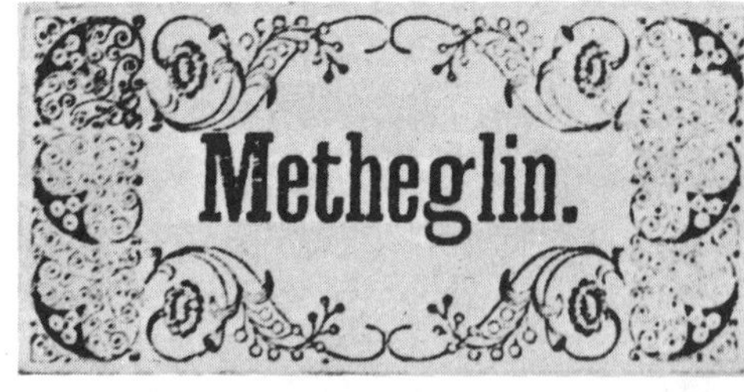
Metheglin.

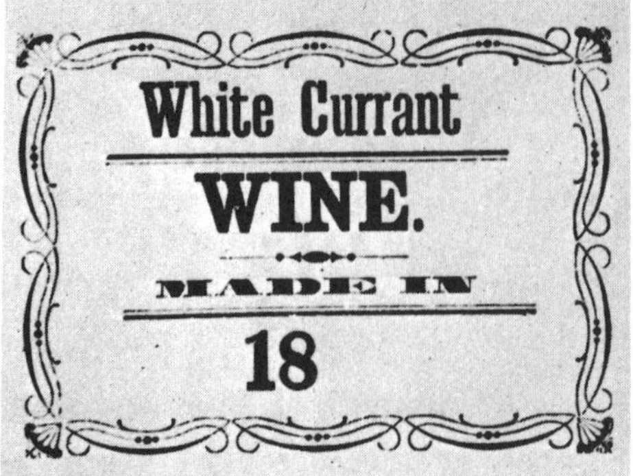
White Currant
WINE.
MADE IN
18

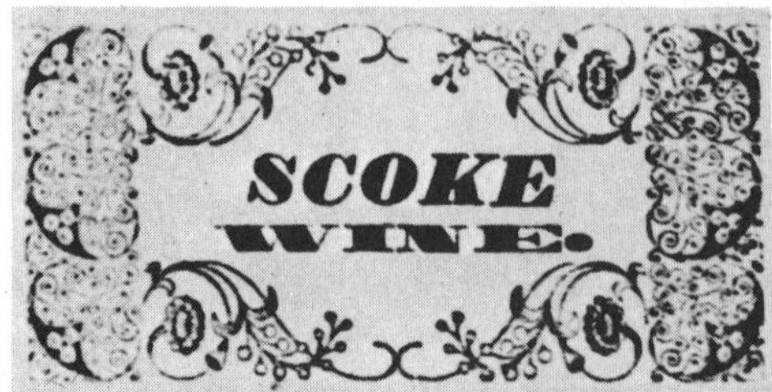
SCOKE
WINE.

Dried sweet corn and dried apples were products that were produced in large enough quantities to involve many members of each family in the preparation and marketing.

Dried sweet corn was a product that was in great demand by outsiders, and its sale became a lucrative industry for the Shakers. The corn, picked at the peak of its growth, was boiled, cut from the cob by the use of a variety of stripping devices which improved in efficiency as the industry grew, and then dried. In the early days the drying was done by spreading the kernels out on sheets in the sun. As the industry became more important to the Shaker economy, drying rooms were built and the quality of the corn became more consistent. Automatic, steam-operated machinery was developed and built, making it possible to strip and prepare the corn in great quantities. Even the barrels could be filled automatically and smaller individual packages as well

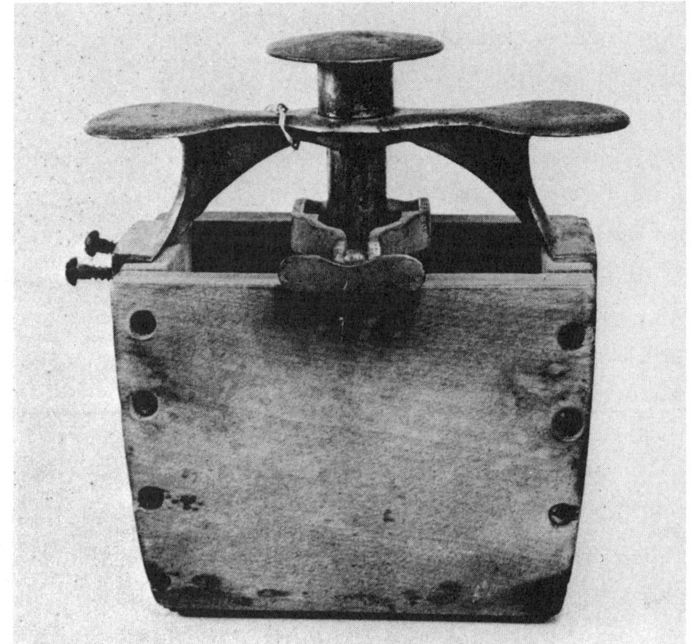

OPPOSITE TOP RIGHT: *Shaker sister cutting bread.*

OPPOSITE: *Shaker printed wine labels. Metheglin was made from fermented honey and water.* OLD CHATHAM.

Butter press for forming butter into blocks. Shakers made butter for sale as well as for their own use. OLD CHATHAM.

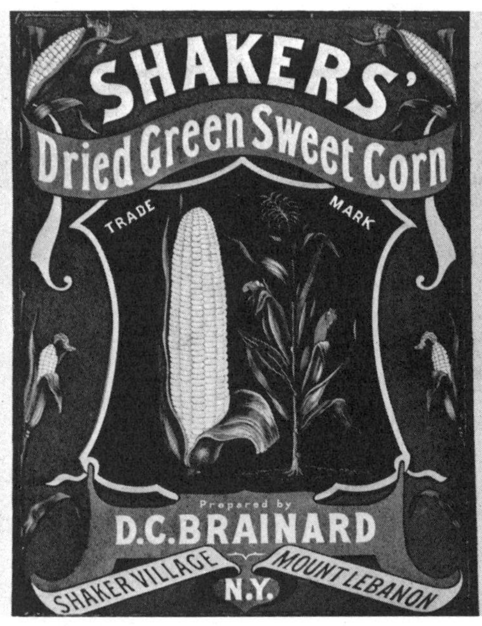

DRIED SWEET CORN

FOR TABLE USE.

WE MAKE THIS A SPECIALTY.

Those who have used it prefer it to the canned corn sold in the market.

It is cut from the cob in its green state, when best fit for eating, and then quickly dried by heated air, being only six to twelve hours drying, thus retaining all its good qualities, being equal to green corn fresh from the field.

It requires to be soaked for six hours in warm water, (milk is better,) and then add milk, butter or cream, and season to suit the taste. Should not be boiled but five minutes, and it is fit to use.

One pint of Dried Corn will make a quart when prepared for the table, thus reducing the price so as to be within the reach of all.

Orders should be sent in as early as August and September, as the increasing demand for it requires our whole stock before early winter.

Prepared and put into barrels, at wholesale by

D. C. BRAINARD,

Mount Lebanon, N.Y.

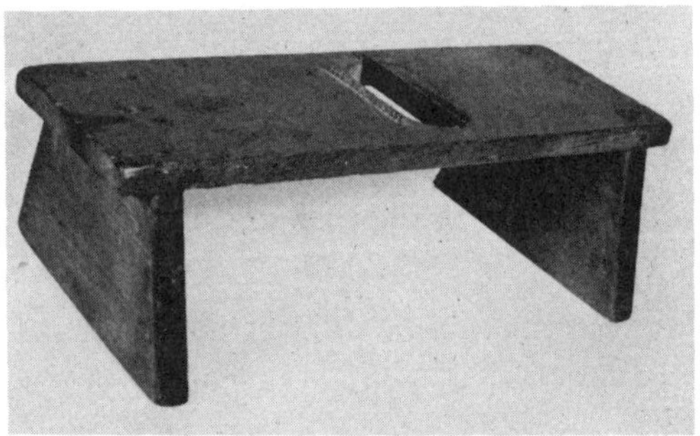

LEFT: *Colorful poster advertising dried sweet corn.* OLD CHATHAM.

TOP RIGHT: *Advertisement for lucrative dried sweet corn industry.* OLD CHATHAM.

RIGHT: *Shaker-made device for stripping corn kernels from cob.* OLD CHATHAM.

as barrels were sent to market with Shaker labels. Directions for cooking the corn for table use were included in the packages.

Although the Shakers didn't grow all the corn that they prepared and sold, they were careful about the quality of the ears that they purchased from outside sources, and surrounding farmers knew their crops had to be superior in order to be sold to the Shakers. Colorful banners and posters advertised Shaker dried sweet corn around 1870, and the business continued throughout the nineteenth century.

The New England and New York Shakers derived a great deal of income and sustenance from the variety of apples they grew. Apple trees were planted on all Shaker farms as soon as land was purchased. Nothing was wasted in the Shakers' use of apples. Shaker applesauce was a well-known product that found a ready market from the time when it was first distributed at Hudson and other New York towns, probably as early as 1814. By 1830 applesauce was delivered to dealers by the barrel, and the applesauce and dried-apple business thrived throughout the nineteenth century. In 1856 Shaker applesauce sold for twelve dollars a barrel.

Apples provided several other food products that were made and marketed to the world by the Shakers. Dried apples were prepared on a rather large scale in the New York and New England Shaker families. Apples were trimmed, peeled, and cored, and dried in large bins in specially built drying rooms. The dried apples were then packed in barrels and sold. Dried apples were also used in the preparation of the famous applesauce, which was made by simmering them in cider.

When the apples ripened in the fall, the Shakers held "paring bees" several times a week. Various tools were

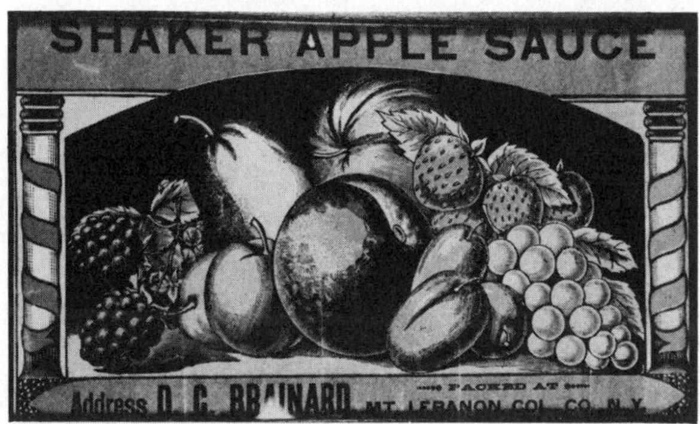

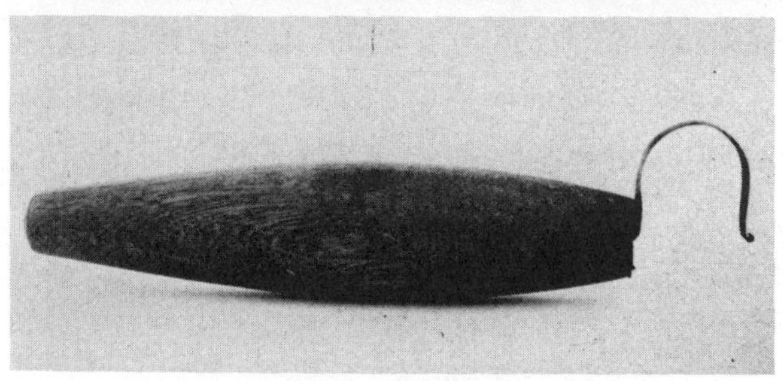

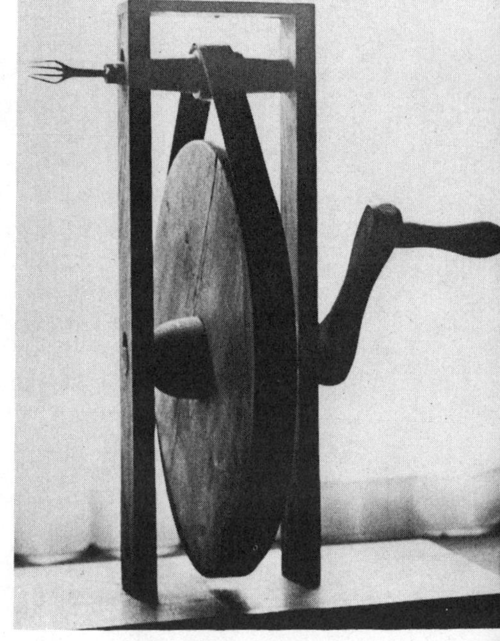

LEFT TOP: *Advertising poster for famous Shaker applesauce.* OLD CHATHAM.

BOTTOM: *Shaker apple corer. Length, 6½ inches.* BELFIT.

RIGHT: *Shaker apple peeler. Apple was stuck on fork and held against knife as wheel was turned.* HANCOCK.

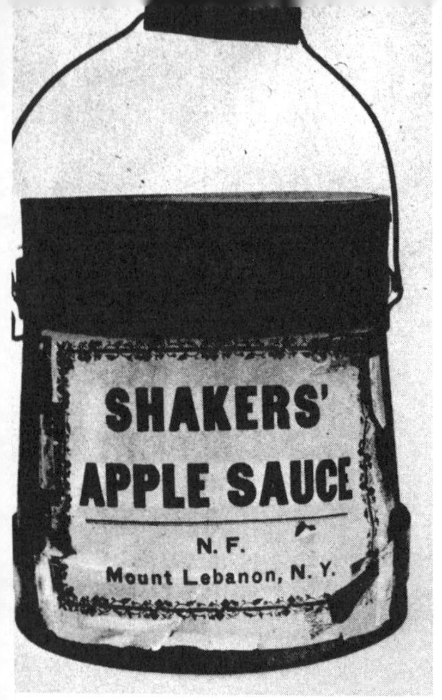

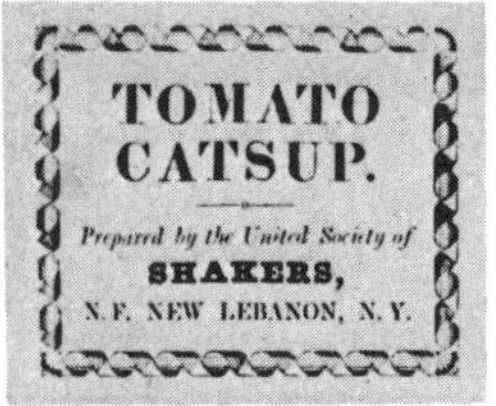

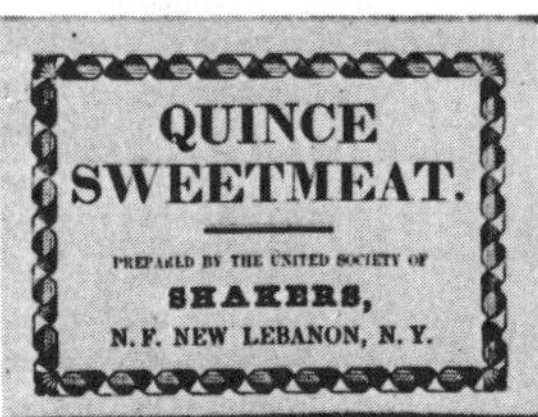

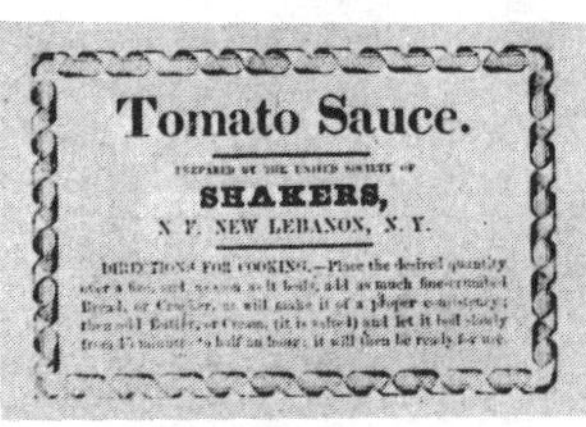

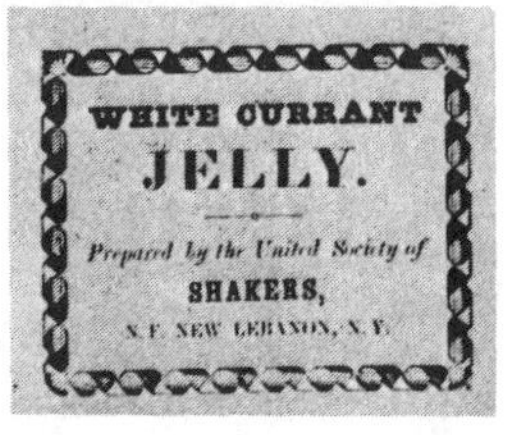

devised early in the nineteenth century to facilitate paring and coring apples. Apple corers and peelers of various designs have survived. As the industry grew, machines were built whereby much of the work could be done automatically.

Only perfect fruit was used for dried apples, but peelings and inferior fruit were used in the manufacture of apple butter. Vinegar and cider were also made from the less than perfect fruit. Apple wine and apple jelly were two other products that were sold.

Besides these major sources of income, other food products were prepared in lesser quantities and sold by the Shakers. Relishes, tomato catsup, pickles, and preserves were well known throughout the regions where they could be purchased. Jellies and jams were also made and sold. Baked goods were another product which the Shakers shared with their customers.

The making of wine was also an occupation of the Shakers, and a great variety was produced, including blackberry, elderberry, cherry, white currant, and grape. Metheglin, distilled from fermented honey and water, was a popular Shaker product. The Shakers also printed their own food product labels, particularly those for wines, although, again, they did not make their own jars and bottles. In the mid-nineteenth century just about every Shaker community was engaged in the wine-making industry.

Maple sugar cakes, with or without butternuts, were prepared in small, tin, Shaker-made fluted molds. The molds were also an item in Shaker shops. Sugared or spiced nutmeats and many other candy products were packaged and available to Shaker customers.

TOP: *Shaker-made wooden bucket in which applesauce was sold. Wood expanded when wet, making bucket leakproof.* BELFIT.
BOTTOM: *Shaker printed labels for some of their food products.* OLD CHATHAM.

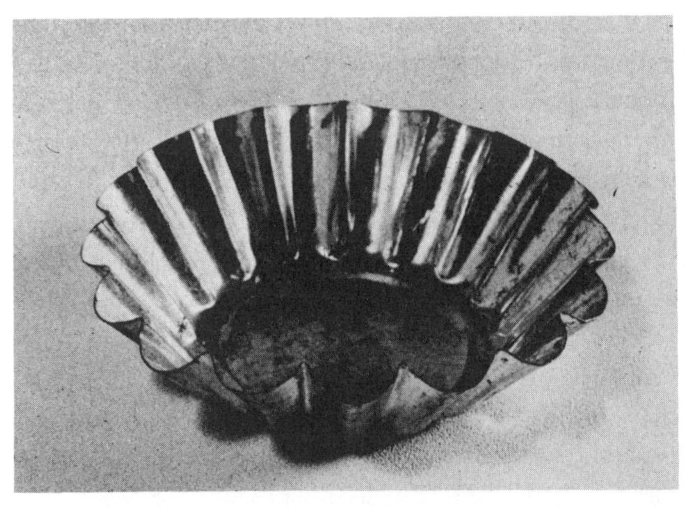

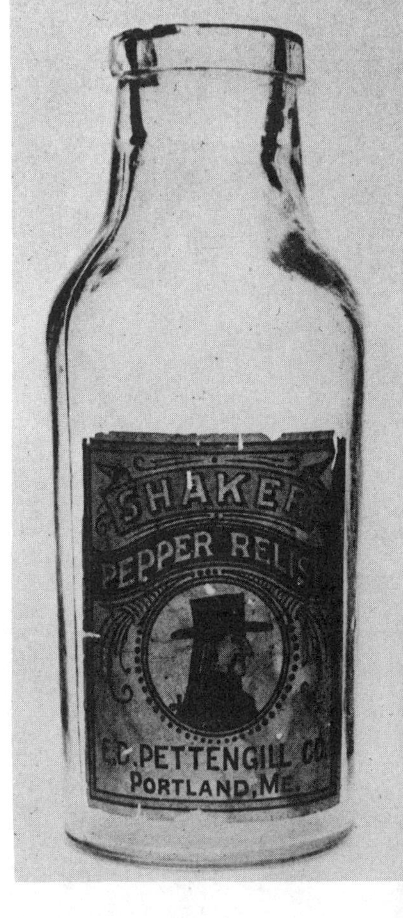

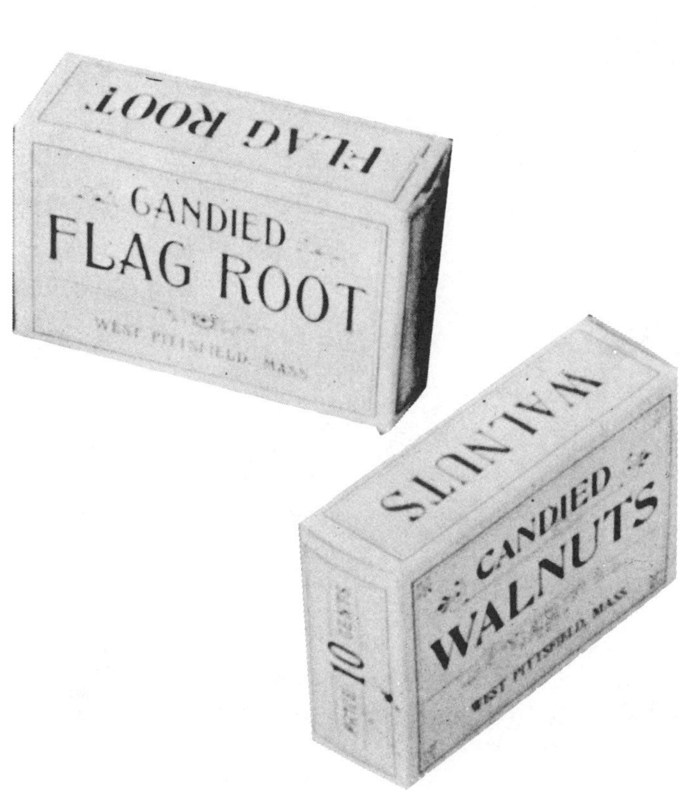

ABOVE RIGHT: *Label and bottle for pepper relish made by Maine Shakers. Shaker men were seldom used in advertising. Aqua glass. Bottle made 1880.* BELFIT.

ABOVE LEFT: *Fluted mold in which maple sugar cakes were made. Many molds were also sold in Shaker shops.* BELFIT.

LEFT: *Shaker sisters also made and boxed many confections to sell in their shops.* OLD CHATHAM.

LEFT: *Cheese press and cheese mold. Cheese and butter were made and sold by many Shaker families.* HANCOCK.

RIGHT: *Tool used for separating milk in the making of cheese.* BELFIT.

The Shakers' reputation for excellence in their food products and cleanliness and care used in preparation, during a period when sanitary conditions elsewhere left much to be desired, led to the success of their many kitchen industries, and there was great demand for their food products. The sisters also made cheese, butter, and sausages, which were sold locally. Dried currants and elderberries were also prepared and sold.

Many families kept bees, as much for their benefit to the orchards as for the honey and beeswax to be had. Honey and maple syrup were two other Shaker products that were sold to the public. A complete list of products made in Shaker kitchens and sold in varying amounts, depending upon the crops and the seasons, would be

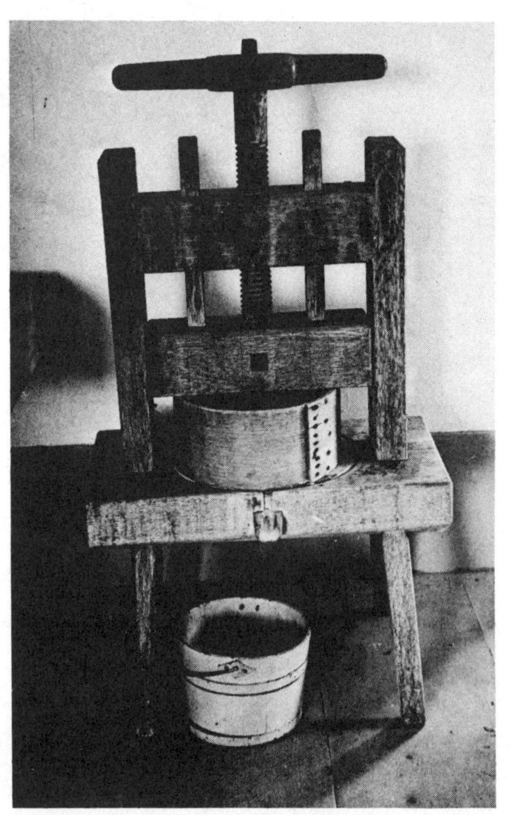

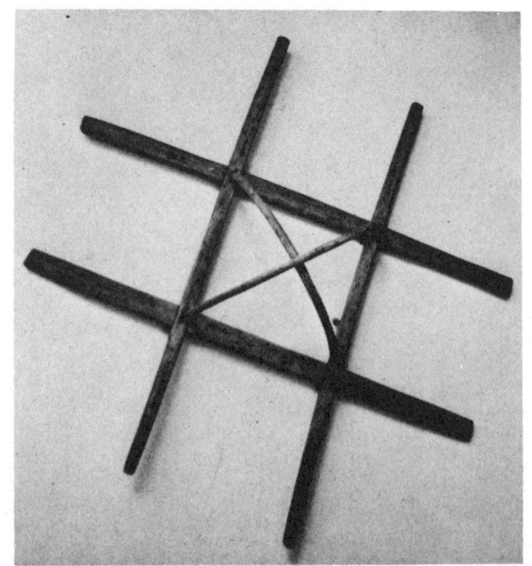

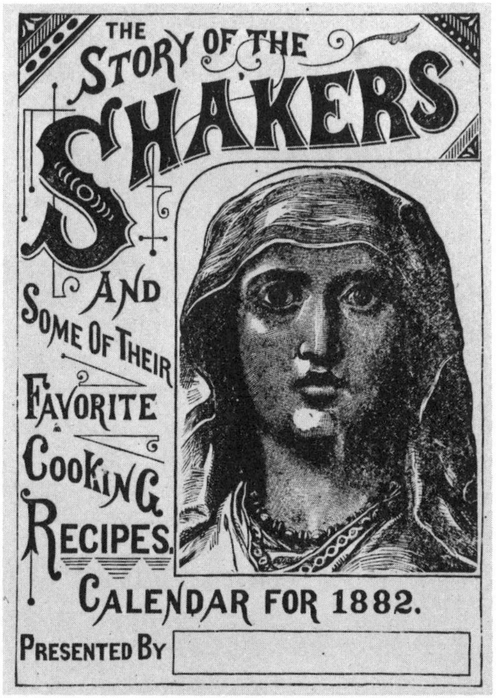

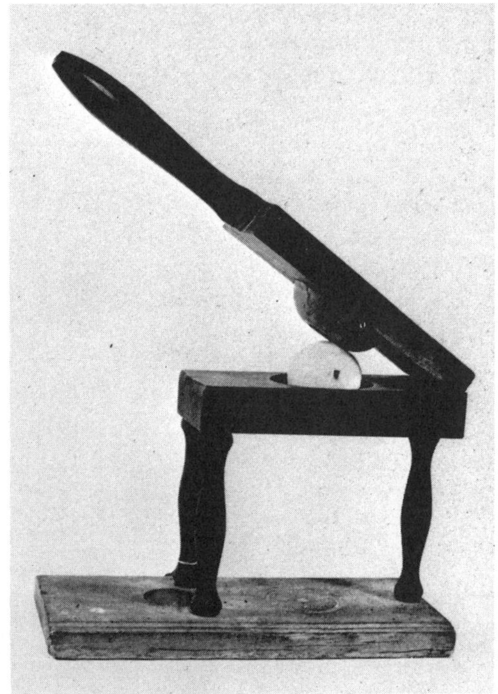

impossible. It is only when labels, packages, or some other form of written or printed record exists that we can be certain of the variety of good food products made and sold by the Shakers. The hand-printed labels and the various types of packages that have survived are, to many, of more interest than the products they held. Shaker wooden applesauce pails, with bail handles and copper rivets, made by the men, are examples of what resulted from perfect separation, but cooperation, between the Shaker sisters, who made the contents, and their brethren. It was necessary to work in perfect harmony in order to achieve the kind of success in business that was typified in many of the Shaker enterprises.

LEFT: *The Shakers were famous for their cooking and used this pamphlet to advertise their food products.* OLD CHATHAM.

RIGHT: *Hand press for squeezing fruit.* OLD CHATHAM.

CHAPTER 7

TEXTILES

—Comfortables should be of a modest color, not checked, striped or flowered. Blankets or Comfortables for out side spreads, should be blue and white, but not checked or striped; other kinds now in use may be worn out.

Window curtains should be white, or of a blue or green shade, or some very modest color, and not red, checked, striped or flowered.
Millenial Laws, 1821, Revised, 1845.

The Shaker sisters were responsible in the beginning years of the sect for spinning and weaving textiles to supply the members with clothing and the households with bedding and other cloth products. Many of the women who came into the Shaker communities were knowledgeable in the arts of spinning and weaving, since this was normally a domestic occupation for women in the eighteenth century.

By the beginning of the nineteenth century a large amount of yardage of various kinds of cloth was necessary and the brethren built looms, spinning wheels, and many other devices to be used in the manufacture of cloth.

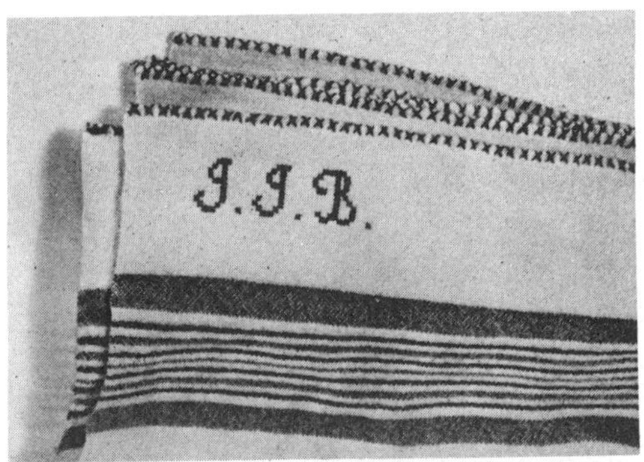

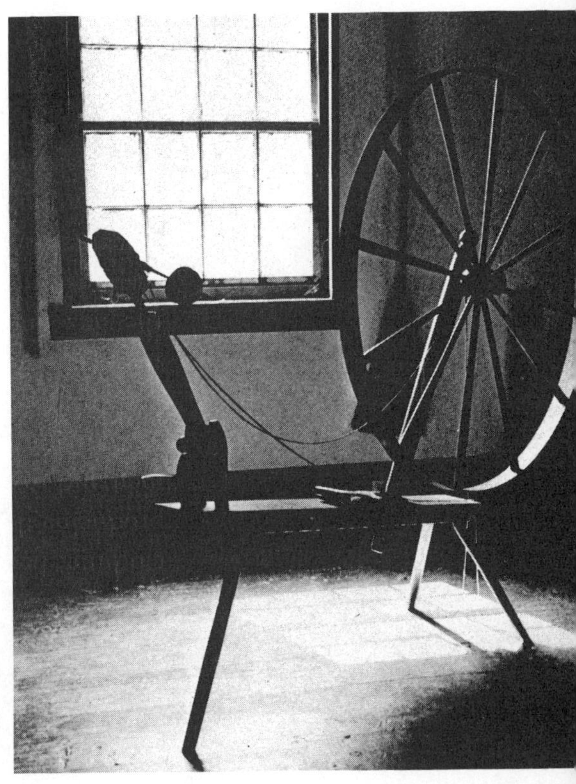

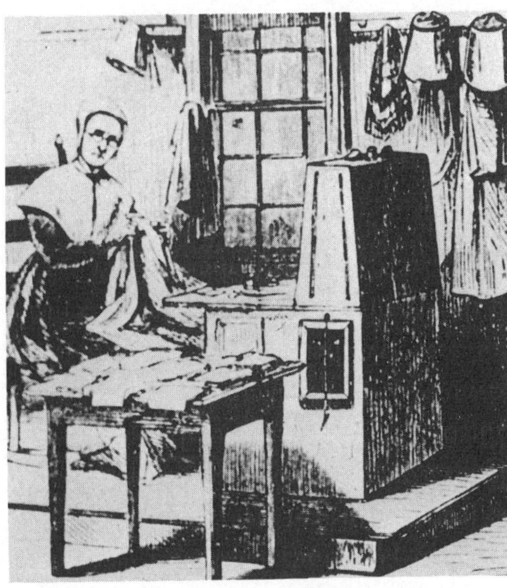

Some of the earliest articles made from Shaker textiles are horse blankets, towels, sheets, straining cloths, ironing cloths, handkerchiefs, and bags for seed and herbs.

In the manner of all colonial households, although on a much larger scale, various textiles were produced, from the raw fibre to the finished product. The most important use for which textiles were made was, of course, the provision of clothing for all members of the group. For this purpose yards of fabric were woven to provide material for such items as boys' trousers, flannel shirts, worsted jackets, drugget linings, drawers, serge for shoe uppers,

TOP LEFT: *Hand-woven white wool blanket with hand-embroidered edging and monogram. Red and blue striped border.* OLD CHATHAM.

RIGHT: *The spinning wheel, symbol of Shaker sisters' industry.* HANCOCK.

A mender of clothing. Note cloaks and bonnets hanging on pegs.

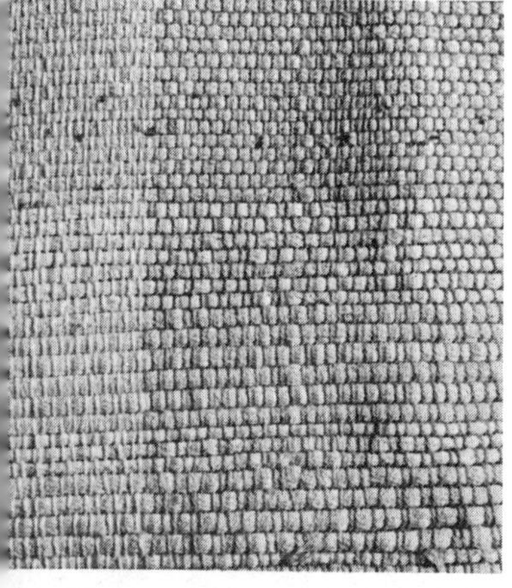

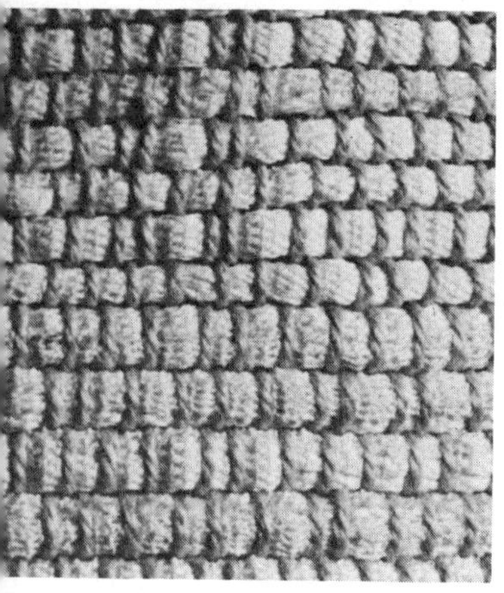

Two details of Shaker-woven homespun coverlet. Blue and white. OLD CHATHAM.

cotton and worsted jackets, serge trousers, and red and blue deacons' frocks. Textiles woven for women's clothing were used to make cotton and linen "open frocks," kerchiefs, gowns, cotton bibs, flannel drawers, drab habits, undercoats and checked aprons. Red and blue worsted was made in quantity for the sisters' dresses. Cloaks and cloak linings were also made from Shaker wool and this item was later to be an important source of income to Shakers who made the cloaks to sell.

The home manufacture of textiles began with the arduous preparation of the fibre, which was then spun into thread. The Shakers were probably the first New Yorkers and New Englanders to grow their own flax for linen cloth. The many processes necessary to prepare the fibre for spinning into thread were difficult and painstaking. From scutching to hatcheling to the finished fabric, the sisters worked to provide thousands of yards of linen cloth. Wool, sheared from their own specially grown sheep, also required many hours of preparation to become yarn from which cloth could be woven.

It is probable that in the first half of the nineteenth century no one in the United States surpassed the Shakers as producers of textiles. Toward the middle of the century, when the great textile industries of New England had become established, the Shakers were, of course, outdone in terms of quantity. However, the quality of Shaker textiles and the variety produced were still superior. Long after machines were developed to turn out endless yards of cloth goods, the Shakers were still hand-weaving many yards of certain textiles that were of exceptional quality and for which there were no machine-made substitutes. By this time, however, they were also purchasing machine-made textiles where a fabric would suit their needs. They concentrated their efforts on the handmade textiles for which they had become known and for which there was a demand on the market. By mid-century, for instance, Shaker chairs were an important item to their economy, and special looms had been developed for weaving the narrow tapes from which the seats and backs of the chairs were woven. Tape was also produced for binding rugs and skirt hems. Blankets, chair cushions, and rugs were also woven on Shaker looms until quite late in the century.

Shaker specialization in textile production was a perfect example of what happened to many cottage industries in the nineteenth century. As machines were developed that could produce textiles that, while not quite as good as handmade, would do for certain purposes, even the Shakers realized the folly of continuing to produce everything by hand, and they purchased their own household textiles and concentrated their efforts on fabrics for which they could find no substitute. By the middle of the century certain Shaker-made products that required hand-loomed textiles had become popular among their customers.

LEFT: *Stack of hand-woven tapes which were made on special Shaker-designed and-built tape looms. Tapes were made in a great variety of color combinations throughout Shaker history and were used for chair seats and backs and for footstools.* OLD CHATHAM.

RIGHT: *Linen dish towels and handkerchiefs initialed and owned by Shakers. They grew their own flax and spun linen thread. At bottom of photo is knitted washcloth which was sold in sisters' shops.* OLD CHATHAM.

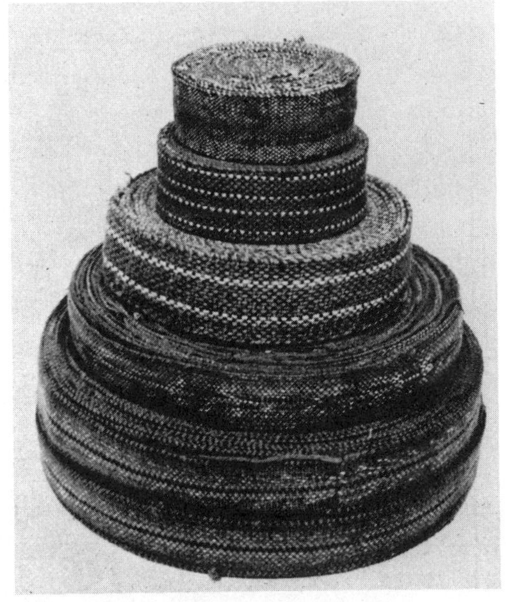

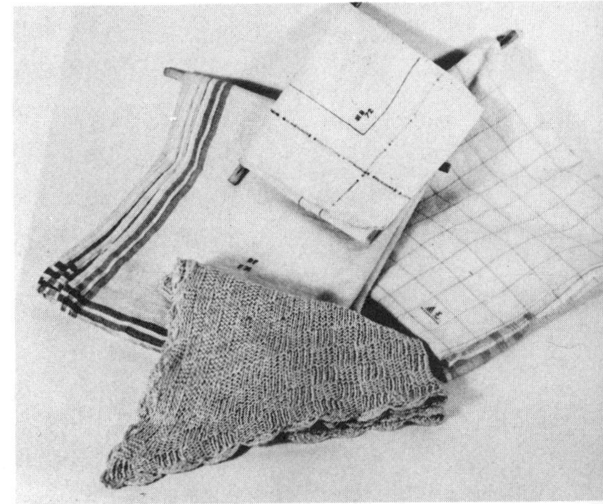

The Shaker finished products that required special fabrics to be woven in the communities were straw bonnets, silk kerchiefs, Shaker cloaks, and many other items of wearing apparel that became fashionable. Certain of the sisters' shops became known for having superior knitted goods, and many household articles made of Shaker cloth. Table mats and coverings for boxes were made on Shaker looms from palm-leaf straw or woven strips of poplar wood. Rugs were woven on large looms specially designed and built by the Shakers. Face braids, cushion linings, silk head nets, baby blankets, wool hats, gloves and mittens were sold by the Shakers. In most cases, especially during the first half of the nineteenth century, the finished products were entirely "Shaker."

As the needs of the Shaker communities for more clothing, bedding, etc., increased, the effort involved in producing the necessary textiles was divided between the men and women. The children and the elderly members of the communities were put to work performing the less arduous tasks. For instance, while the brethren and the sisters shared much of the work involved in growing the flax and caring for the sheep, the brethren were responsible for designing and building the spinning wheels, looms, and many other tools necessary in the preparation and manufacture of textiles.

The sisters were responsible for the preparation of yarn and the weaving and spinning. The women also had charge of bleaching and dyeing the fibers, and in the early days the sisters of the New Lebanon community prepared textiles for the other Shaker communities as well as their own.

The earliest dye that seems to have been used was indigo. Logwood, copperas, camwood, madder, red tartar, fustic, and sumac leaves were also made into dye. The Shakers also used hemlock and butternut, which were common New England dye materials. The dyeing

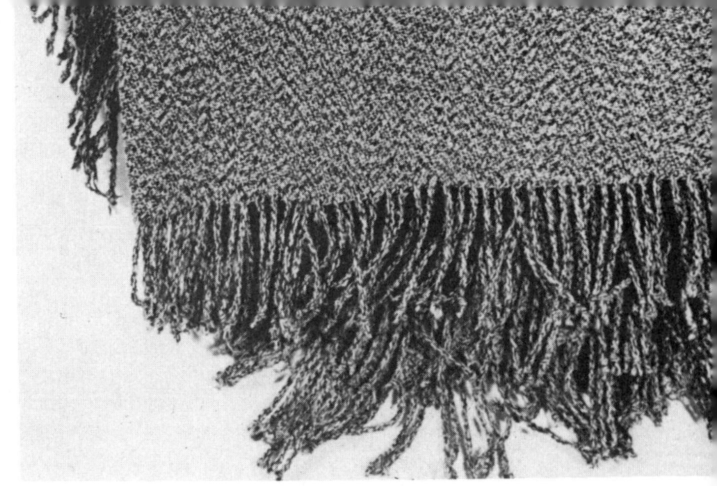

of textiles was a seasonal occupation for the Shaker women. The process usually began in the early spring after the textiles and yarns made during the winter had been sorted, boiled, and bleached. Various ingredients used in making the dyes were gathered and prepared. "The first week in this month," wrote one sister in New Lebanon in June 1840, "we put the butternut bark to soak." This same sister later reported, "We put the wool into the butternut dye about the middle of the 2nd week in June and finished colouring butternut the 14th of July."

Exact quantities of worsted dyestuffs were prepared. The sisters figured earlier the amount that would be needed for the clothing each year. "Eleven lbs. for stockings, some grey and some white," were prepared in 1840. That same year in New Lebanon only sixty-one pounds of wool for "cloak head linings" were needed. It was also figured in advance how many yards of wool should be dyed in each color; fifty-two pounds of wool were colored blue and ten pounds colored black "for boys' frocks." The early Shakers did not believe in using bright colors for their own clothing and the dyes were, for the most part, of subdued shades. Rug dyes, especially in the Midwestern communities, were often of more brilliant shades. Blue dye was used for textiles to be made

Detail of Shaker shawl. Grey and black woven fringed material. OLD CHATHAM.

into pocket handkerchiefs, linings, window curtains, trousers, and jackets. Thread for sewing the finished articles was dyed along with the textiles so that it matched perfectly.

As successful as the Shakers were in producing textiles for their own use and later for sale to outsiders, records show that they were always willing to learn more about their crafts. In 1850 it was recorded at New Lebanon that "An English man named John Robbins, resided at Tyringham [the site of a small Shaker community in Massachusetts] comes to teach us about bleaching and colouring. He stays till Friday noon and is very helpful. I wrote 33 receipts from his own mouth. He colours blue, yellow, purple and orange on silk, wool and cotton, bleaches a little linen and cotton cloth, makes several preparations such as Nitrate of Iron, Nitro Sulphate, Lac Spirit, Blue Spirit, etc."

From the above it is obvious that the Shakers who were expert in a particular craft or industry traveled to teach new techniques to their brethren and sisters. The date of this journal is also of interest, since by 1850 the New Lebanon sisters were already considered the experts in spinning, weaving, and dyeing. They were always willing to learn more, however. Thousands of yards of textiles per community were made up to the Civil War. Following the war more and more textiles were purchased on the "outside."

All fabrics for Shaker use were woven and dyed to order according to projected needs. Different weights, weaves, and colors of textiles were made for various articles of clothing, and since the Shaker laws dictated that all must dress alike and all must have the same amount of clothing, it was not a difficult matter for the sisters to figure rather closely how much of each fabric would be needed to get through a season.

Although at first the women were in complete charge

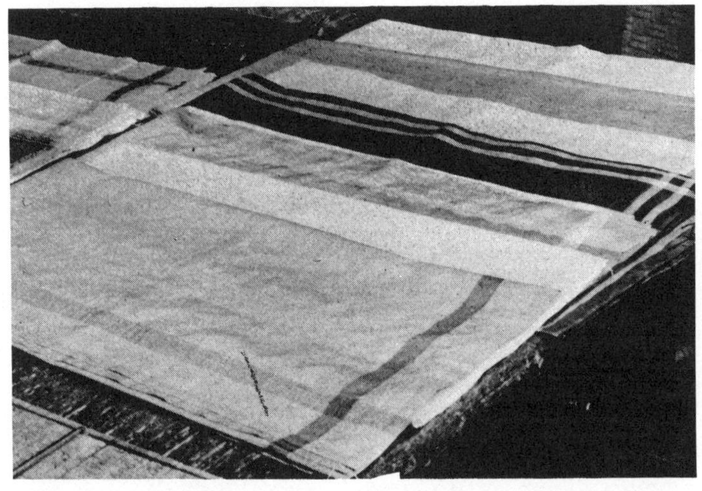

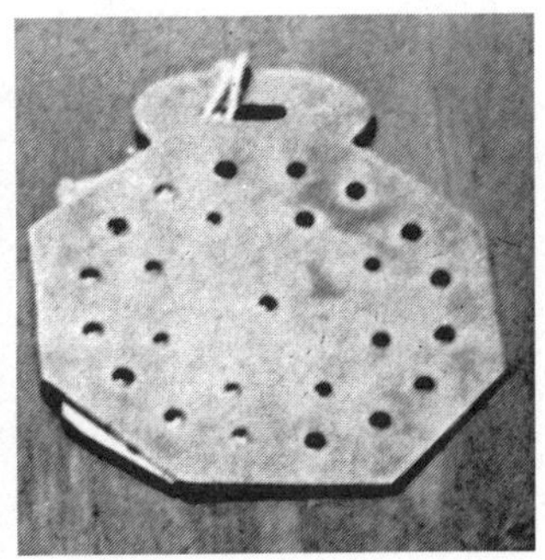

of textile manufacture and the making of clothing for their own use, as time went on, and more and more textiles were needed, carding mills, dye houses, and very sophisticated looms were devised and built to facilitate the manufacture of the textiles. The Shaker looms were in constant use until the Civil War. However, certain kinds of textiles were made continuously until the twentieth century. Bird's-eye linen, sold for baby's diapers, was a Shaker invention, and this product was popular enough among the Shakers' customers for the continuation of its manufacture until late in the nineteenth century. The Shakers also are credited with developing the first wrinkle-free textiles. The cloth was placed between layers of chemically treated papers and pressed in a Shaker-invented screw press, using heat underneath. This process produced a shiny surface on one side of the material (usually silk) and a dull watered-silk effect on the reverse.

Another rather special fabric made by the Shakers deserves attention. Silk was produced in 1822 by Shakers in South Union, Kentucky, and some Ohio Shakers, also. Mulberry trees, necessary to the cultivation of silkworms, could be grown with some success in these more temperate climates, and silk that was produced was sold to all the Shaker communities in the East. The most popular item made from Shaker silk was a magnificent iridescent

LEFT: *Assortment of colorful silk kerchiefs made from silk grown in Midwestern Shaker communities.* OLD CHATHAM.

RIGHT: *Shaker-made needle gauge.* OLD CHATHAM.

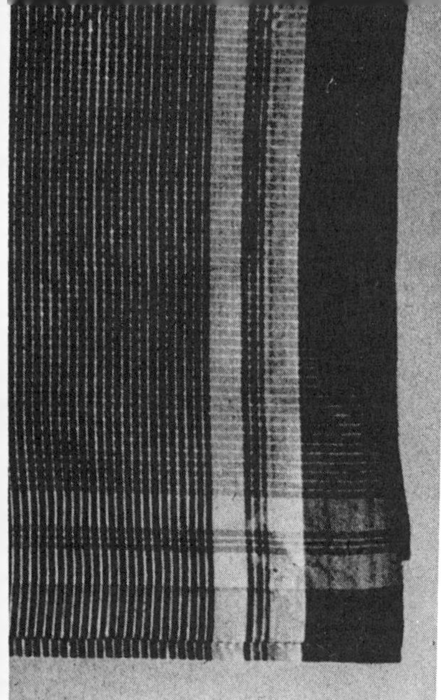

kerchief, produced in a variety of weaves and colors. The kerchief was worn as a shawl or bodice covering by the Shaker sisters, and it was also sold in the sisters' shops. These shawls were woven with contrasting borders and hemmed by hand in minute overcast stitches. Although early cultivation of silkworms had been attempted in Connecticut, the Shakers seem to have been the only Americans to have carried on this industry with any real success.

Nineteenth-century Shakers were considered to be experts in every area of textile manufacture. What had started as a typical cottage industry in the eighteenth century provided the sisters with income during the first half of the nineteenth. Just as important were the many inventions and innovations of the brethren in their successful attempts to supply the sisters with convenient tools for their textile production. "Great" (or oversize) spinning wheels, reels, swifts, foot-wheels for flax, skarns, hatchels, shears, reeds, temples, and shuttles were all necessary to the art of spinning and weaving, and these items were all made by the brethren in quantity. In 1809 a machine was made for cutting cloth, and this was an early Shaker invention. An almost staggering amount of paraphernalia necessary to the occupation of producing textiles in quantity was made by the Shakers, and many of them are inventions that were later copied by commercial textile manufacturers.

The many "special" kinds of textiles that kept Shaker looms producing throughout the nineteenth century can still be found. Chair tape and Shaker-woven handkerchiefs are just two of these later items. Carpeting and plush for the later chairs and footstools were also made rather late.

Detail of woven silk kerchief. Pincheck in iridescent grey and blue. Hand hemmed. OLD CHATHAM.

CHAPTER 8

SHAKER CLOTHING

If brethren desire any garments or fixtures to garments, as pockets, etc. etc. or new articles of manufacture, that come in the sisters line of business, which are not common to the brethren in general, they must apply to the Elders.

Silk hat bands, may not be worn, save on fur hats, for nice use.

Dark colored hat bands may not be worn, on summer hats.

All should remember that these are not the true heirs of the Kingdom of Heaven, who multiply to themselves, needless treasures of this world's goods. Millenial Laws, 1821. Revised, 1845.

Shaker dress was uniform and purposely different from worldly costume. After the first few dreary years, when survival was the only important issue for the Watervliet Shakers, Sabbath costumes and work clothes for weekday use were made for each member of the community by the sisters from textiles they wove themselves. By the beginning of the nineteenth century, dress styles and textiles were already uniform. The winter Sabbath costume for the sisters included long dresses made of butter-

Shaker sisters' workbench with table swift attached. HANCOCK.

nut-dyed worsted with blue and white checked aprons, blue cotton or linen neckerchiefs, white linen or lawn caps, and cloth shoes.

The earliest women's shoes were made on the same pattern as shoes the sisters wore before entering the communities and were high heeled. By 1810 the heels were lowered. About the same time, white neckcloths were worn with white high-collared stocks underneath, and until the time of the Civil War the Sabbath costumes for women under fifty were white cotton dresses. Corsets were discarded rather early in the century. It is obvious that corsetless Shaker sisters who walked about in low-heeled shoes were physically better off than their more fashionable worldly sisters.

The Millenial Laws dictated the Sabbath costume. All were told that they "should be dressed in uniform, as near as consistent, when assembled to worship God."

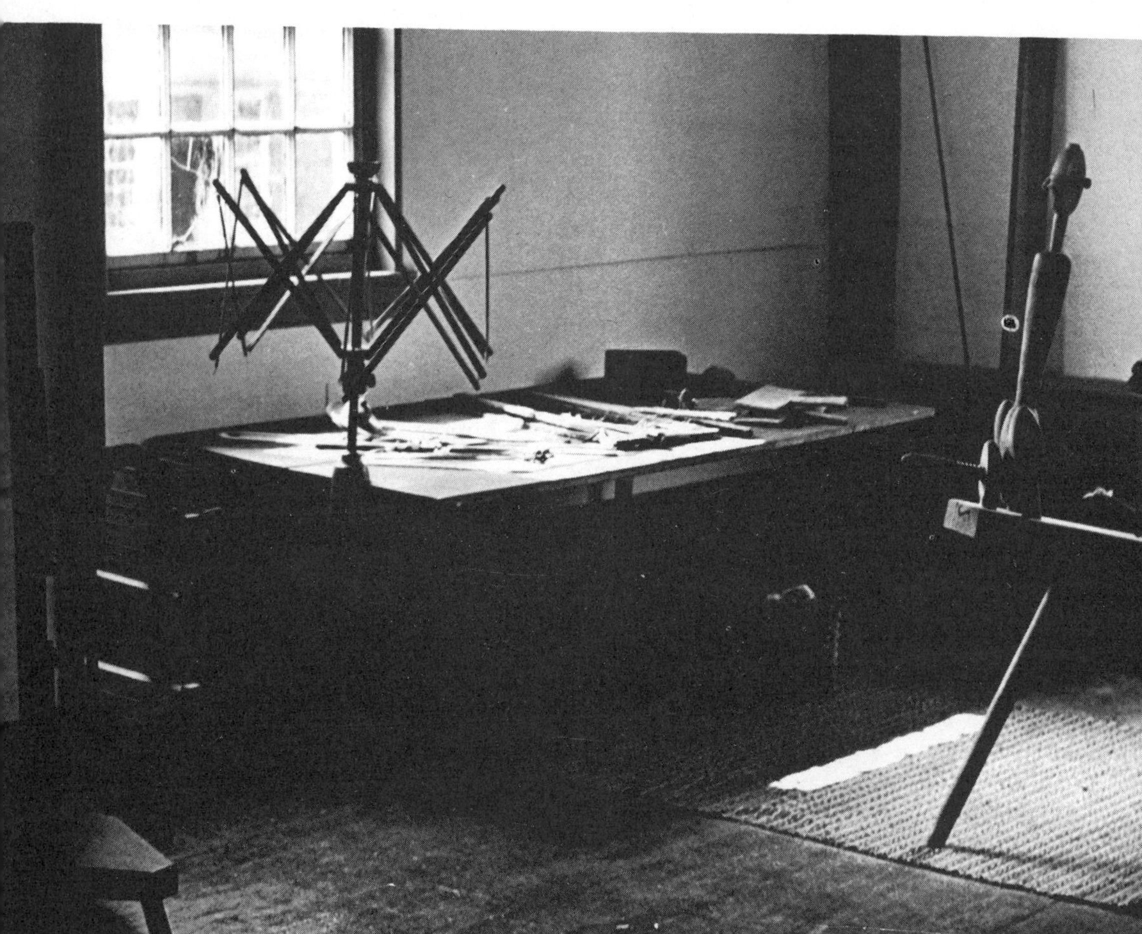

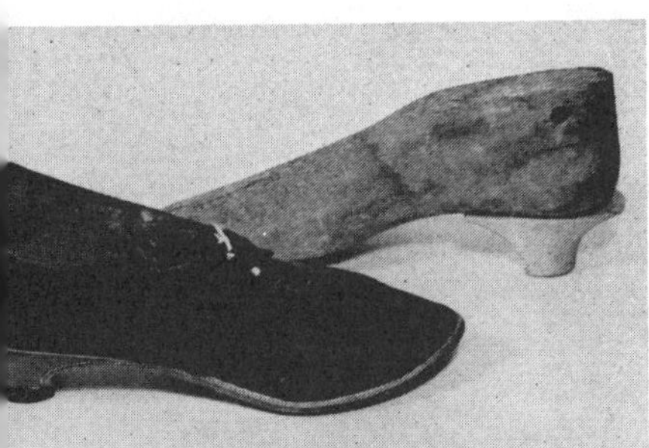

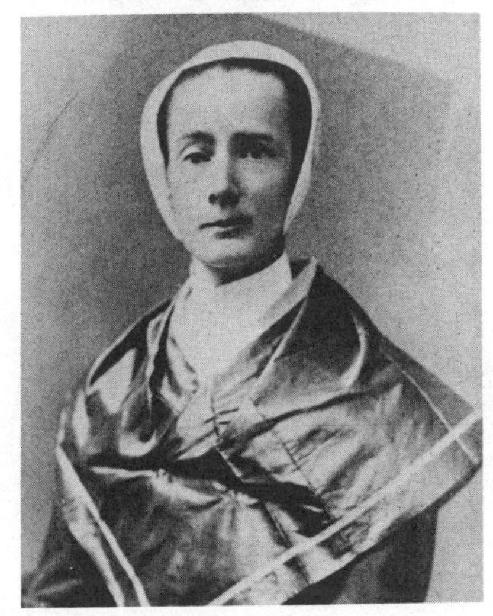

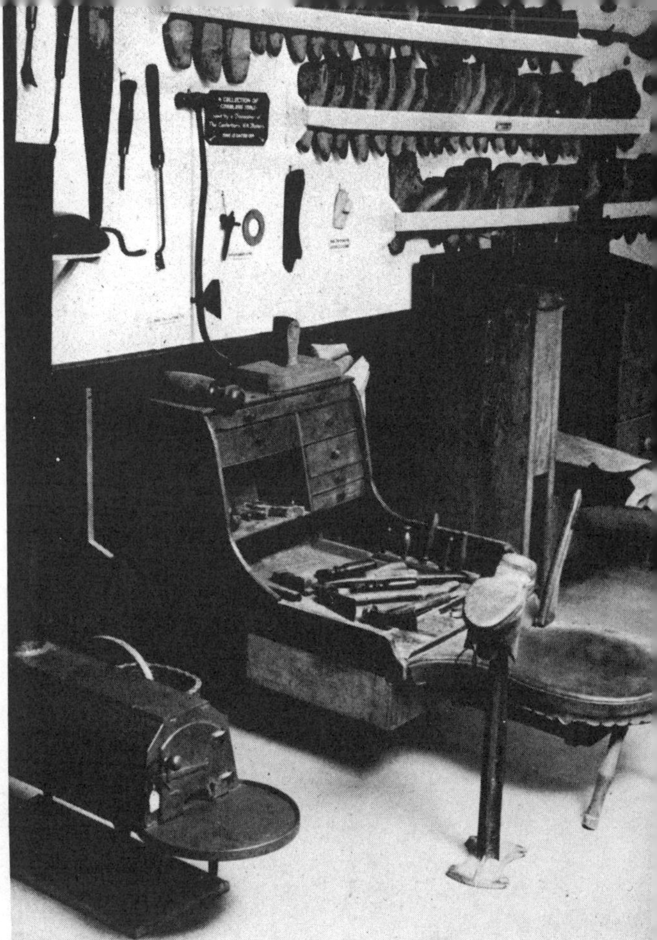

Another Millenial Law stated that "No one should wear very ragged clothes, even about their work, if it can consistently be avoided."

The early nineteenth-century costume for brethren consisted of coats made of blue fulled cloth with capes, jackets, or vests of the same material and a white stock. Blue sleeve strings, without which a Shaker could not go to Sunday meeting, black or blue breeches, long hose, and shoes with brass buckles completed the Sabbath costume. After 1810 the brethrens' coats were made of a grey material. Five years later, cotton trousers, dyed with nutgall, were replaced with a blue and white striped material. Drab jackets became the men's costume around

TOP LEFT: *Shaker sister's shoe with leather-covered wood heel and cloth upper. Wood form is in background, resting on carved wood heel. Shoes for left and right feet were not made before the Civil War.* OLD CHATHAM.

RIGHT: *Cobbler's bench, shoe forms, and tools. Bench is from Canterbury, New Hampshire, and is dated 1842.* OLD CHATHAM.

BOTTOM LEFT: *Photograph of Shaker sister wearing linen cap and silk kerchief (1900).* OLD CHATHAM.

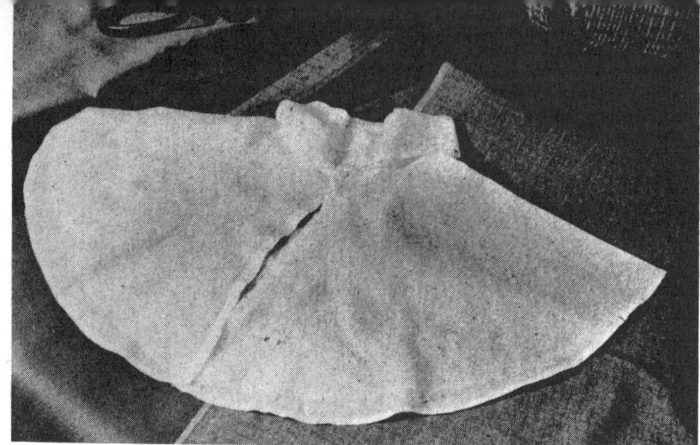

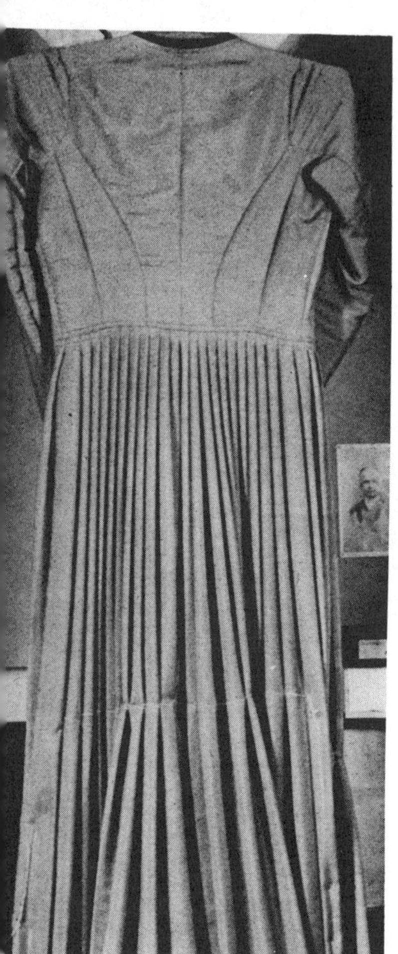

LEFT: *Shaker sister's dress with pleats basted down for pressing (1880).* OLD CHATHAM.

RIGHT: *Shaker sister's linen high collar. Note embroidered initials. At top of photo is pair of Shaker-made shears and sister's net-covered bonnet.* OLD CHATHAM.

this time, also, but in 1832 blue cloth jackets were once again the style. Drab jackets were to appear once again in 1840, and by 1854 "pursley blue jackets" were being worn on the Sabbath. Blue and white striped pantaloons made of linen cloth were worn later in the nineteenth century.

From the very beginning of the establishment of most Shaker communities, textiles were woven and clothing was made in the clothier shops that were set up by the brethren. Originally clothes were for use by the Shakers, who provided first for their own "families," second for less fortunate or newly organized Shaker families, and finally, for sale to the world. A tailoring shop was one of the earliest occupations set up at New Lebanon. It was managed by David Slosson, who was a tailor by trade. As early as 1789, New Lebanon records list clothing sold to outside customers. Surtouts, coats, breeches, "trowzers," shirts, and drawers were all made to order. As well as supplying clothes to outsiders, the Shaker tailoring shop also made clothing for all the families then settling in the New Lebanon community.

As has already been noted, all fabrics were woven to order according to projected needs. Different fabrics were made for the various articles of clothing. The width and weave, as well as the colors of the textiles made by the Shakers, were all governed by the eventual use for which the textiles were made. The sisters were in charge of making all their own clothing as well as manufacturing the many articles that they sold in their shops.

Special furniture for cutting and sewing the clothing was designed and built for the sisters' sewing rooms. Long and wide cutting tables, where cloth could be conveniently laid out and cut, were built in the carpenters' shops. The height and size of these tables were carefully figured so that minimal bending would be required. Many drawers were built into the tables for easy access to sewing tools and equipment. Small sewing desks and cabinets were built. Often the sewing desks could accommodate two sisters at one time, and drawers were placed at the ends of these desks and on both sides, for the convenience and access of both workers.

The Shaker sisters made articles of clothing that required more than the usual tailoring provided by the men's shop. For instance, stockings, socks, shoes, mittens, gloves, pocket handkerchiefs, shirts, and even some coats

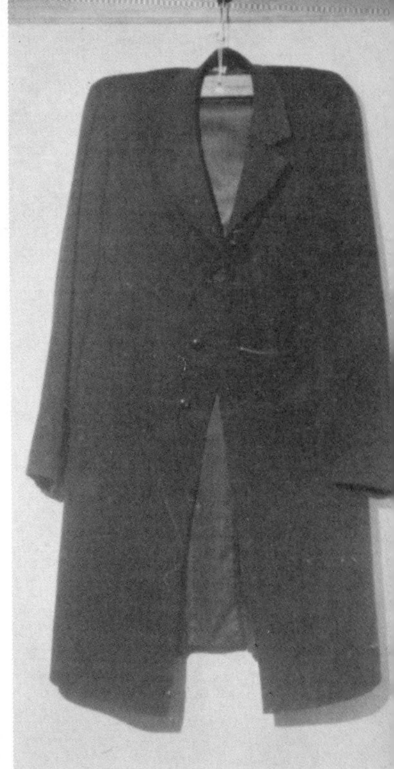

ABOVE: *Shaker brethren's long coat on Shaker hanger.* OLD CHATHAM.

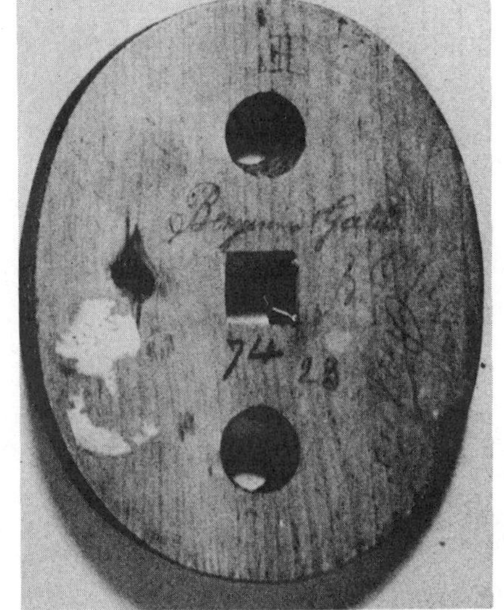

LEFT: *Each Shaker man had his own hat form. This one belonged to Benjamin Gates, a tailor.* OLD CHATHAM.

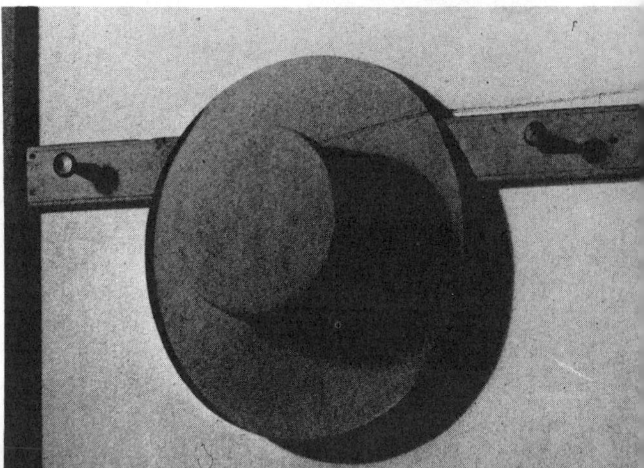

BELOW: *Shaker man's felt hat. Men's hats were also made to sell to outsiders.* OLD CHATHAM.

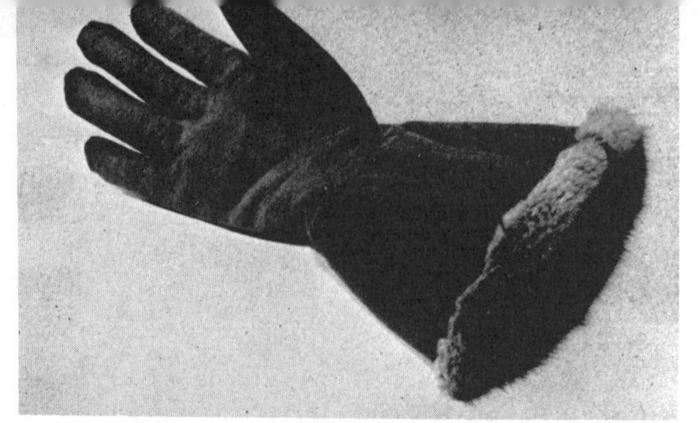

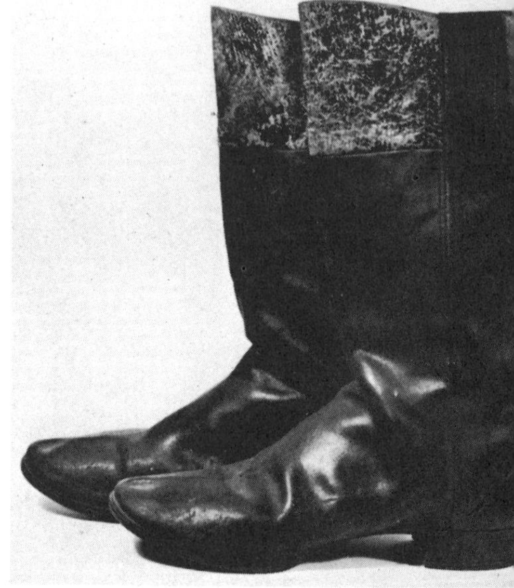

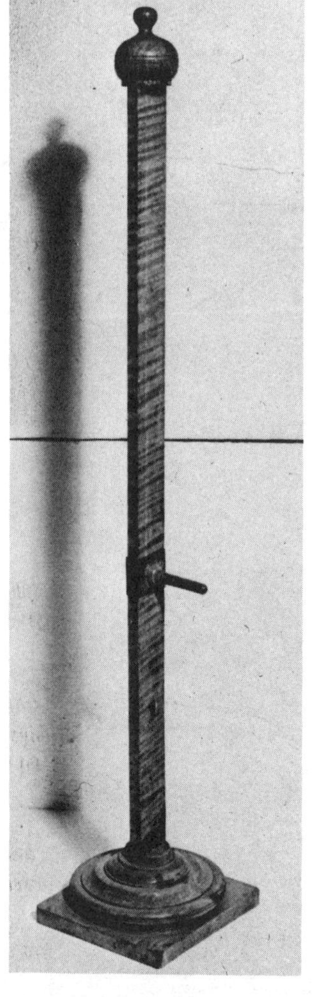

TOP LEFT: *Warm glove made of blue cotton suede-cloth with muskrat fur. Hand sewn.* OLD CHATHAM.

and trousers were made for the men by the sisters. For their own use they made dresses, gloves, underwear, silk handkerchiefs, bonnets, and cloaks. Because the bonnets and cloaks became popular and fashionable items that the Shakers made in quantity to sell, they will be treated in a separate chapter.

Each sister was allowed a limited number of articles of clothing, and when each item was finished, the initials of the owner would be hand-embroidered somewhere on the garment. A Millenial Law stipulated that "The initials of a person's name, are sufficient mark to put upon any tool, or garment, for the purpose of distinction." It was also "considered unnecessary to put more than two figures for a date on our clothes . . . "

In 1840 in New Lebanon an order gave to each female under twenty-six "2 outside gowns, 2 worsted gowns, 3 common summer gowns, 3 common winter gowns, 1 white gown, 2 cotton and worsted gowns, 2 light colored gowns, 2 cloaks, 2 winter petticoats, 1 white petticoat,

3 summer petticoats, 2 checked aprons, 2 good winter aprons, 6 kitchen aprons, 9 shifts, 3 palm bonnets, 1 pair of leather shoes, 1 pair wash shoes, 6 pairs cloth shoes, 2 pairs of socks, 8 white neck handkerchiefs, 16 caps, 12 collars, 3 pairs undersleeves, 8 underjackets, 2 white handkerchiefs, and common handkerchiefs as many as needful." It is obvious that no one did without during this period of relative Shaker affluence.

According to the Millenial Laws, no new fashions in manufacture, clothing, or wares of any kind could be introduced into the Shaker sect without the sanction of the Ministry. Therefore, although the style of Shaker clothing changed somewhat through the nineteenth century, certain features such as the pleated skirts on women's dresses, collarless blouses, and kerchiefs worn over the bodice remained a part of Shaker sisters' costumes throughout.

A great many objects of dress were knitted by hand by the sisters to sell in their shops. Women learned to

OPPOSITE RIGHT: *Shaker brother's boots made of black leather.* OLD CHATHAM.

OPPOSITE BOTTOM: *Stick for measuring skirt hems.* OLD CHATHAM.

BELOW LEFT: *Many Shaker items of clothing were made for sale to the world. This is an advertisement from catalogue of Shaker goods.* OLD CHATHAM.

BELOW RIGHT: *Mailing label for Shaker-made knitted goods and other products.* OLD CHATHAM.

SHAKER KNIT GOODS.

Manufactured at East Canterbury, N. H.

These comprise Gents half hose and Sweaters. The latter are used by athletes, particularly in Boating Base Ball, etc. These are made of the best Australian wool in three grades. Heavy, Medium and Light, designated as Nos 1, 2, 3. We make White, Black and Blue in the above grades. And make Tan, Garnet, Brown and Gray in the medium only. We sell these goods at wholesale and at retail.

We also make Gents all-wool half hose, widely known as the David Parker, silver mix. These we sell at wholesale, $5.00 per Doz. or at 50 cts. per pair.

Send all orders to Hart and Shepard, East Canterbury, Mer. Co., N. H.,—and send special directions for size, length and quality.

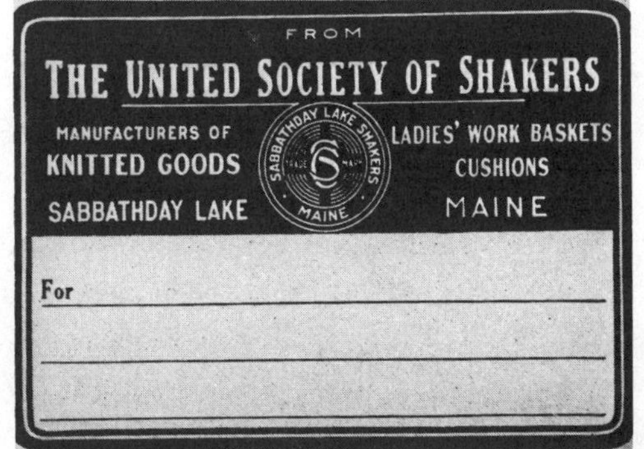

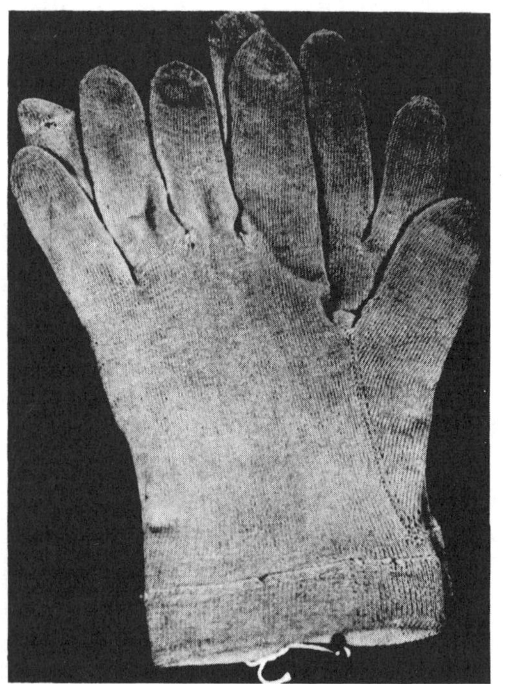

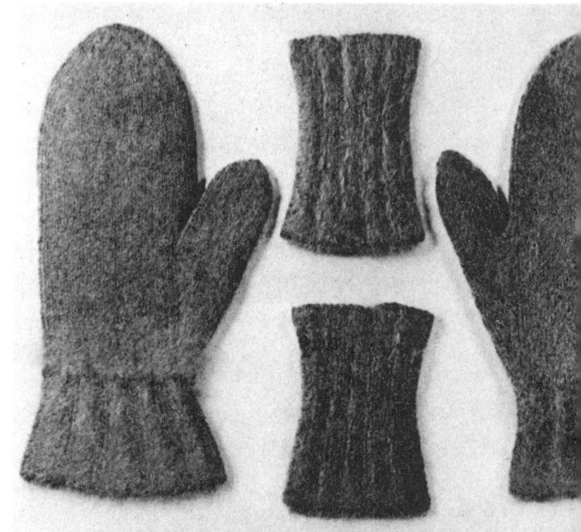

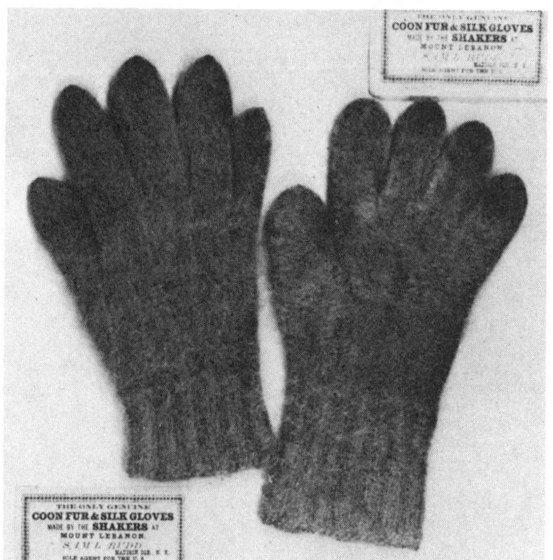

LEFT: *Knitted goods of thin yarn and a very fine stitch were also made by Shaker sisters to sell. These are men's gloves.* OLD CHATHAM.

TOP RIGHT: *Coon fur and silk hand-knit mittens and wristlets made by Mount Lebanon sisters.* OLD CHATHAM.

BOTTOM RIGHT: *Coon fur and silk gloves were made from scratch by sisters. Fur fiber had to be pulled from racoon pelts and spun into thread with silk fiber. Gloves were then hand knit. These gloves, mittens, and wristlets were popular shop items.* OLD CHATHAM.

knit at a very early age, and very young girls and the elderly sisters who could not do more strenuous work made a variety of knitted articles to sell. There was always a market for the variety of needlework made by the Shakers. Socks and gloves, especially, were turned out in large quantities.

Because the Shakers made their own textiles and clothing, certain styles they adopted were somewhat ahead of their time. Aprons were often made from the same bolt of fabric as the dresses with which they were to be worn. Cloth uppers for shoes were also made to match the dresses.

An important part of the Shaker sisters' dress was the kerchief worn over their bodices. These were made at first of black silk, but eventually white lawn or linen became the Shaker style. In 1818 drab colored silk was used for the kerchiefs. When the silk industry became established in Kentucky and Ohio, the sisters began to wear kerchiefs made of Shaker silk in many bright iridescent colors.

At no time was the dress of the Shakers entirely uni-

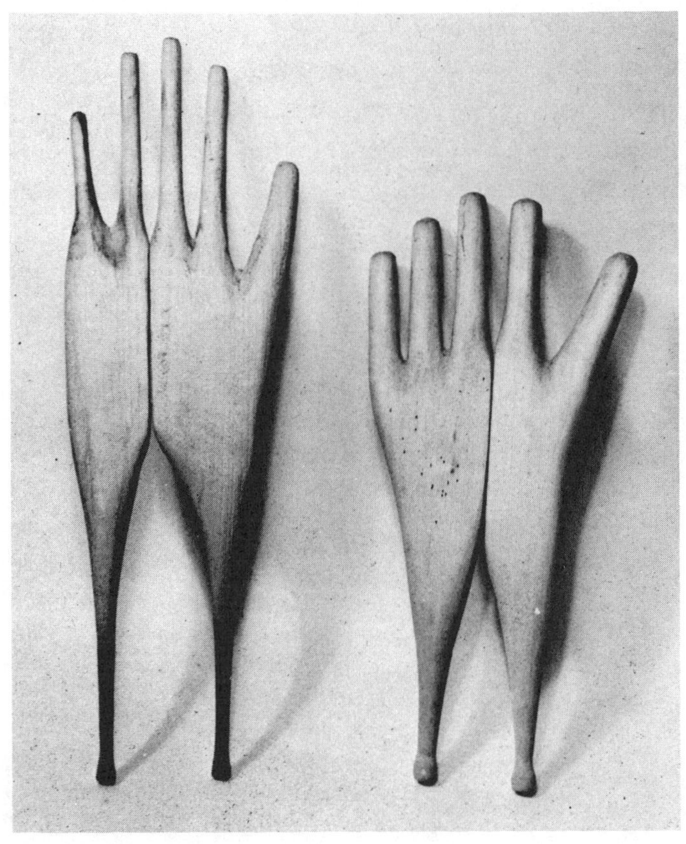

Wood stretchers for blocking knitted gloves. Forms are Shaker made and fold in half when not in use. OLD CHATHAM.

form, with the possible exception of Sabbath clothes. The general styles were always followed, but colors and small details could vary from family to family. Certain styles or colors were not allowed at given times in Shaker history. Anything superfluously trimmed or ornamented was against Shaker rules. In 1821 Millenial Laws dictated against the Shakers' owning and using "gay silk handkerchiefs, green veils, bought dark colored cotton handkerchiefs or lace for cap borders."

The major purpose in dictating uniformity of clothing among the Shakers was to continue the feeling of oneness in the sect and separation from the world. In a community where everyone dressed alike, no one could be jealous of what another wore.

Shorter dresses made of flowered print material are the last innovation in Shaker women's styles. The flowered prints were a great departure from nineteenth-century Shaker styles. The dresses conformed with contemporary styles. The surviving Shaker sisters still wear the bonnets for which they had become known from the earliest Shaker times.

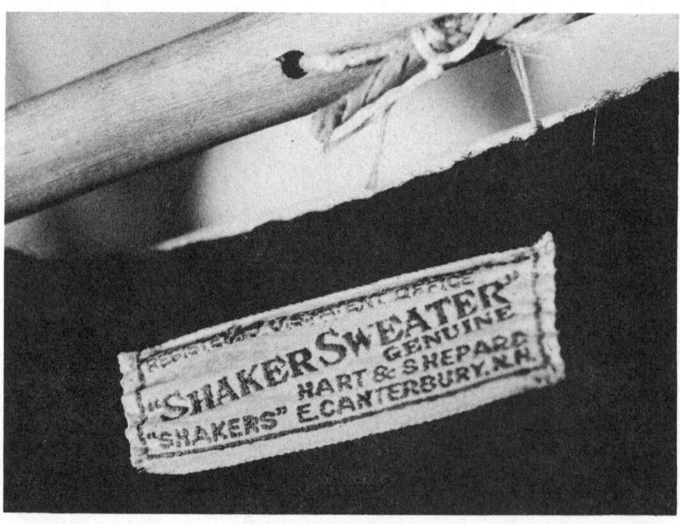

Shaker sweaters became so popular that the name became generic for slipover, hand-knit sweaters. Photograph shows label used by Shakers. OLD CHATHAM.

CHAPTER 9

BONNETS AND CLOAKS

Believers may not in any case or circumstances, manufacture for sale, any article or articles, which are superfluously wrought, and which would have a tendency to feed the pride and vanity of man, or such as would not be admissable to use among themselves, on account of their superfluity. Millenial Laws, 1821. Revised, 1845.

Two articles of clothing that the Shakers made for their own use became popular and fashionable among more worldly women in the nineteenth century. Palmleaf or straw bonnets were worn by the world's women and children from the late 1820s until the Civil War, and their manufacture and sale became an important Shaker industry. Shaker hooded cloaks were fashionable and in demand by the "carriage trade" in the latter part of the century.

The earliest Shaker bonnets were made of braided straw that was covered and lined with black silk. Plaited silk covered the crown, which was about one inch deep. Silk ribbons were attached to the crown and brought

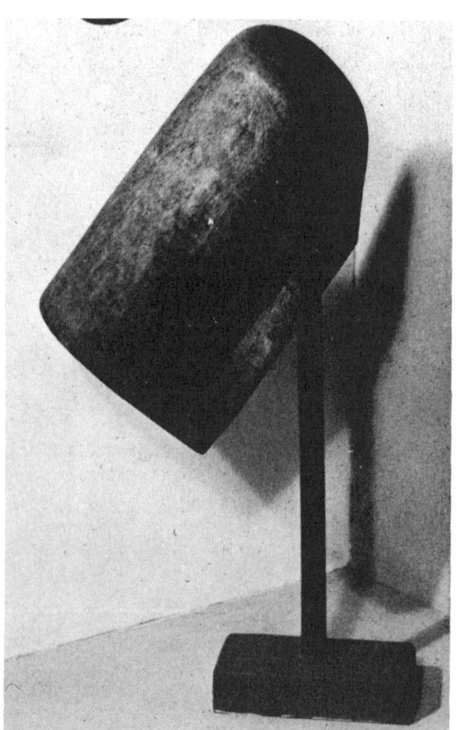

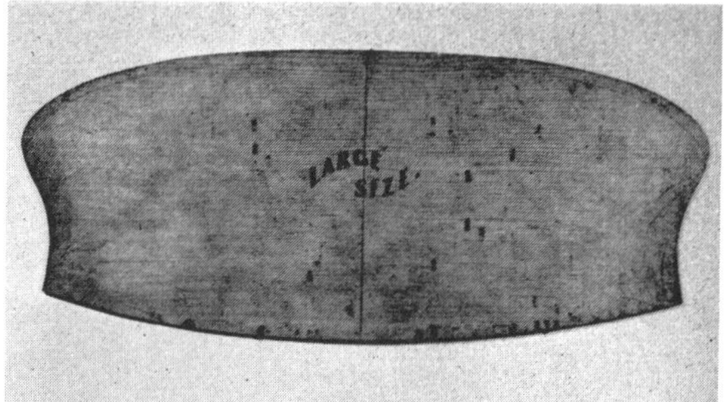

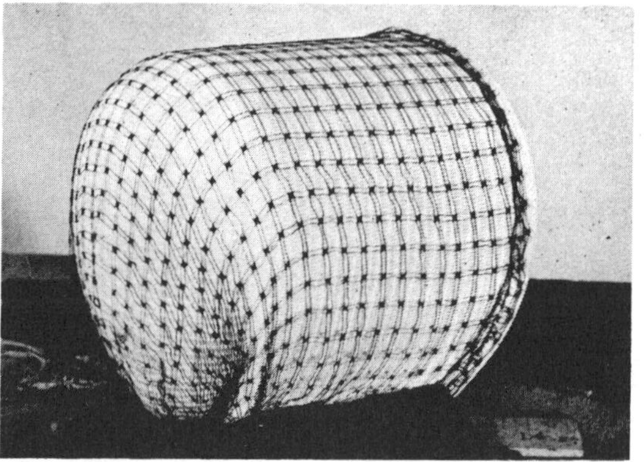

TOP LEFT: *Bonnet form used in shaping Shaker sisters' bonnets.* OLD CHATHAM.

TOP RIGHT: *Wooden pattern for Shaker bonnet.* OLD CHATHAM.

BOTTOM: *Shaker straw bonnet covered in black net.* OLD CHATHAM

down over the brim. The ribbons tied in the back of the neck. Called "chip hats," these narrow, crowned bonnets had brims that were about six inches deep. "Chip hats" were worn toward the end of the eighteenth century.

About 1800 the style of Shaker bonnets changed, as did the method of making them. Bonnets at this time were made of pasteboard and were covered in light-colored silk. The crown was made of soft fabric with no solid base. These hats were similar to those worn by the Quakers during the same period. By 1827 Shaker bonnets were made of palm-leaf straw and were trimmed with a short silk cape and ribbons that tied under the chin. These straw bonnets became a part of the standard wearing apparel for Shakeresses and many of their customers throughout the nineteenth century.

Palm leaf for the early straw bonnets was purchased from Cuba. After it was sized and dampened, the pieces of straw were split and tied to hand looms and woven with thread. Patterns were made of wood, and bonnet forms were produced in various sizes. The hats sold well until the Civil War, and the price was always around a dollar. Children's bonnets, made in the same manner, were half the price.

Following the Civil War, rye or oat straw was used in the manufacture of Shaker bonnets. Canterbury sister Eliza A. Stratton, in an undated journal, wrote instructions for preparing straw for making bonnets and other articles:

The time for gathering the straw is when the grain commences to ripen or turn yellow. Gather in the field, the grain standing; as the best straws, those freest from mildew, can be more easily selected. Cut just above the upper joint on the stalk for bonnets, the next two are shorter and may be used for table mats and small fancy articles. It is preferable to gather the straw a little too young, than too old.

Have ready, water boiling hot in which to scald the straw. When scalded sufficiently, the joints will make a snappy sound. The next process is to whiten it in the sun: three days are usually a sufficient length of time. Do not leave it out overnight after the first. Unsheathe it the second day. Bleach it in the same manner that woolens are bleached, repeating the burning of the brimstone two or three times. Rye and oats produce the best straw of any of the grains. Rye straw is the strongest; oat straw the whitest.

Brimstone causes steel to rust; palm leaf and straw being bleached with this, should not be cut with scissors or knives that are good, as it ruins them.

It is a good idea to varnish wire that is used in making bonnets, to prevent rusting.

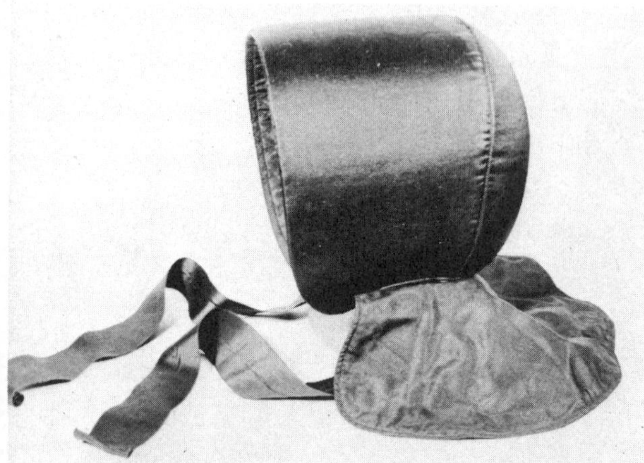

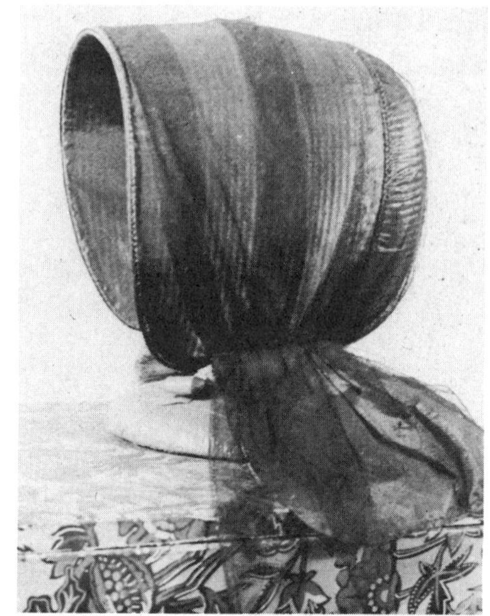

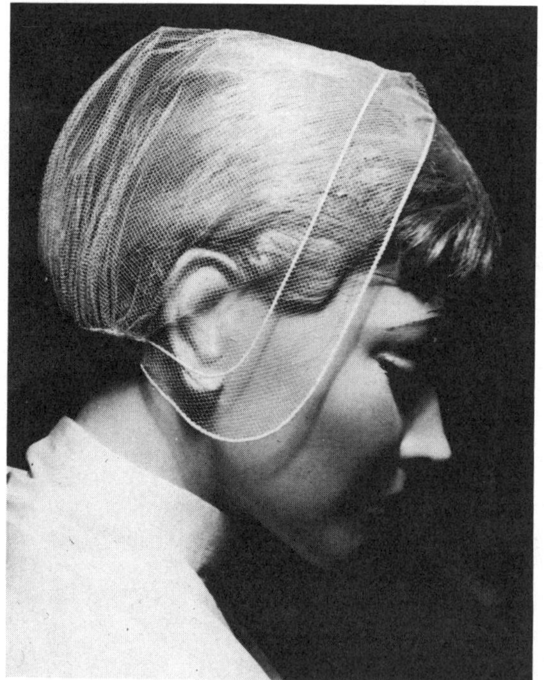

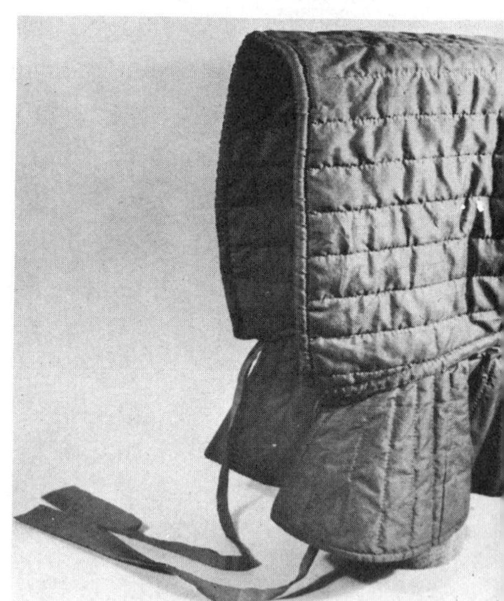

TOP LEFT: *Shaker bonnet made of straw and covered in black silk.* OLD CHATHAM.

Straw bonnets were worn in summer by the Shaker women and many were sold to their customers. The bonnets became as popular as the Shaker cloaks did at a later date. Winter bonnets made of silk that was hand quilted, filled and lined, were worn during cold weather.

Girls' sunbonnets with a soft crown and a wide brim were made as a shop item in the early part of this century. These sold for a dollar.

There still exist many Shaker bonnets covered with a variety of materials. Net covering was used that tied

OPPOSITE TOP RIGHT: *Shaker straw bonnet covered in black net. Paper-covered box is for storing bonnets.* OLD CHATHAM.

BOTTOM LEFT: *White net bonnet was worn indoors by Shaker sisters.* OLD CHATHAM.

BOTTOM RIGHT: *Winter bonnet is filled and quilted waterproof silk.* OLD CHATHAM.

LEFT: *At the turn of the century, bonnets in this style were made by Shakers for young girls and sold in the shop or by mail.* OLD CHATHAM.

BELOW: *A measuring table for cutting sizes of Shaker clothing, possibly cloaks. Board folds in half when not in use.* OLD CHATHAM.

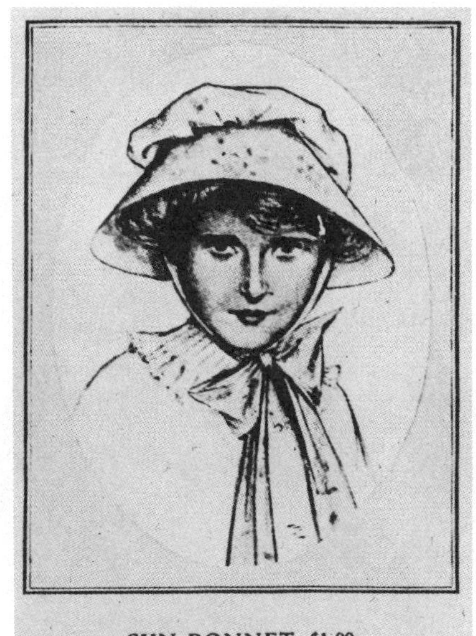

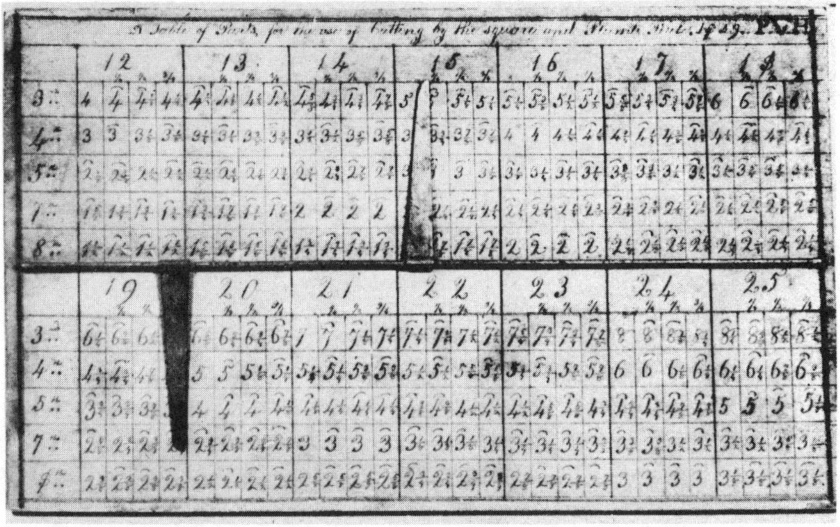

under the chin, and this same style is worn today when Shakeresses venture out in the summer. Although Shaker bonnets made during various periods of the nineteenth century differ somewhat in material, method of manu-

Pages from brochure advertising Shaker cloak. OLD CHATHAM.

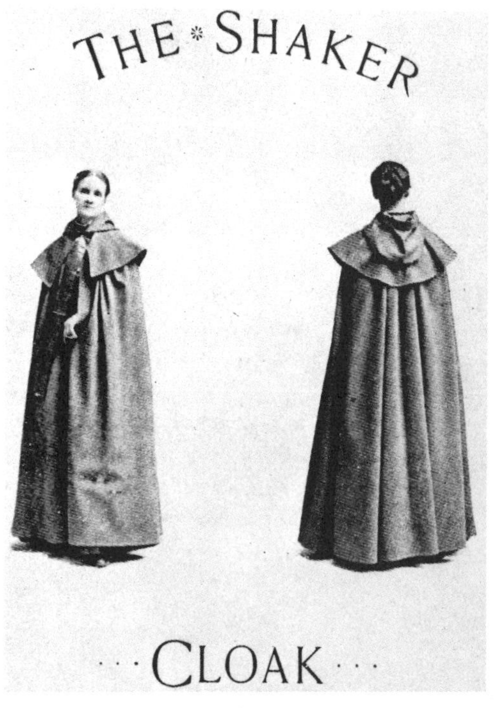

INTRODUCTION

IN presenting this little catalogue to the general public, it is our aim to show in a concise way a few of the many articles made at the present time by the Shakers of Mount Lebanon, Columbia County, N. Y.

For more than a century past various productions from the Shaker work-rooms have been before the public, always receiving therefrom much commendation for thoroughness of construction, simplicity of character, and originality of design

Making the SHAKER CLOAK, which is an unique and comfortable garment, is one of the principal industries carried on at the present time, and commands large patronage.

The hand-made boxes which are shown in this catalogue, are made from the wood of the poplar tree and woven in a style to resemble basket work. They are a combination of neatness and utility, and will commend themselves to lovers of the beautiful.

On the last page of the pamphlet will be found a specific price list of the different sizes of illustrated articles, also a list of miscellaneous articles *not* illustrated, but equally desirable for gifts or souvenirs.

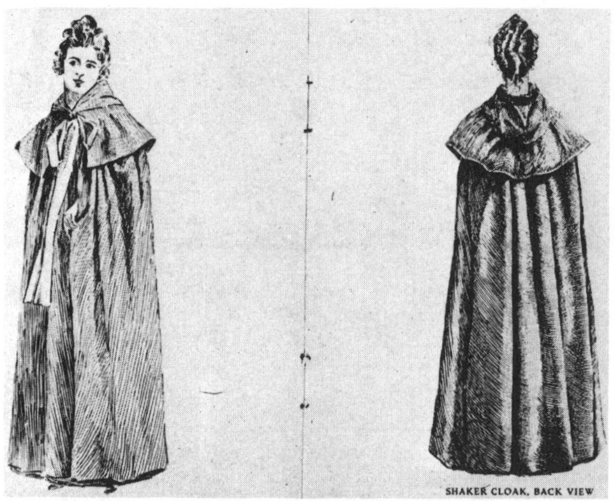

facture, or color, the general appearance is similar and all have a "poke" effect that somewhat hides the face. They were practical in that they were light in weight, kept the sun out of one's eyes, and the short capes found on many of the bonnets covered and protected the neck.

It is interesting that some clothing styles chosen by the Shakers because they were practical and different enough to set them apart would appeal strongly enough to non-Shakers to make them fashionable. Such was the case with Shaker cloaks. They were warm and ample and the hoods, made large enough to cover Shaker bonnets, fitted comfortably over the elaborate hair styles of more worldly late nineteenth-century ladies.

The "Dorothy" Shaker cloak, named for its originator, Eldress Dorothy Durgin, of Canterbury, became fashionable in the last quarter of the nineteenth century. The cloaks were made in sizes ranging from tiny white cloaks for babies and small girls to adult sizes. Cloaks exist today that were made by the Shakers in a variety of colors. Mauve pink, blue, green, maroon, and dove grey cloaks were a lucrative and popular product of the Shaker sisters. Fine French broadcloth replaced hand-woven Shaker wool when the manufacture of cloaks first became an industry. One Shaker sister, writing in this century of the Canterbury industries, said that "although the fine

LEFT: *Advertisement for Shaker cloaks made by Emma J. Neale.* OLD CHATHAM.

RIGHT: *Measuring sticks were made for many purposes in shops. Since these were often made to serve just one purpose, measurements were not written on them.* BELFIT.

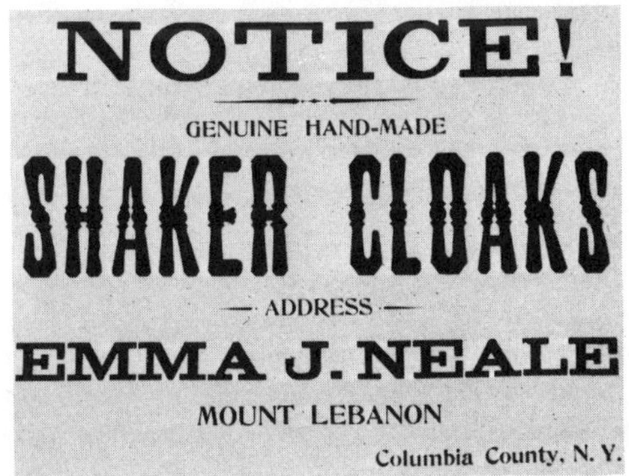

RIGHT: *Certificate of trademark given to Emma J. Neale in 1901 for Shaker long cloak.* OLD CHATHAM.

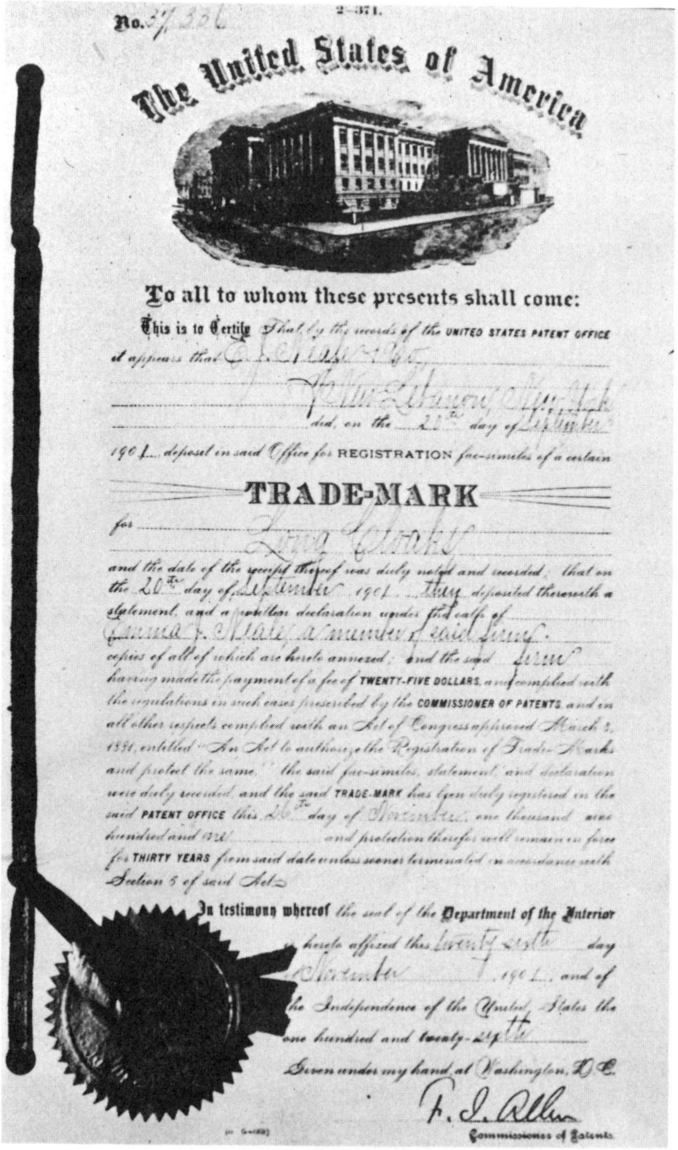

No. 37,336 2-371.

The United States of America

To all to whom these presents shall come:

This is to Certify That by the records of the UNITED STATES PATENT OFFICE it appears that E. J. Neale & Co. Mount Lebanon, N.Y. did, on the 20th day of September 1901 deposit in said Office for REGISTRATION fac-similes of a certain

TRADE-MARK

for Long Cloaks

and the date of the receipt thereof was duly noted and recorded; that on the 20th day of September 1901 they deposited therewith a statement, and a written declaration under the oath of Emma J. Neale a member of said firm copies of all of which are hereto annexed; and the said firm having made the payment of a fee of TWENTY-FIVE DOLLARS, and complied with the regulations in such cases prescribed by the COMMISSIONER OF PATENTS, and in all other respects complied with an Act of Congress approved March 3, 1881, entitled "An Act to authorize the Registration of Trade-Marks and protect the same," the said fac-similes, statement, and declaration were duly recorded, and the said TRADE-MARK has been duly registered in the said PATENT OFFICE this 26th day of November, one thousand nine hundred and one and protection therefor will remain in force for THIRTY YEARS from said date unless sooner terminated in accordance with Section 5 of said Act.

In testimony whereof the seal of the Department of the Interior is hereto affixed this twenty sixth day of November, 1901, and of the Independence of the United States the one hundred and twenty-sixth

Given under my hand, at Washington, D.C.

F. I. Allen

Commissioner of Patents.

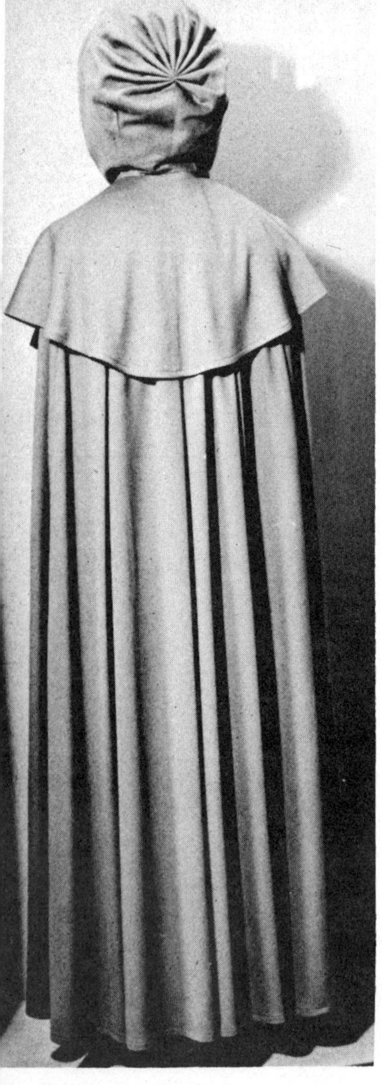

LEFT: *Shaker cloak made for Mrs. Grover Cleveland to wear to husband's second inauguration. Because of defect, this cloak was never sent and another was made in its stead. The fabric is dove grey wool broadcloth.* OLD CHATHAM.

material of earlier days cannot be found, the cloaks are still an acquisition to milady's wardrobe."

The early Shaker cloaks, made of hand-woven wool, were usually either blue or grey. Later, when the cloaks were manufactured for sale at Mount Lebanon, under the name of Emma J. Neale and Company, French doeskin and other quality fabrics were used. Eldress Neale received a patent in 1901 that covered the design of her Shaker cloaks. Shaker cloaks were so attractive and practical that Mrs. Grover Cleveland ordered one in dove grey to wear to her husband's second inaugural in 1893. The cloak that was made to fill this order is on display at Old Chatham Shaker Museum and was never sent, due to an imperfection, the whereabouts of which is still a secret. Another cloak was quickly made to take the place of the first and reached Washington in time for the inauguration.

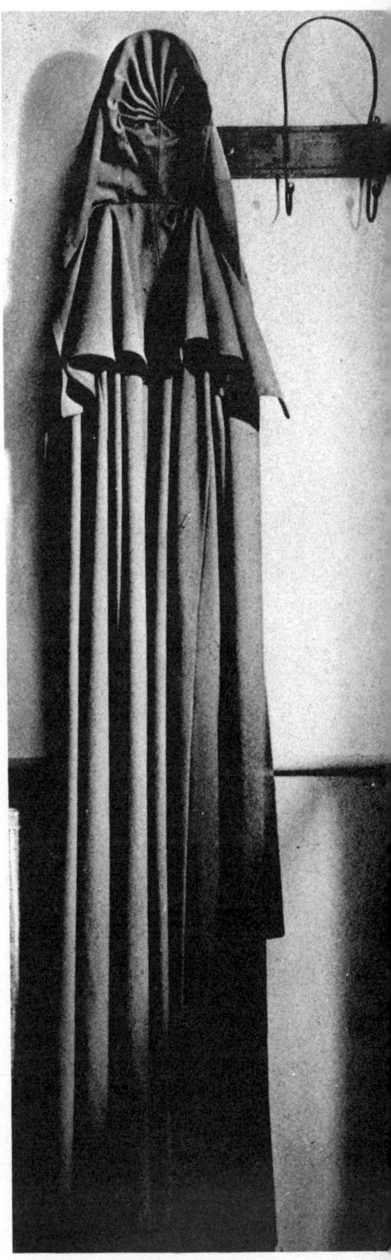

A special wire hanger was designed and made to hang cloaks so that they kept their shape. OLD CHATHAM.

A great advantage of Shaker cloaks is their ample hood and a wide cape collar that adds extra warmth on the shoulders. The body of the cloak was cut so that the back formed perfect uniform drapes from the shoulder to the hem. No patterns have been found for the original cloaks, and although similar garments are currently being made (not by the Shakers), the pattern was formed by taking apart an old cloak and tracing the parts.

The cloak business was terminated in 1929. When dresses cut to the floor were no longer fashionable, there were no orders for the long cloaks. Before the flapper era, however, women could send their measurements to Eldress Neale at Mount Lebanon, choose from a selection of beautiful wool fabrics, and receive a warm and attractive garment that they knew would be superbly draped and tailored.

One Shaker product, associated with the cloak business, has erroneously been considered by collectors as having been originally used for advertising. This is the

EMMA J. NEALE & CO.,
COLUMBIA COUNTY, MOUNT LEBANON, N. Y.

Mount Lebanon, 191

FRIEND:

Replying to your letter we enclose samples of cloaking in various weights and colors, with price of cloak in usual finish attached to each. If cloak is lined throughout the price of silk and $2.00 for extra work is added. Repairing cloaks from January to September only. Please return samples not used and oblige, Yours respectfully,

EMMA J. NEALE.

ORDER.

EMMA J. NEALE & CO.,

Dealers in GENUINE SHAKER CLOAKS,

Mount Lebanon, Columbia Co., N. Y.

Please make me Shaker Cloak like enclosed sample by following measures. Price $.

Length from top of collar at back to exact length desired when finished, inches.

Bust, over arms, inches.

Neck Measurement, over dress collar, inches. (we making necessary allowance in size.)

To be sent by express.

To

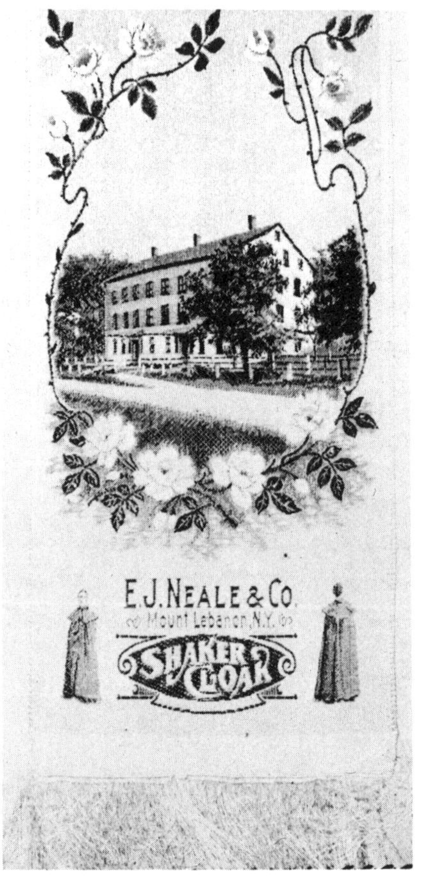

LEFT: *Order blank for Shaker cloaks from beginning of this century when they were stylish article of clothing for world's women.* OLD CHATHAM.

RIGHT: *Woven silk bookmark, made in Lyons, France. Advertising on bottom was an error and bookmark was never sold.* OLD CHATHAM.

woven silk bookmark that is illustrated in this chapter. The Shakers were constantly searching for small gifts and souvenirs to sell in their shops, and in the late nineteenth century woven ribbons, called "stevensgraphs" after the man who invented the process of weaving minutely detailed silk pictures on ribbon, were popular as bookmarks. The loom that Stevens used was an adaptation of a jacquard ribbon loom that had been invented in France as early as 1801. Because Stevens, who sold many of his ribbons to be used as giveaways at fairs or as inexpensive advertising items was English, it was generally thought that all these ribbons had been made in England.

Sometime around the turn of the century, the Mount Lebanon sisters ordered a quantity of ribbons from a maker in Lyons, France, with the woven picture of one of their buildings and garlands of flowers. An assortment of pastel silk colors were used for the background. Unfortunately, the sisters used stationery for the order that had Eldress Neale's letterhead advertising her famous cloak, and the French weavers, who were used to designing ribbons with advertising, included Emma Neale's trademark. The ribbons were never sold and were simply put away until the stock was offered to friends and customers shortly before the shop closed permanently. Many of these ribbons have disappeared. A few have shown up and have been sold by antique dealers for very high prices, usually under the impression that they were created for advertising, which, as we have seen, was never the intention of the Shakers.

The woven silk bookmarks are interesting from several viewpoints. First, they were not made in England, but in France. Second, they were never sold as planned, due to the error of weaving the letterhead on the bottom. The instructions for making the ribbons were probably sent in English and were not understood by the French weavers. Most interesting of all is that the Shakers did not often look abroad for items to sell in their shop and it is probable that this experience discouraged them from ordering foreign objects again. The few Lyons bookmarks that do exist in private collections are, therefore, unique Shaker items that are probably the most un-Shakerlike collectables that exist.

CHAPTER 10

RUGS AND CARPETS

When brethren and sisters go up and down stairs, they should not slip their feet on the carpet, or floor, but lift them up and set them down plumb, so as not to wear out the carpets or floor unnecessarily. Also when they turn at the head or foot of the stairs, they should not turn their feet on the floor, lest they wear holes in it. Millenial Laws, 1821. Revised, 1845.

Rugs and carpets were made by the Shakers for use in their own dwellings and to sell in their shops or through the mail. Rug looms were built rather early in the nineteenth century, and runners were woven on them as well as chair mats and coverings for footstools. There was also a variety of handmade rugs and mats, many of which were made by methods and techniques that seem to have been peculiar to the Shakers.

In some of the existing Shaker-made rugs can be seen the thriftiness typical of many New England women in using scraps of textiles. Rags were employed in making braided and hooked rugs. Small area rugs were made in a variety of techniques and patterns.

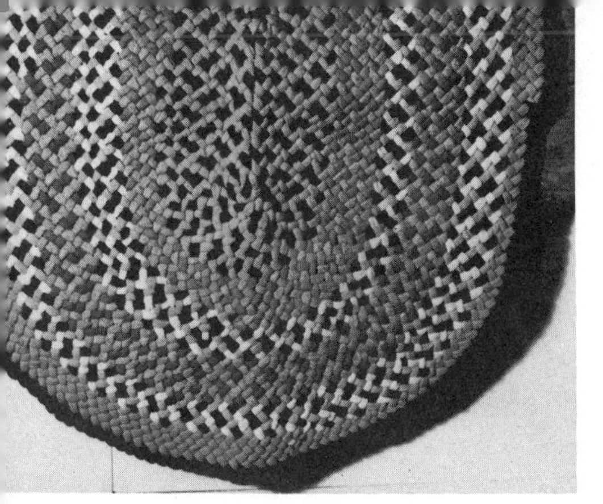

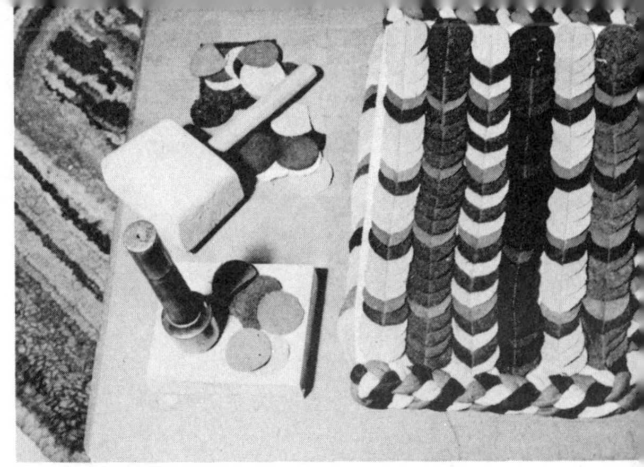

One type of rug made by the Shakers that utilized scraps of wool is the "dollar mat." It was made of discs cut about the size of a silver dollar, from wool fabric left from the manufacture of Shaker cloaks. The discs were cut by stamping them out with a special cutting tool that resembles a cookie cutter. Probably several layers of cloth could be cut at the same time. The wool circles were then strung together according to color. Rugs were made by overlapping the discs and sewing them to a backing. Colors were alternated to form a pattern. It is probable that this simple version of the "dollar mat" was made by children.

A more sophisticated method of using the wool discs in rugmaking was to fold the circles into quarters and sew them to a backing. The quarter circles were placed closely together, forming a rug that had a rather high pile. The mats were finished by edging them with one or two rows of braided fabric.

TOP LEFT: *Braided rugs were made in quantity for Shaker use and for sale.* OLD CHATHAM.

TOP RIGHT: *"Dollar mat" probably made by Shaker child. Illustration shows tool for cutting discs out of wool fabric scraps. Rug in background is more common Shaker hand-loomed rug.* OLD CHATHAM.

LEFT: *"Dollar mat" made in 1952 at Mount Lebanon.* OLD CHATHAM.

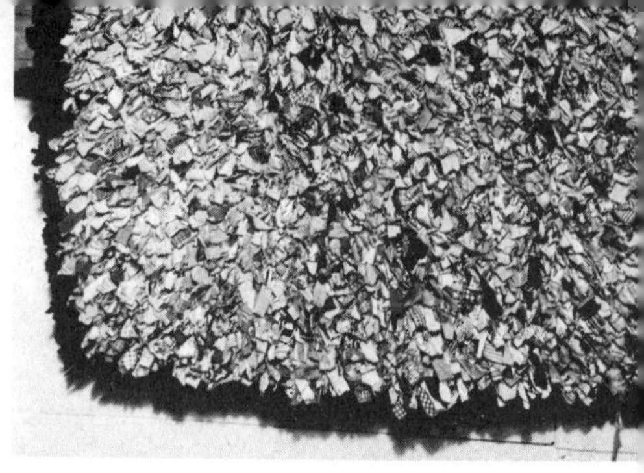

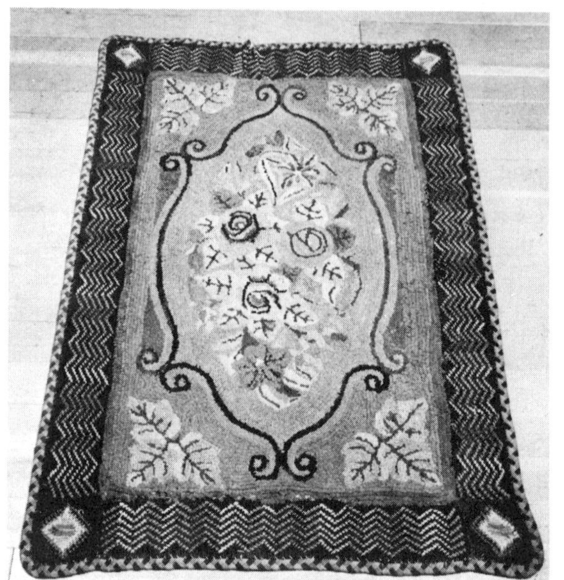

LEFT: *Hooked rug in bright floral pattern made from narrow strips of cloth. Borders are knitted and edge is braided.* OLD CHATHAM.

RIGHT: *Brightly colored rug made from strips of silk at Hancock by Sister Jennie Wells in 1953. Probably not made for Shaker use.* OLD CHATHAM.

Often two or more needlework techniques were used in making a Shaker rug. Hooked rugs might have a knitted border, for instance. Round rugs were made by knitting strips of increasing widths and sewing these strips one around the other until the rug was the desired circumference. The circles were then sewn to a backing and edged with a single or double fabric braid. In order that the knitted rugs would lie flat, careful stretching and blocking had to be employed. The geometrical patterns of contrasting colors, often a different pattern for each knitted strip, make these round rugs distinctive.

An interesting rug at the Old Chatham Shaker Museum is one made of silk rags that were cut into strips about an inch wide and about three inches long. These strips were then doubled over and either hooked through or sewn to a backing. As many varicolored strips as could fit were crowded onto the rug and the myriad of colors in the silk gives an appearance of confetti. The rug has a deep pile and a shaggy, colorful appearance. The border is made of black silk strips.

Braided rugs seem to have been made in quantity by the Shakers. They were another means of using up scrap textiles and utilizing worn-out clothing. Sister Sarah Collins of Mount Lebanon was the best known of the Shaker rugmakers, and two magnificent large oval braided rugs made by her are on display in the Sitting Room at Old Chatham.

Rugs made from tightly looped fabric strips that give the appearance of having been hooked were made in runner and L-shapes to fit around the worktables in Shaker buildings. The technique of making these rugs seems to have been peculiar to the Shakers, and when new, the rugs must have been cheerful and practical.

A rather atypical Shaker-made patchwork quilt is on display at Old Chatham Shaker Museum. The quilt was made in high Victorian style by Mount Lebanon Shakers on special order from the outside world. It dates around 1890 and possibly was a group effort rather than made by one person. It is composed of twenty-five colorful velvet and silk patchwork squares sewn together and edged in a border of maroon velvet. The quilt exhibits a large variety of embroidery stitches, and many of the patterned or plain silk patches were over-embroidered

Shaker rugs knitted in strips and sewn into round shape. Edges are braid. Rugs are from Hancock. OLD CHATHAM.

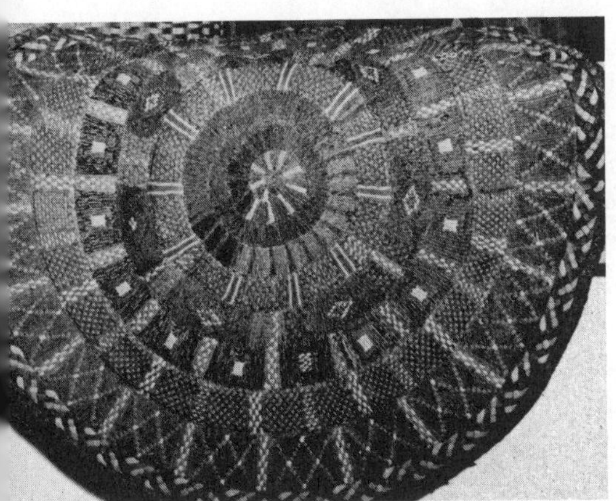

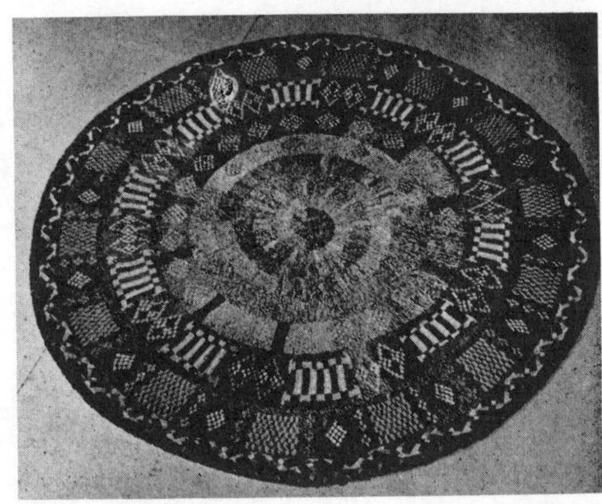

RIGHT: *Varicolored crocheted rug resembles braided rugs.* OLD CHATHAM.

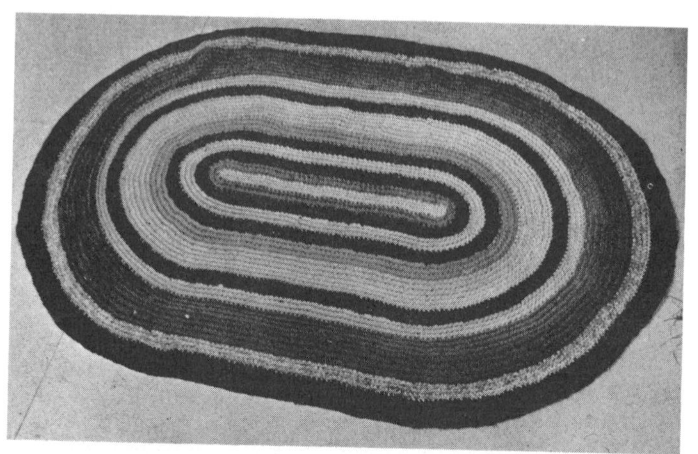

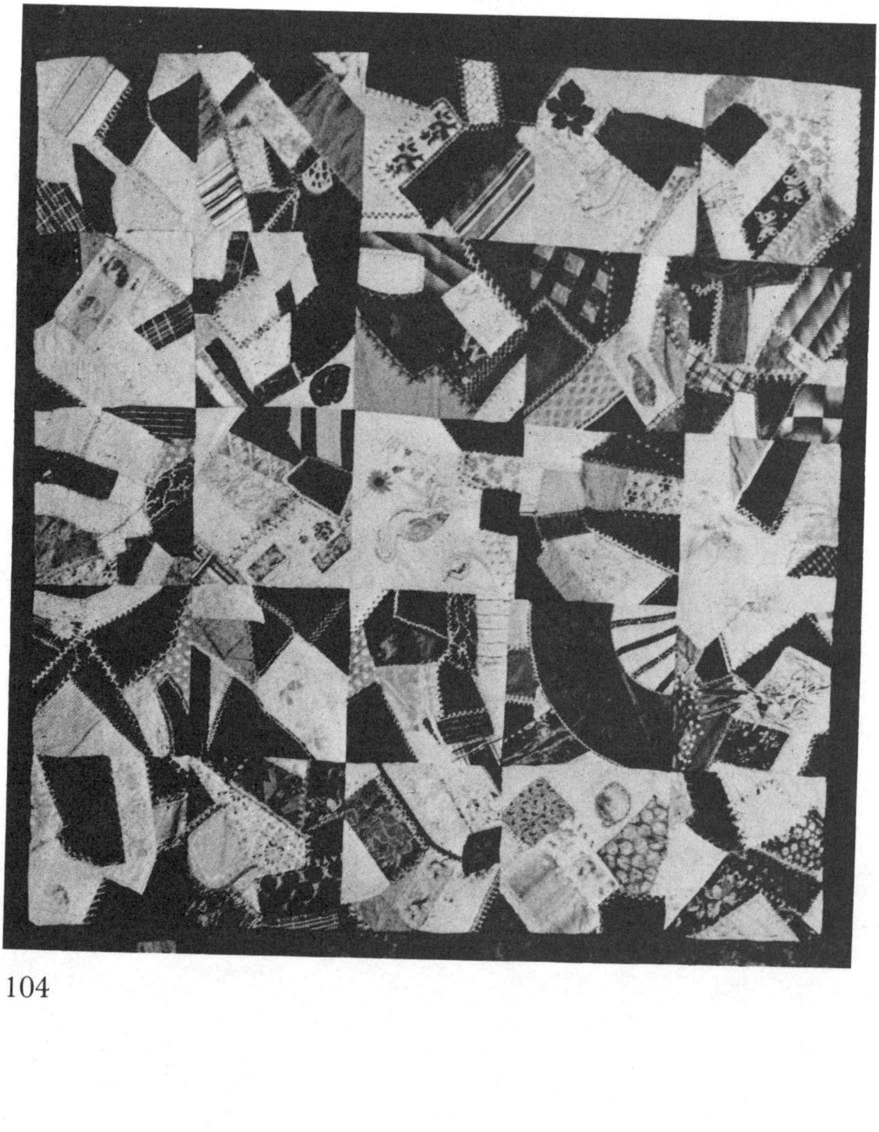

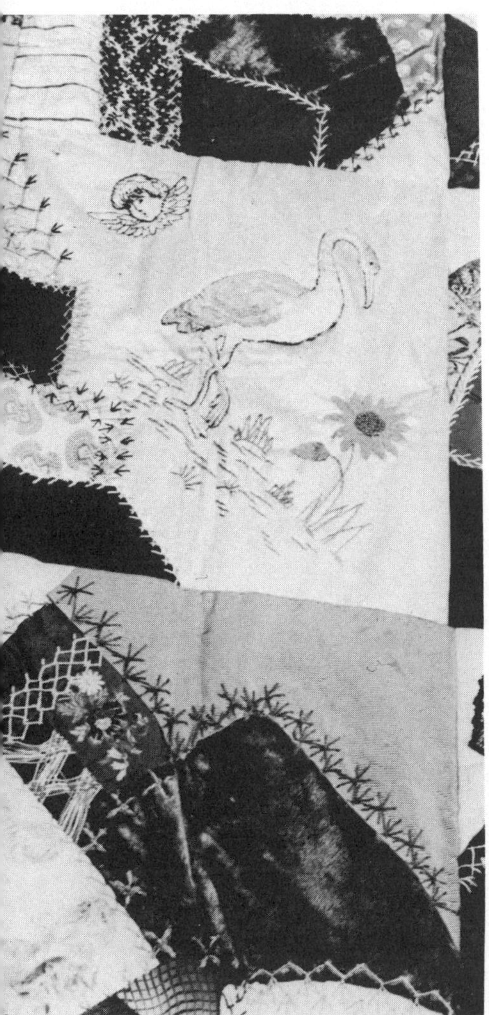

BOTTOM OPPOSITE PAGE AND THIS PAGE: *Shaker-made silk and velvet patchwork quilt, heavily hand embroidered. Quilt was made around 1890 on special order from outside customer. Illustrated are quilt and two details.* OLD CHATHAM

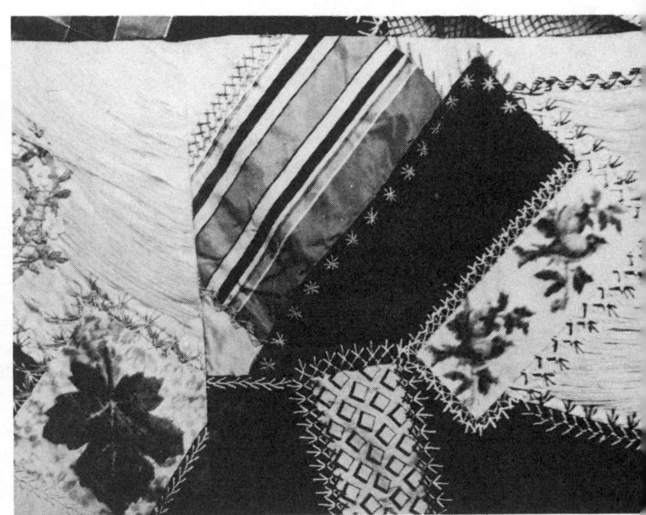

by hand. A variety of motifs can be found in the embroidered patches. The center square has a large silk patch embroidered rather whimsically with an angel's head, a crane, and a few flowers. There is little repetition of fabric in the quilt, and the patches are edged with a variety of fancy needlework stitches. The quilt typifies the willingness of the Shakers at the end of the nineteenth century to use their skills to make articles for sale that they would never have used themselves.

CHAPTER 11

THE CHILDREN'S ORDER

Children should be kept in an order by themselves, where it can be done consistently. And as a general rule, boys should remain in the children's order, until sixteen years of age, and girls until fourteen.

No one but such caretakers as are appointed, should interfere in the dictation of children.

Children should never be made equals and playmates of, by those who are older. All should be sociable with children, but not familiar. Millenial Laws, 1821. Revised, 1845.

Many children were brought into the Shaker communities by parents who chose the Shaker way of life. Other children were taken into Shaker families as orphans. Still others were indentured to the Shakers by agreement with their parents or guardians so that the children would be taught a useful trade. It was not unusual for a child in the nineteenth century to be indentured to artisans at an early age, and nine was thought not to be too young for a boy to begin to learn a trade. Since there was a rotation of labor among adult Shakers, the children placed under their care often became versatile in their talents also.

In communities where there were large enough groups of boys and girls, a caretaker was appointed to oversee their welfare and industry. Thus the boys were introduced to many skills and occupations in which the Shakers were involved and could choose the work for which they were most suited. During periods when there were too few boys to make it practical to house them together, each one might be indentured to a particular artisan. Many of them stayed on and continued their trades as Shakers throughout their adulthood.

Education of a practical nature, other than that of learning one or more trades, was not neglected either. In the indenture agreements, which differed depending on the Shaker families concerned, each child was given schooling in "Spelling, Reading, Writing, Composition, English Grammar, Arithmetic, Mensuration, The Science of Agriculture, Agriculture Chemistry, a small portion of History and Geography, Architecture, Moral Science, Good Manners, and True Religion." In 1845 these subjects were considered sufficient as general studies

Minerva Langworthy made this cross-stitch sampler or "example" at the age of twelve. OLD CHATHAM.

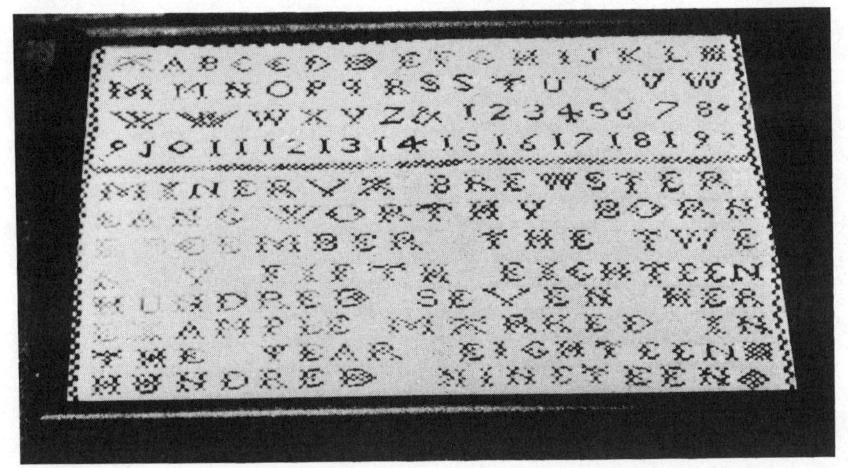

RIGHT: *Doll dressed in Shaker costume could be purchased with either straw bonnet or cape. Late nineteenth century.* OLD CHATHAM.

BELOW: *Pair of early dolls dressed in Shaker costume.* OLD CHATHAM.

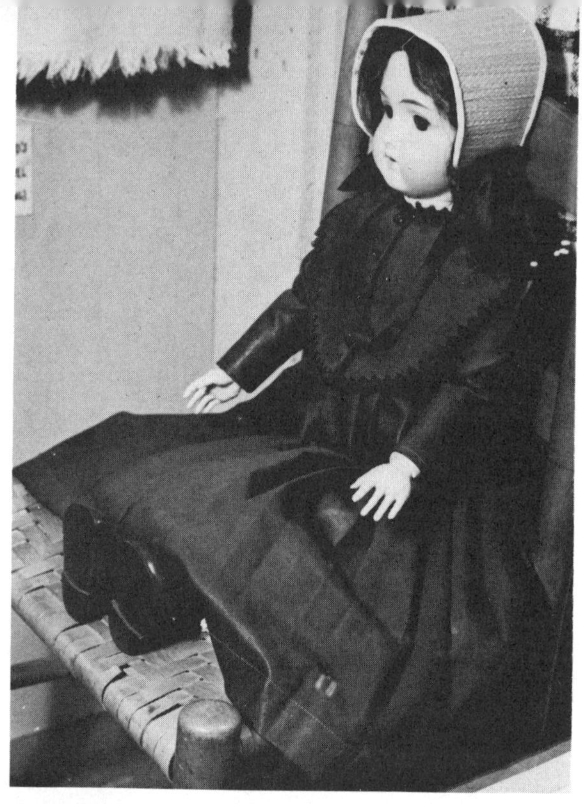

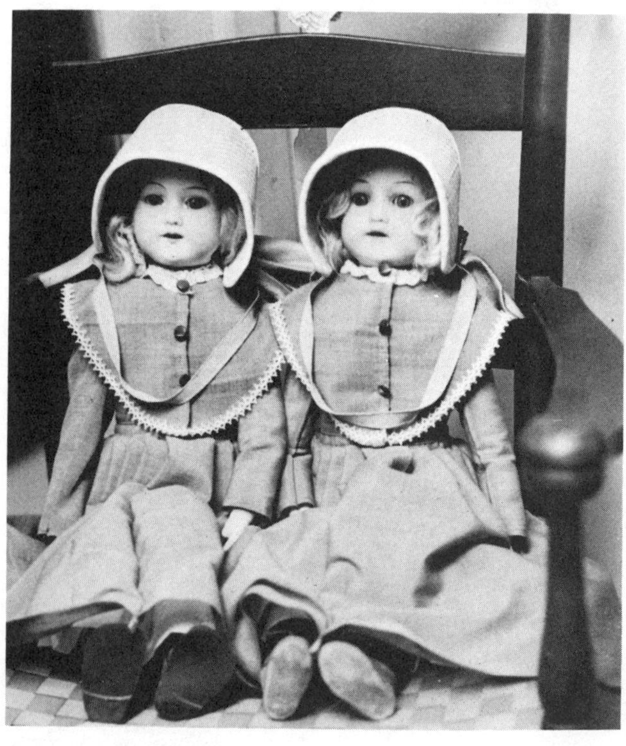

for children among Believers. Each child who attended Shaker schools was given a strong indoctrination into the religion that was the basis of the Shaker way of life. A great many of the children, thus exposed to an early education in Shaker religion, stayed on in the communities and lived the protected and comfortable life to which they had become used.

Taught skills by master craftsmen at a young age, many of the boys became expert in more than one craft and continued to make objects in the Shaker style. Children were taught that there was only one way to work and salvation would be theirs if they "put their hands to work and their hearts to God." It was in part because of this indenture system that the Shakers continued for such a long period of time to make products for sale that were continuously of superb quality. When shortcuts in manufacture could be devised that would not lead to the making of inferior products, they were introduced and shared among the Shaker communities. If innovations in any way cheapened the product, they were not used.

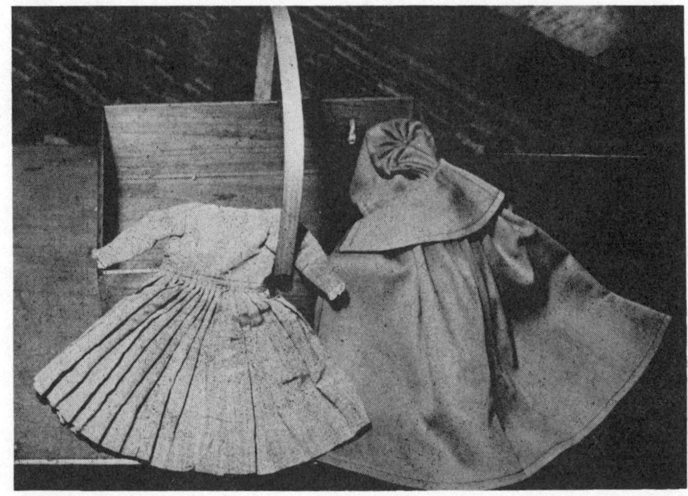

Doll dresses and cloaks were made of the same fabric and with as much detail as adult-sized clothes. Shown here with Shaker carrier. OLD CHATHAM.

Education for the young girls who came under the care of the Shaker communities was not neglected, either. Separate classes taught them the same basic subjects as the boys learned. The girls' school was kept in the summer and the boys attended classes in the winter. Children of both sexes were never taught together.

Occupations thought suitable for girls were taught by the Shaker sisters. Thus, a young girl of the age of nine or ten might be taught dressmaking as a trade. However, she would also learn other occupations by helping with the many other industries with which the Shakeresses occupied themselves and supported their families. The preparation of food products that were sold, planting, harvesting, and preparing herbs, spinning, weaving, and the many other occupations of the sisters were shared with the young. The girls dressed in smaller copies of their elders' costumes.

It must have been an easy matter for children to fit

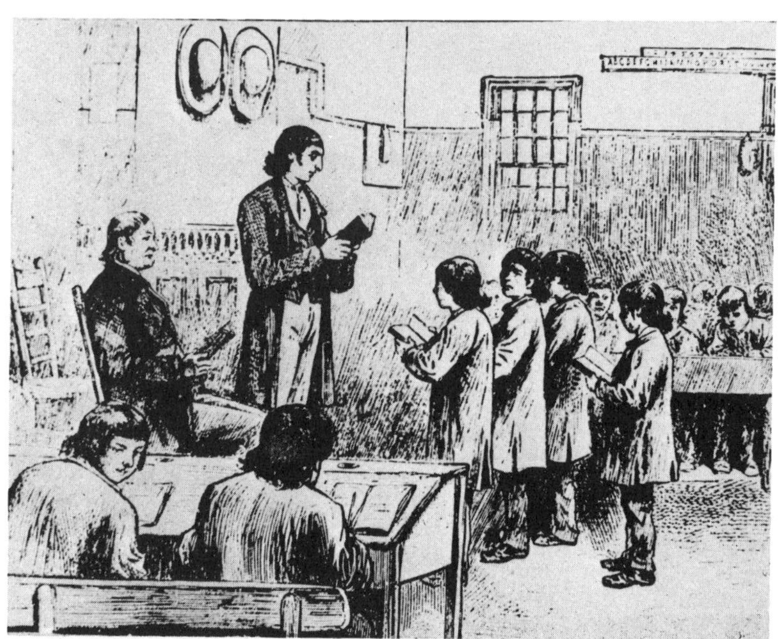

Boys' schoolroom, Niskayuna Community.

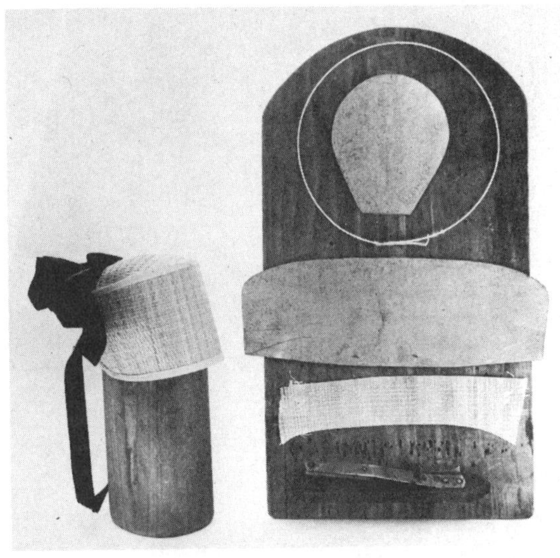

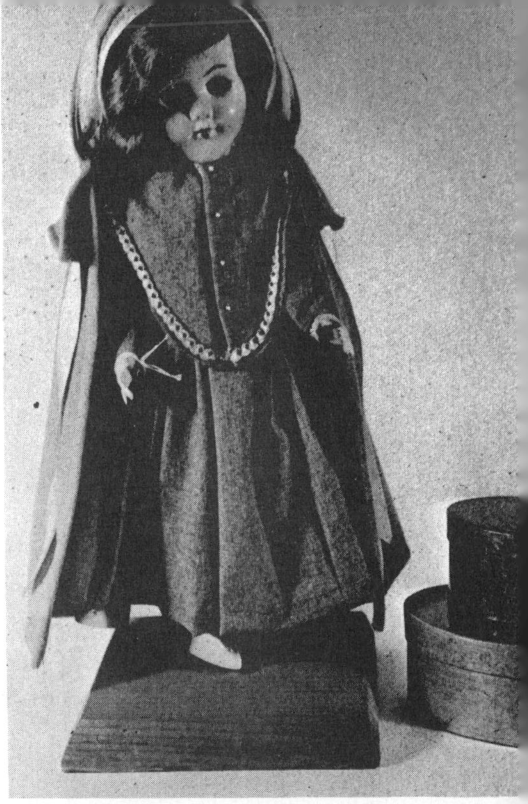

into the Shaker way of life, and most certainly they were treated with the firmness and warmth to which children respond. Brought up in an atmosphere of careful regulation, children would soon learn that the same rules governed all and that there was not one set of regulations for them and another for the adults. Everyone worked and everyone shared in the fruits of his labor. To be "seen and not heard" applied to adults as well as children, and those Shakers who could not conform to the rules were not made to feel welcome no matter what their age. It was not allowed for sisters to make pets of any of the children, and rules were written so that the presence of a child still did not license the meeting between a single male and female adult.

Among collections of Shaker-made objects one can find evidence of the importance of the children who came under the care of the Shakers. Scaled-down brooms and

LEFT: *Doll bonnets were made in same manner as adult Shaker bonnets except that woven poplar straw was used. Illustrated here is wooden form and patterns for doll bonnet. Tool on bottom right is straw splitter for shredding poplar wood.* BELFIT

RIGHT: *Doll on display stand as shown in Shaker sisters' shops at beginning of this century. Shaker boxes are miniature size. Dolls were not made by Shakers.* OLD CHATHAM.

Wooden top with metal tip made by Shaker brethren. OLD CHATHAM.

rakes and other household and garden tools are indications that the children worked, but at their own level. It is obvious that the young Shakers were in no way used to do the work of adults, but worked alongside the grown-ups at their own pace.

Articles of clothing made for children show the same fine workmanship and loving care that indicate the young did not go unattended or uncared for.

Scaled-down furniture, made in the simple utilitarian Shaker styles of the nineteenth century, allowed the children to sit comfortably at table or in classroom. Children's chairs were made for sale to the world as well. The chairs were designed in graduated sizes, so that no child should have to sit with his feet dangling while he worked. Highchairs were also made in Shaker style, probably just for Shaker use, since so few still exist. The chairs were made without trays, and the very young child was probably pulled to the table and fed with the group. Revolving stools were also made for sale and for use in Shaker schoolrooms.

In a clean and healthy atmosphere, where the youth were given excellent care and training in the practical arts, their toys were small replicas of adult tools. However, the Shakers made some frivolous playthings for sale to the world, and it is not unlikely that some of these toys were used by Shaker children, also.

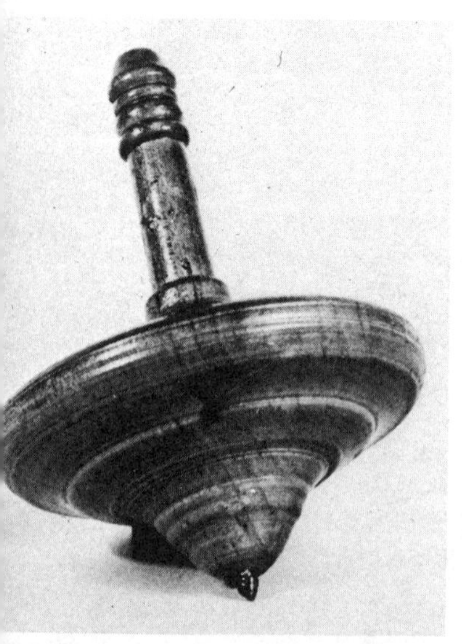

Throughout the latter part of the nineteenth century, commercially purchased dolls were dressed in Shaker costume and sold in the sisters' shops. Most amazing is the care with which the miniature Shaker doll clothing was made. The dresses, straw bonnets, and Shaker capes in which the dolls were dressed are duplicates of adult Shaker women's costumes, and the needlework is as carefully done as for the grown-up version. The patterns and textiles used for Shaker doll bonnets, dresses, cloaks, and underclothing were scaled-down duplicates of their maker's clothing.

Doll-sized oval boxes were made and sold for holding doll's clothes. Turned-wood tops of superb quality were made in the woodworking shops by the brethren. Small fitted sewing baskets for young girls were also made in duplicate of the adult product, and miniature sewing stands were used by Shaker girls and also sold to the world. If learning by imitation and indulgent instruction were Shaker beliefs that dictated the manner in which their wards were brought up, many of the tools were made in miniature for the Shaker children's comfort.

Some of the most charming Shaker objects that can be seen in collections today are the products made by the young. Examples of corkwork, a kind of simple knitting done on a spool in which four nails have been inserted, can be found. Small and simple rugs, and samplers made in simple stitches can also be found. Particularly charming are the small versions of the "dollar mats" made from round pieces of wool fabric and sewn to a backing.

Rather than setting impossible tasks for young fingers, it is obvious that easy stitches were tolerated while children learned the discipline of working on and completing tasks that were set before them by what must have been somewhat indulgent taskmasters or task mistresses. If little time was spent by young people in play, adult Shakers did not play either. Release came for all in the songs and dances that were a part of Shaker worship. While the appointed caretaker was the closest most Shaker children came to having a substitute parent, and Shakers were forbidden to make favorites of the children placed in their care, it is highly probable that religion and work, which could not be separated in the Shaker philosophy, were also, when it came to the young, tempered with a certain amount of general indulgence, attention, and affection.

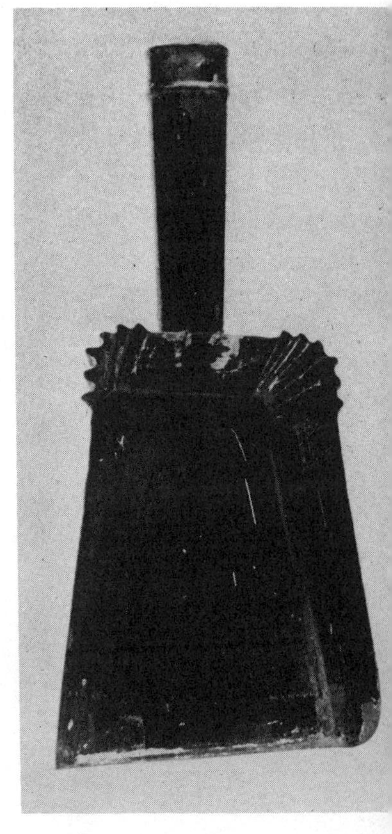

Small dustpan, painted black.
BELFIT

CHAPTER 12

BROOMS AND BRUSHES

No kind of filthy rubbish, may be left to remain around the dwelling houses or shops, nor in the dooryards, or streets in front of the dwelling houses or shops.

Brethren and sisters should turn out in the spring and clean the dooryards and street.

No one should carelessly pass over small things, as a pin, a kernel of grain, etc. thinking it too small to pick up, for if we do, our Heavenly Father will consider us too small for him to bestow his blessing upon. Millenial Laws, 1821. Revised, 1845.

For many Americans in the early nineteenth century "a new broom" meant a Shaker-made broom. The Shaker's penchant for cleanliness and order led to the manufacture of their own brooms, and by the beginning of the nineteenth century they were making brooms and brushes for others to use.

Broom corn, a type of sorghum, was grown in the East, and brooms and brushes were manufactured as early as 1798. Theodore Bates of Watervliet is credited with having invented the first flat broom. A variety of shapes and sizes of brooms and brushes was produced, and as usual with all early Shaker products, the brooms soon were in demand for their excellent quality and reasonable price.

It is probable that the Shakers were the first to have grown broom corn in the New England and New York areas for the purpose of manufacturing brooms and brushes. By 1805 brooms and brushes were made for sale at Watervliet and New Lebanon. Broom and mop handles for other Shaker colonies were made at New Lebanon also.

While it is obvious today that a flat broom is a more efficient tool for cleaning than a round broom, because the flat broom can reach more easily into corners and under low furniture, until the flat broom was invented, brooms were made of a bunch of broom straw tied around a handle.

Brooms and brushes of many shapes and sizes were

LEFT: *Straw splitter designed and made by Shakers and used in manufacture of brooms.* OLD CHATHAM.

RIGHT: *Unfinished broom stands against window in broom shop at Hancock.*

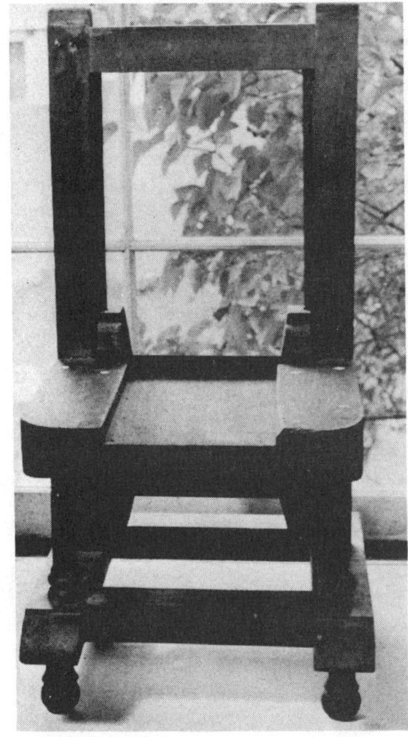

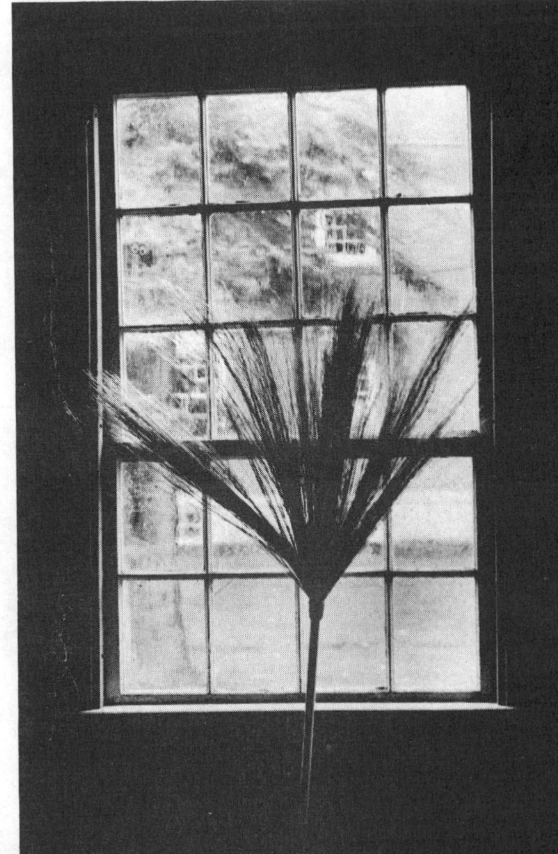

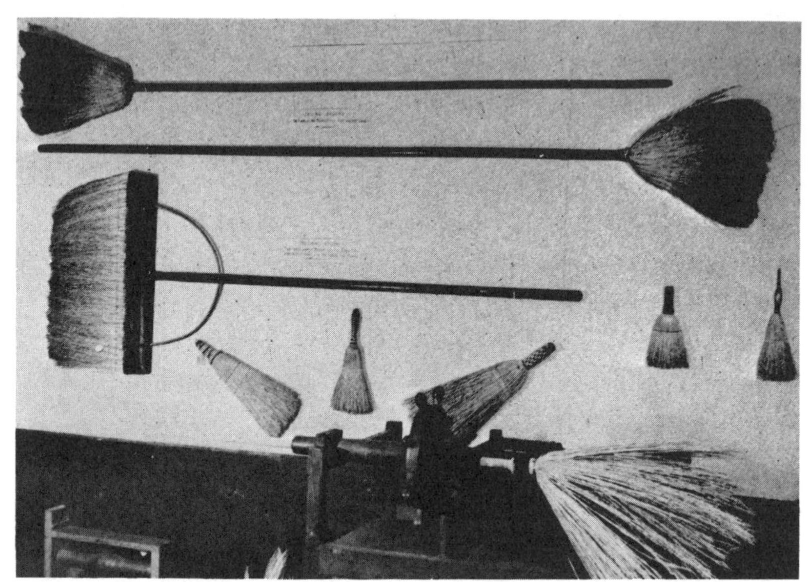

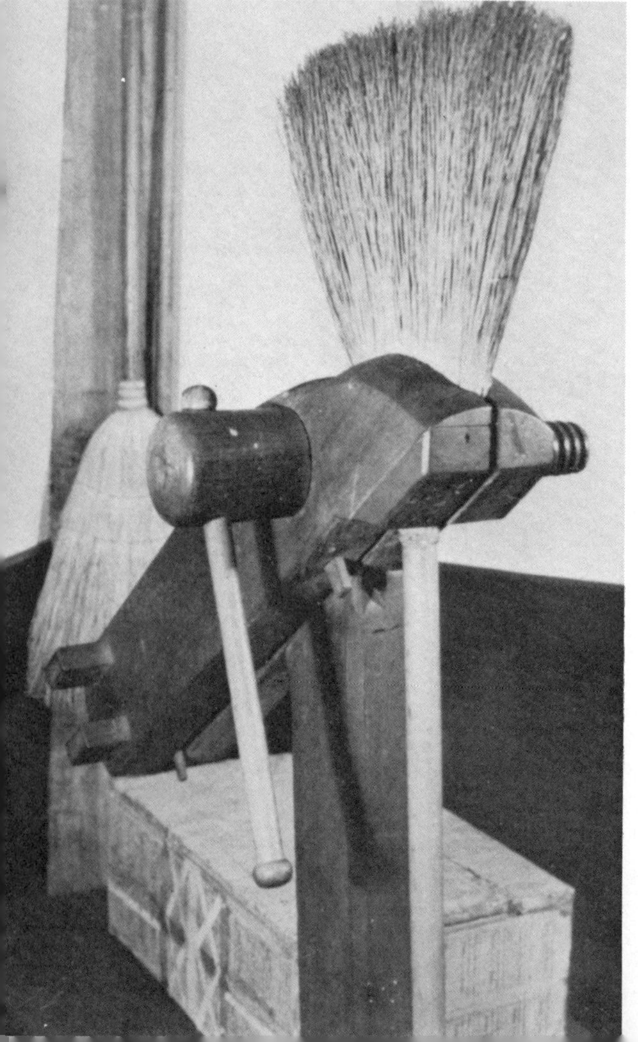

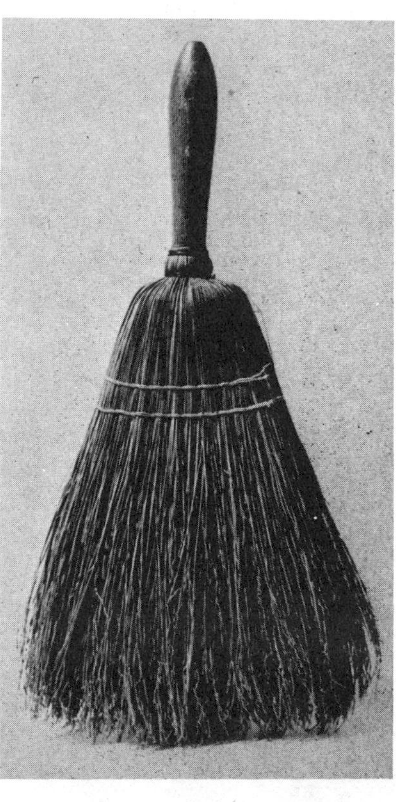

made by the Shakers. They invented, or developed for manufacture, long-handled brooms for cleaning walls and ceilings, and the sisters made white cotton covers for brooms which were used for dusting difficult-to-reach places in Shaker houses and outbuildings. Push brooms, dust brushes, and floor mops were also included in lists of early Shaker products made for sale to the world. Shoe brushes, lather brushes, scrubbing brushes, clothes brushes, and whisk brooms were made in a variety of sizes. Daniel J. Hawkins, a trustee of New Lebanon, inspected these early brushes and his initials were set into the bristles of some of the brushes.

The broom and brush business seems to have prospered well into the 1860's, and as with most Shaker industries, fell off at that time because of the Civil War and a reduction in Shaker population. From the variety and amount of Shaker brooms that still exist in good condition, it is probable that the Shakers continued to make brooms, mops, and brushes in a limited amount throughout the remainder of their history. Following the Civil War the growing of broom corn was abandoned, and it was purchased from outside sources.

At its peak, the broom and brush industry involved just about every Shaker family. Lathes were developed and built to make the maple handles, and apparatus for tying the corn on the handles, at first a simple wheel and shaft, became more sophisticated as the industry grew. Vises were invented and made that both flattened the broom and held it while the corn could be sewn in place.

Brooms were fitting symbols for the Shakers and they were conveniently hung in full view in almost every room and shop where they were used with frequency. If the Shaker sisters worked hard to keep their buildings spotless and free from dust, they were always provided with the proper tools with which to perform that task.

OPPOSITE TOP: *A variety of brooms and brushes were made by the Shakers to sell to the world. The long brooms are for cleaning high ceilings.* OLD CHATHAM.

BOTTOM LEFT: *Shaker broom vise to flatten and hold broom while it was being sewn.* OLD CHATHAM.

BOTTOM RIGHT: *Shaker whisk broom. Broom corn was grown by early Shakers.* BELFIT.

CHAPTER 13

SHAKER FURNITURE

Beadings, moldings and cornices, which are merely for fancy may not be made by Believers.

It is the duty of those who are placed as caretakers in the rooms, to see that the furniture is used carefully, the room kept clean and decent, and to know that good order is maintained therein; And if the inmates deviate therefrom it is their duty to kindly admonish them, and if they do not receive the admonition, they should make the case known to the Elders, and there leave it.

If a brother or sister desires to make any change of furniture, in the room, it must be done by the union and consent of those who have the charge therein. Millenial Laws, 1821. Revised, 1845.

So much attention has been given in the past thirty years to Shaker furniture and its importance to American furniture design that it would be impossible to pursue the entire subject within the limitations of a single chapter. The most noteworthy scholars to pursue the subject are Edward Deming Andrews and his wife, Faith.

In the Andrews' books, Shaker furniture is discussed in full in relationship to Shaker beliefs concerning their work with wood and the restrictions of style pertaining to certain extraneous features of worldly furniture. Belief that the sect would continue indefinitely justified superbly and carefully made furniture that would serve "forever."

Whereas Shaker chairs were manufactured for sale to the world, and therefore required uniformity of style and quality, furniture made to be used by the Shakers was more individual and each piece was made to order to fit into its place in the dwelling and to serve functions that might be peculiar only to a particular family or community. Constructed of simple design with superb materials and excellent workmanship, Shaker furniture is now recognized as being the best quality of American country furniture ever made. American "country style" furniture can often mean shoddy workmanship and inferior materials. However, when the term is applied to

Although Shaker candle stands were made in a variety of styles, this particular shape is thought to be the most typical and the most graceful. It is currently being reproduced by crafts guilds. In the background is an example of Shaker built-in chest and cupboards. HANCOCK.

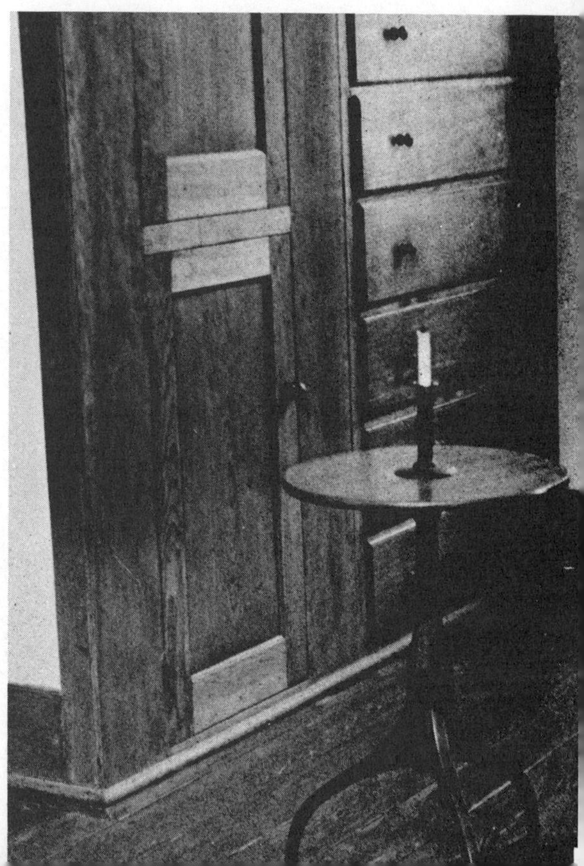

Trestle dining table is from Hancock, Massachusetts, and slat-back dining chairs are from Watervliet, New York. Desk on right is from Watervliet also. The pine cupboard in rear from same community is circa 1810. Table is set with English china, made in 1880. It was used at Hancock. OLD CHATHAM.

Shaker-made furniture it conjures up a vision of beautiful native wood and functional styles that are honest and free of any extraneous decoration. Seen against the white walls of a Shaker dwelling, the furniture has a serene and handsome appearance that enhances but never dominates its surroundings. It is obvious that Shaker furniture is the most perfect example of belief in the saying of Mother Ann, "Put your hands to work, and your hearts to God." Intelligence in the proper choice, seasoning, and handling of native woods can be found in the most functional of Shaker furniture pieces. Each object is designed to do the work for which it was intended. All the furniture was intended to lighten the burden of housekeeping, which freed the sisters for their many other tasks and for the hours spent in worship.

Important to the understanding of Shaker furniture is the simple peg which can be found in quantity in every Shaker dwelling and workroom. Anything, including chairs, that could be made to hang on the walls of Shaker rooms, was designed with that purpose in mind.

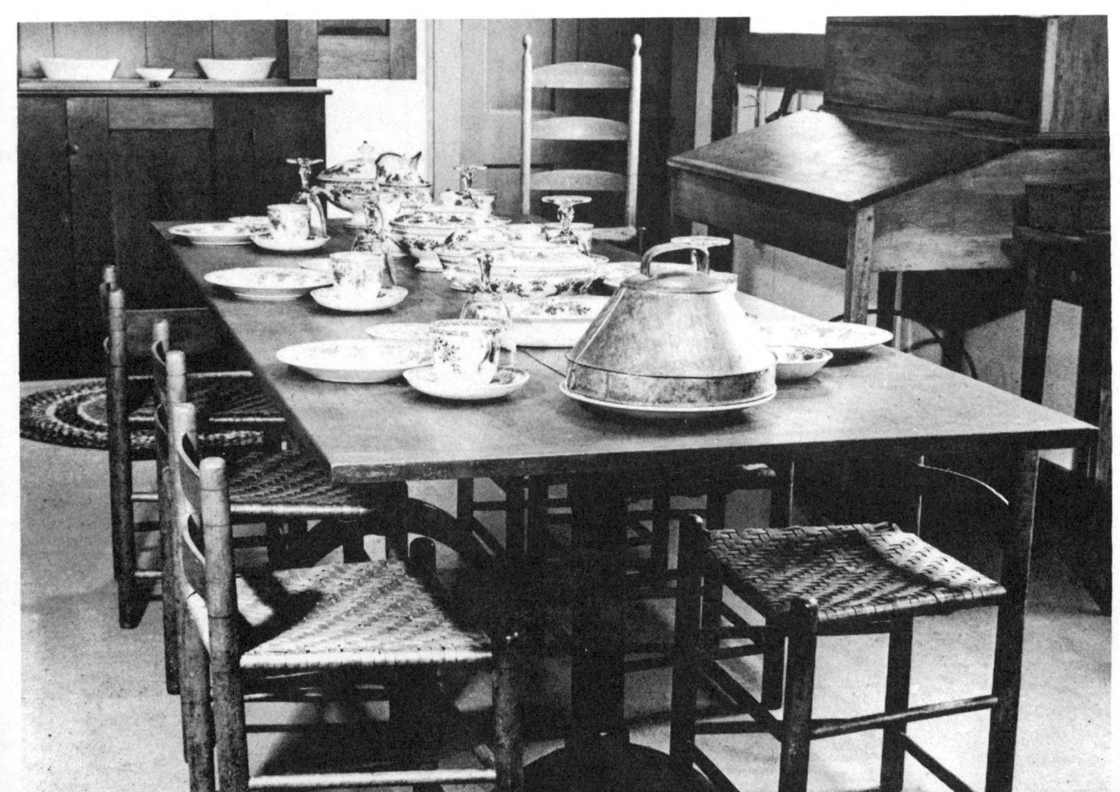

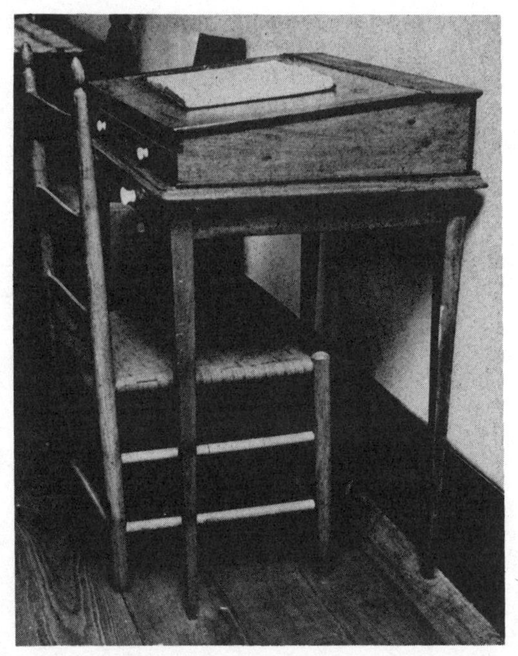

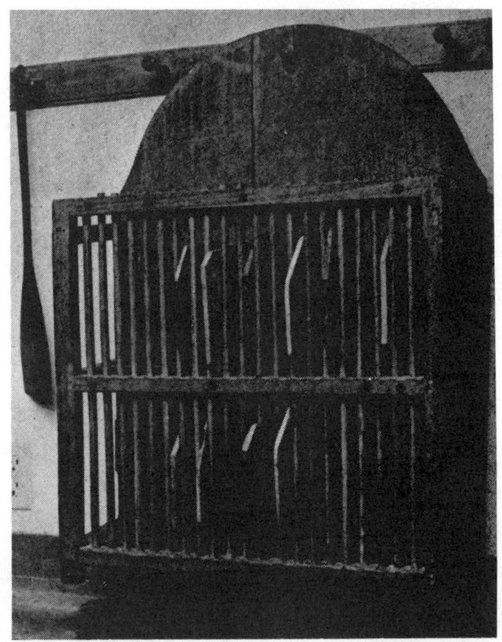

Clocks, mirrors, clothes hangers, utensils, and a variety of racks for holding small objects were made to be hung on the pegs and out of the way to facilitate cleaning. Beds were made with wheels to ease the burden of dusting and sweeping the floors. Meeting rooms had double rows of pegs to hold hats and coats. Chests were built with legs that were high enough to make it a simple matter to fit the Shaker mops and brooms under them. Some case furniture was built to the floor so that dust could not collect underneath. As we have seen, furniture for children's quarters was scaled down so that small feet did not dangle uncomfortably as the boys and girls pursued their studies or learned the crafts taught them by their elders.

The very fact that children were apprenticed to Shaker craftsmen at an early age accounts for the fact that beautifully made furniture could be produced for each family as needed. The furniture styles that are exclusively

LEFT: *Child's desk and chair. Only those who had a need could own a desk. Elders, ministry, and deacons were allowed to own desks. The Shakers also made some school furniture.* HANCOCK.

RIGHT: *Rack for storing wooden table mats in Shaker kitchen. Table cloths were not used and surface of table was protected by use of wood mats.* HANCOCK.

TOP LEFT: *Sisters' sewing table made by Elder Henry Blinn of Canterbury, New Hampshire. Predominate wood is butternut. Drawer pulls are white porcelain and not made by Shakers.* OLD CHATHAM.

Shaker can be laid to the cultural isolation that brought about the aura of orderliness and simplicity that entered every facet of Shaker life. Because all furniture was made to suit certain purposes and was built to perform special functions in Shaker dwellings, there are many unusual and unique pieces to be found. Sewing tables for the sisters' workrooms had many drawers, ample worktops,

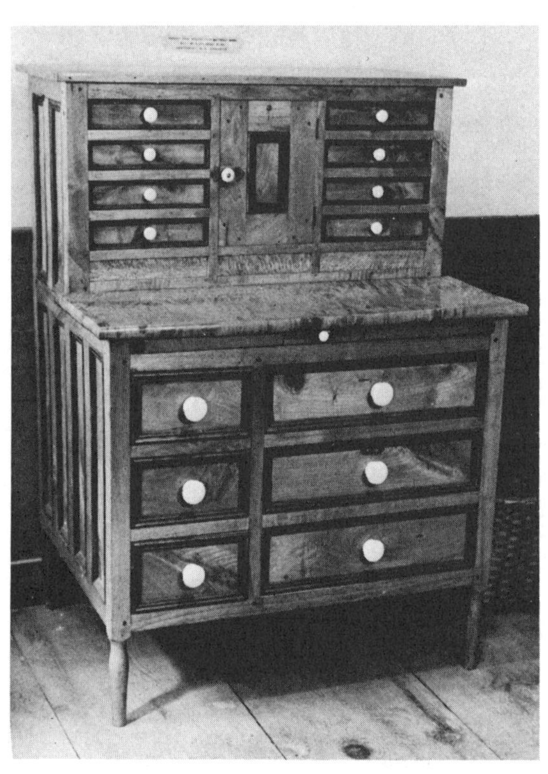

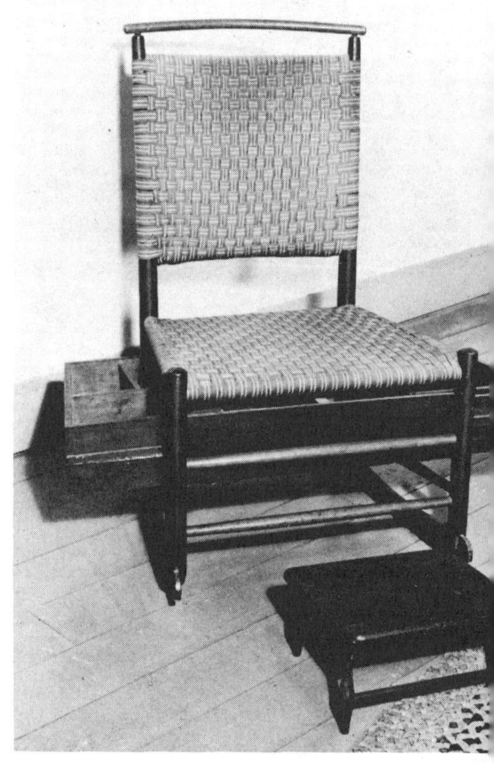

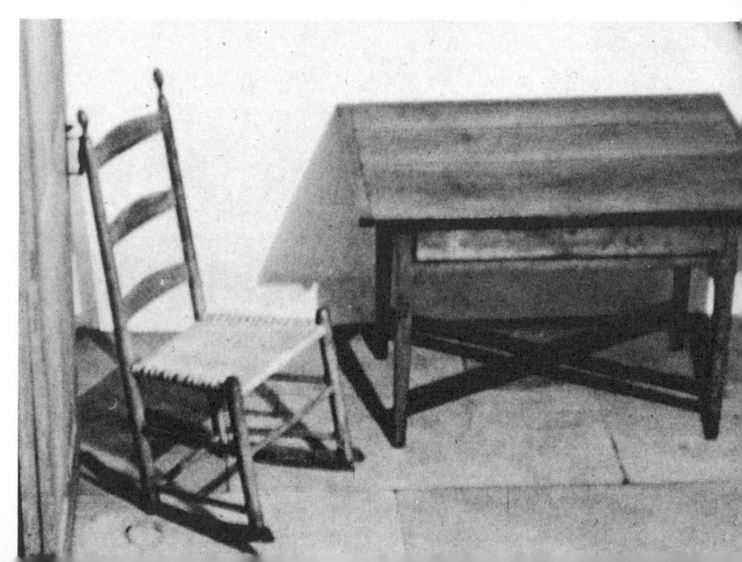

and often could accommodate two sisters. Frequently, matching pairs of sewing desks were made that fitted back-to-back. Surfaces of cutting tables and kitchen work counters were placed at heights so that the sisters did not have to bend. Spool chests to hold the large amounts of thread for many needlework projects were designed so that messy objects could be kept out of sight and dust free. Graceful candle-stands were constructed as early as 1805 from the many kinds of local lumber. Trestle tables and back-slat benches for community dining were also made by Shaker craftsmen. Cupboards to hold the many household objects and keep them clean and out of sight ranged in size from huge communal closets to small corner cabinets. Ironing tables with high stools were designed so that the sisters could sit down while performing this arduous task.

Function, simplicity, and excellent workmanship with fine seasoned woods all added up to provide the Shaker communities with furniture for the ages—country furniture, perhaps, but built with a distinct style and obviously much talent, patience, and love. No space was wasted, and drawers were installed in every piece that could accommodate them.

Case furniture, the first institutional furniture to be made in America, held all the belongings of brethren or sisters. Many of these immense chests were built to fit perfectly into certain areas of rooms and looked as though they were built in. Blanket chests, painted and in natural wood, were made in quantity, some with bone keyhole escutcheons. Chests of drawers and drop-leaf tables were also Shaker products.

There were washstands and wood boxes, step stools and sill cupboards, sideboards and candle-stands. Many chairs were made and some still exist that were different from standard Shaker chair styles intended to be sold to the "world's people." One especially serviceable chair

OPPOSITE TOP RIGHT: *Unusual Shaker rocking chair for sewing, with drawers beneath for storage of materials.* OLD CHATHAM.

OPPOSITE BOTTOM: *Worktable and rocker at Hancock Shaker Village. Photograph also shows large slabs of slate used for basement floor in brick dwelling, which was built to house one hundred Shakers.*

can be seen at Old Chatham. It is a sewing chair with drawers that pull out from underneath the seat. Footstools were made for Shakers as well as for sale. Some of these are padded and upholstered, while others are taped or caned.

Ornament on Shaker furniture did not exist. However, as with the chairs, there is a difference in some of the furniture that can definitely be attributed to the Ohio and Kentucky settlements. While all Shaker furniture might look similar to the untrained eye, no two pieces are exactly alike. American country furniture styles were simplified and refined by the Shakers in a manner unlike any other domestic furniture of the nineteenth century. As the country turned to mass-manufactured products, the Shaker craftsmen kept to their old methods of furniture building, with the exception of the chair industry in which they depended on methods of mass production when it did not interfere with the quality of the product.

Departures in the forms of Shaker furniture can be found, however. Traces of the Victorian styles crept into the later pieces. The bentwood chairs made for sale around the time of the centennial exposition in Philadelphia are certainly an adaptation by the Shakers of a more worldly style. While glass was seldom used in cabinet or secretary doors, there are several known examples in existence. One secretary in a private collection, is dated as early as 1849. Another, in the collection of the Sabbathday Lake, Maine, Shakers has arched glass panels set in the doors. Made by Elder Henry Green of Alfred, in 1884, this piece has a definite Empire influence. Few pieces of Shaker furniture are signed and dated, and where something does exist that can definitely be attributed to one craftsman and to a particular year, it is often an aid in attributing similar pieces.

Shaker furniture craftsmen, especially in the early days of the sect, were somewhat itinerant. Many of the early brethren visited other communities to help others learn the trade and to make suitable furniture for the newer settlements. Although most eastern Shaker furniture is similar in general style, the differences in the Kentucky- and Ohio-made pieces can be attributed to the fact that these areas were settled later, and whatever the general local styles were at the time, these were accepted in the Shaker communities. Although the Midwestern pieces are still functional and plain, there are details on many of them that cannot be found on furniture made in the East.

The woods used in making all Shaker furniture were usually local. Fine wood, such as cherry and maple, was often left in natural grains and varnished. Western Shakers had a greater variety of high-grade woods and used cherry, walnut, oak, and butternut. Often several different kinds of wood were used on the same piece of furniture. Less desirable woods, such as pine and poplar, were usually stained or painted.

Shaker-made furniture suits perfectly the architecture of Shaker-designed buildings. The complete harmony of furnishings with each room accounts for the air of serenity that imparts much concerning the Shaker way of living, working, and worshipping. The Shakers have left an inheritance of magnificent simplicity in their furniture. This inheritance will speak for the Shakers long after the sect, itself, has become a part of American social and religious history.

CHAPTER 14

SHAKER CHAIRS

One rocking chair in a room is sufficient, except where the aged reside. One table, one or two stands, a lamp stand may be attached to the woodwork, if desired. One good looking glass, which ought not to exceed eighteen inches in length, and twelve in width, with a plain frame. A looking glass larger than this, ought never to be purchased by Believers. If necessary a small glass may hang in the closet, and a very small one may be kept in the public cupboard of the room.

No one should lean back against the wall, bed, or ceiling of dwelling rooms. It is also wrong to sit with the feet on the rounds of chairs. Millenial Laws, 1821. Revised, 1845.

Of all Shaker-made furniture, the form that is most familiar is the straight chair with the slat back and cane or woven-tape seat. Chair manufacture was another of the early Shaker industries and one of the last to have been abandoned in this century. It is not generally known, however, that the Shakers were probably the first commercial manufacturers of chairs in America, and that as far as is known, every Shaker community was engaged in the manufacture of chairs at one time or another in their history.

The earliest Shaker chairs were fashioned after the common slat-back chair which dates to Colonial times. While the form was adapted, the Shakers refined it by using carefully seasoned wood that could be turned and shaped into narrower legs and posts without losing strength. The lines of the earliest Shaker chairs are more pure and delicate than the later ones. Yet, these early handcrafted chairs are deceptively strong despite their fragile appearance.

LEFT: *Early Shaker rocking chair. The Shakers were ostensibly the first Americans to manufacture rockers for sale.* OLD CHATHAM.

RIGHT: *Early Shaker chair from Hancock Shakers. Three-slat side chair is one of finest Shaker forms.* BELFIT.

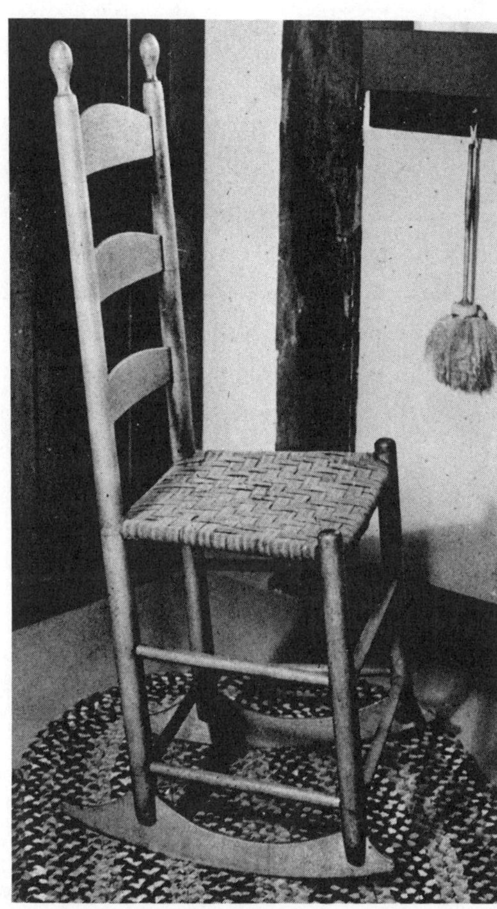

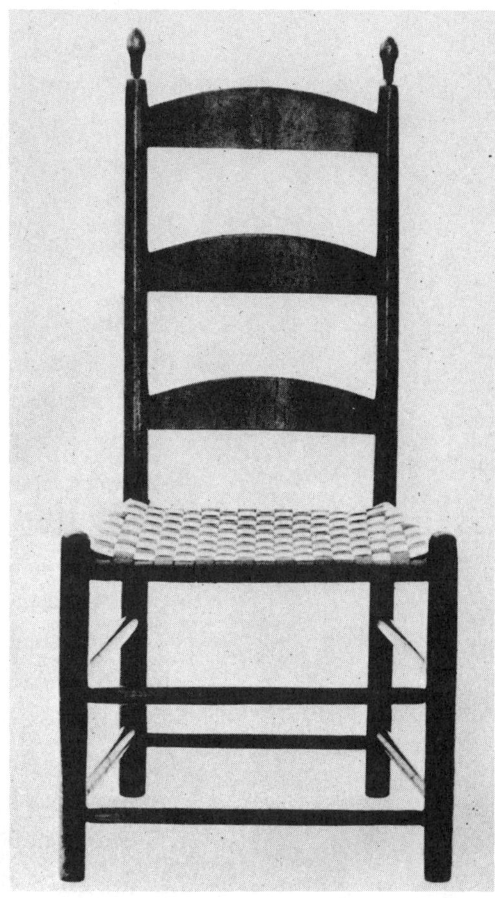

Shaker chairs were made to suit every need and purpose in the late eighteenth and throughout the nineteenth century. The Shakers were probably the first to make rocking chairs in America, and they manufactured armchairs for sale that were handsome and durable. Originally, rocking chairs were placed in communal rooms for use by invalids and the elderly.

Other individually shaped chairs were made for the Shakers' use, with obvious thought having been given to the function which they must serve. At this date it is difficult to separate the chairs made for their own use from the chairs that were made for sale to the world. At first, benches were used in Shaker dining rooms and these were later replaced with individual low-back chairs that could be pushed under the tables when not in use. Revolving highchairs were designed for various tasks, and many child-sized chairs were also made.

New Lebanon records show that as early as 1789 chair seats were being replaced to order and that chairs were sold in small quantities, usually six or a dozen at a time. Within a few years the community at New Lebanon was selling them in much larger quantities, and between the years 1805 to 1807 two hundred and eighty-six were made and sold. While a few were "wagain seats" and "rockin chairs," most were "common chairs." These were the three-slat armless chairs which have become identified with the Shakers. At the time, the price of the "common chairs" was six shillings apiece.

The chair business continued throughout the early years of the nineteenth century, most orders being rather small. Customers for the early Shaker chairs were local. The largest order, written on February 12, 1806, from Hudson, New York, was for thirty-four chairs. Chairs in those early days also went to Albany, Poughkeepsie, Troy, and Granville, New York.

As early as 1806 Shaker goods were also being sold

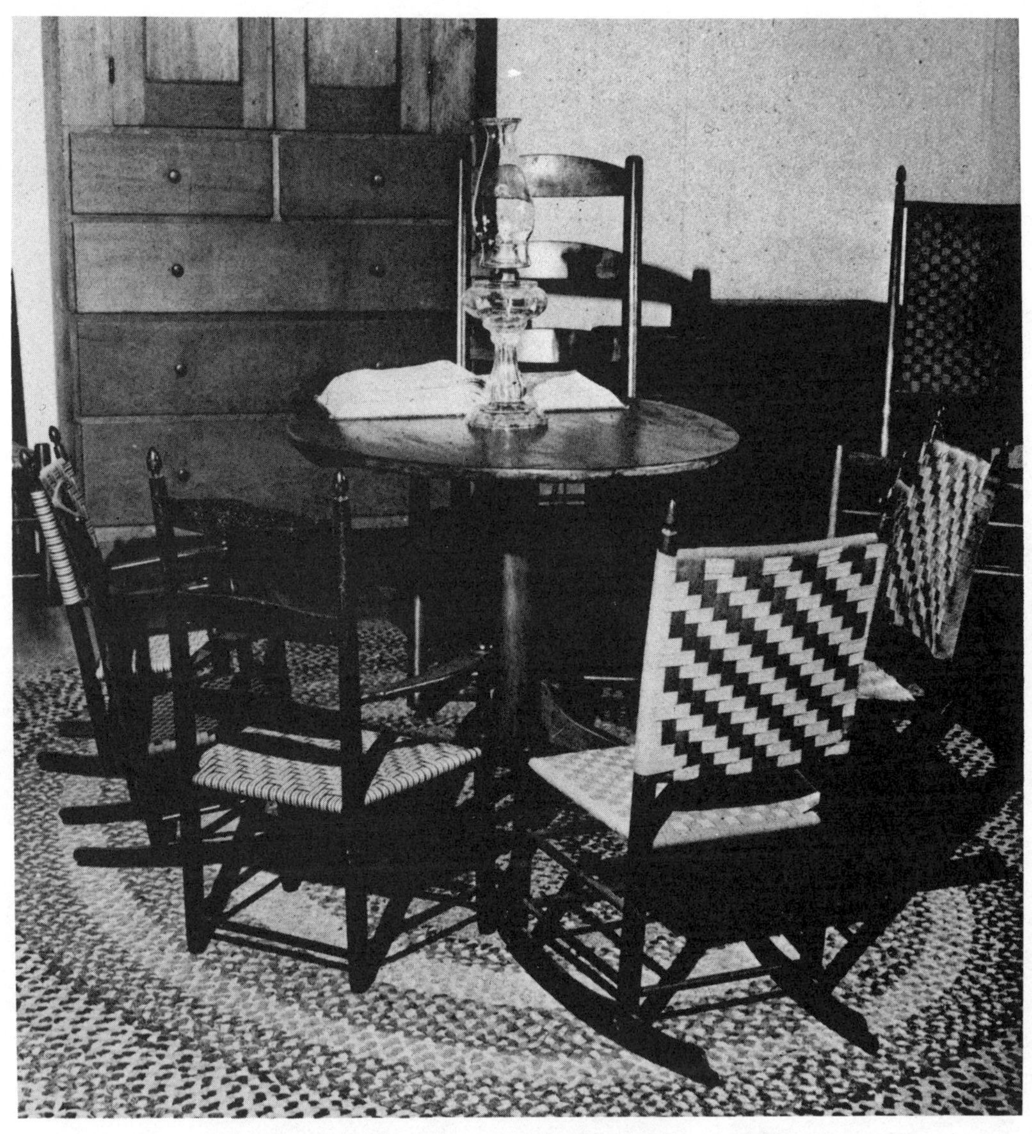

in Boston and New York City, and it is highly probable that chairs were among the many items brought by Shaker peddlars to these centers to be sold to the public. One or two members of a Shaker community were assigned to drive the wagonloads of merchandise to the cities and conduct the business of selling the goods and the purchasing of items needed by the Shakers that they

Group of children's chairs of various sizes and styles. OLD CHATHAM.

RIGHT: *Child's highchair, one of six made at Mount Lebanon around 1880.* OLD CHATHAM.

BOTTOM RIGHT: *Footstool with rush seat.* OLD CHATHAM.

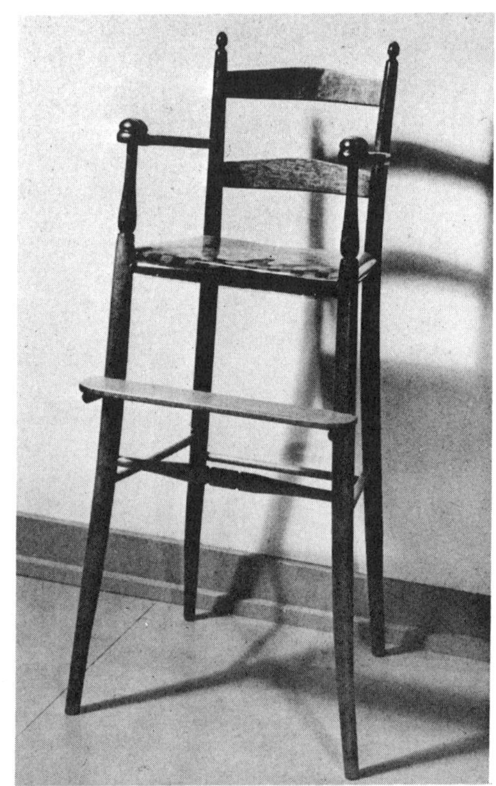

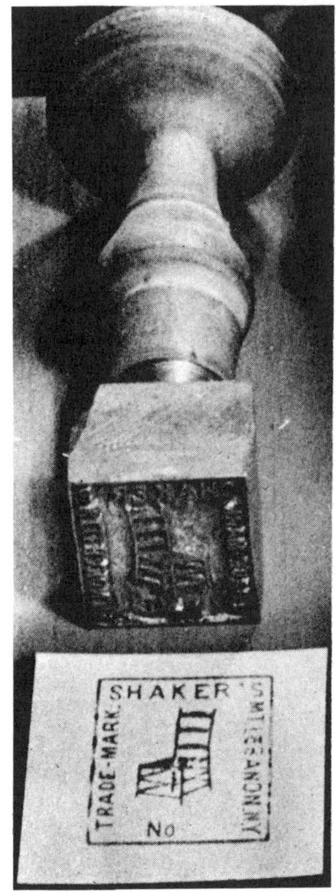

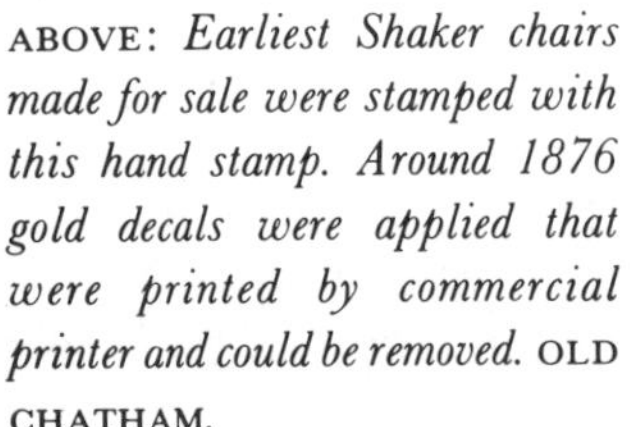

ABOVE: *Earliest Shaker chairs made for sale were stamped with this hand stamp. Around 1876 gold decals were applied that were printed by commercial printer and could be removed.* OLD CHATHAM.

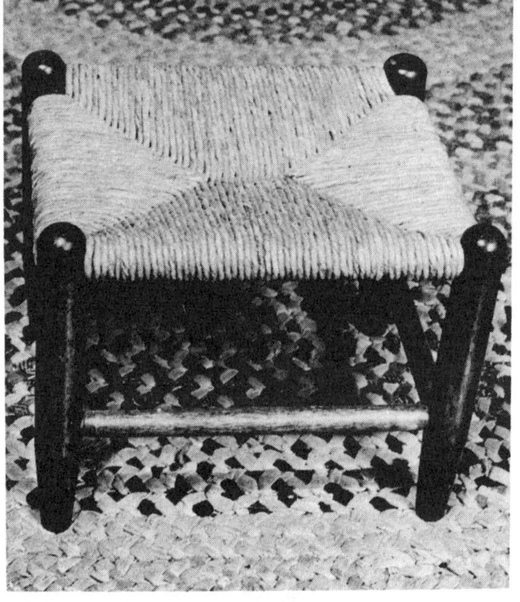

did not themselves produce. All business was transacted for cash.

Not only were chairs made for outside sale by the Shakers at New Lebanon, but eventually just about all Shaker communities were engaged in this occupation. The Church family at New Lebanon appears to have been the earliest group concerned with chair manufacture. Soon the South and Second families at New Lebanon and the Canaan family were engaged in the chair business.

It was not until 1852, however, that the manufacture of Shaker chairs became a major industry. An early patent taken out by George O'Donnell of the South Family of New Lebanon was for a type of chair equipped with a ball-and-socket device in the rear feet, which allowed one to tip back without damaging the chair or the floor. Since O'Donnell left the Shaker community shortly after acquiring the patent, it is not known how many of this type of chair were produced.

By mid-century the Shakers began to manufacture chairs that were sold to other Shaker communities, and by 1863 the South Family at Mount Lebanon was given exclusive rights to the chair manufacturing business. They continued to manufacture chairs almost solely for Shaker use until 1867, when the chairs were made to be marketed to the world. The South Family was the exclusive manufacturer and distributor of many chairs in various styles that were sold by mail order. The bulk of the inventory, however, went to furniture dealers and department stores in the large cities. Among these were Lewis and Conger, John E. Hubbell, Newman and Capron, and Marhesius and Frey of New York City, as well as other firms in Providence, Boston, Troy, Albany, Philadelphia, Racine, and Chicago.

Shaker chairs became widely known for their simplicity, beauty, comfort, and sturdiness. The styles were cop-

ON TWO FOLLOWING PAGES:
Pages from 1875 catalogue for Shaker chair. OLD CHATHAM.

AN

Illustrated Catalogue

AND

PRICE LIST

OF THE

Shakers' Chairs,

FOOT BENCHES,

FLOOR MATS, Etc.

Manufactured and Sold by the Shakers, at Mt. Lebanon, Columbia Co., N. Y.

LEBANON SPRINGS, N. Y.:
B. F. REYNOLDS, BOOK, CARD AND JOB PRINTER.
1875.

---

8 Catalogue and Price List of the

No. 5.

THIS size is well adapted for dining or office use, when an arm chair is desirable. We have a smaller size, with only two back slats and plain top posts, for table use, and without arms.

We do not have this chair without the arms.

We insert an engraving of our new chair factory erected in the summer of 1872. The increasing demand for our chairs has prompted us to increase also the facilities for producing and improving them. We have spared no expense or labor in our endeavors to produce an article that cannot be surpassed in any respect, and which combines all of the advantages of durability, simplicity and lightness. Our largest chairs do not weigh over ten pounds, and the smallest weigh less than five pounds, and yet the largest person can feel safe in sitting down in them without fear of going through them. This is owing to the care we take in our thorough selection of materials which are put into the chairs, and the excellent workmanship which is applied to their construction. Since the establishment of our new factory we have been using a very expensive and durable material in the seating of our chairs, with a great variety of the prettiest colors which can be produced.

Shakers' Chairs, Foot Benches, Etc. 9

No. 2.

THIS is a trifle smaller than the No. 3 in the seat, but in every other respect it is the same. We do not have this size with arms, but with or without rockers.

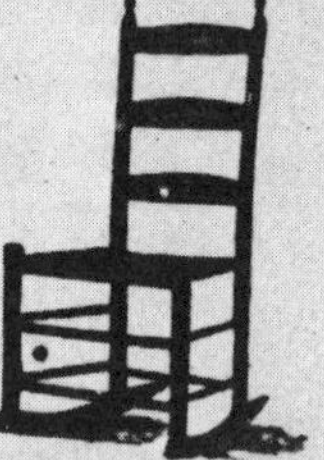

them at the nearest or most accessible place of shipment, and there take a receipt for them, showing that they were received in good order, when our obligations end.

The principles as well as the rules of the Society forbid the Trustees or any of their assistants doing business on the credit system, either in the purchase or sale of merchandise, or in making bargains or contracts. This we consider good policy, and a safe way of doing business, checking speculative or dishonest propensities, and averting financial panics and disasters. We sell with the understanding that all bills are to be cash on receipt of the goods.

Look for our trade mark before purchasing—no chair is genuine without it. Our trade mark is a gold transfer, and is designed to be ornamental; but, if objectionable to purchasers, it can be easily removed without defacing the furniture in the least, by wetting a sponge or piece of cotton cloth with *aqua ammonia*, and rubbing it until it is loosened.

---

10 Catalogue and Price List of the

No. 1.

THIS is a small chair, calculated to suit small persons or grown-up children. We make this chair with arms, and with or without rockers.

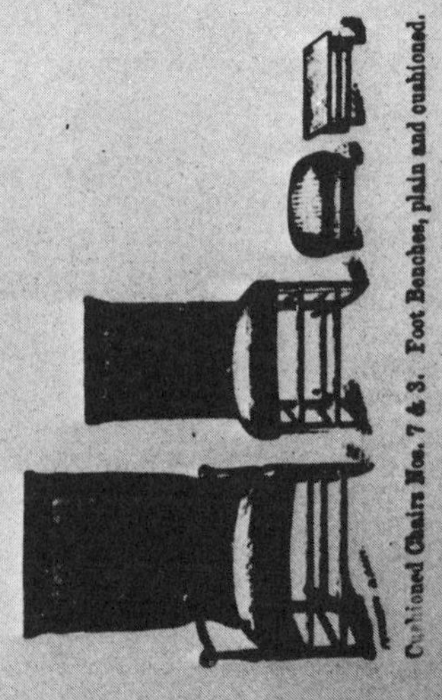

Cushioned Chairs Nos. 7 & 3. Foot Benches, plain and cushioned.

Shakers' Chairs, Foot Benches, Etc. 7

No. 4.

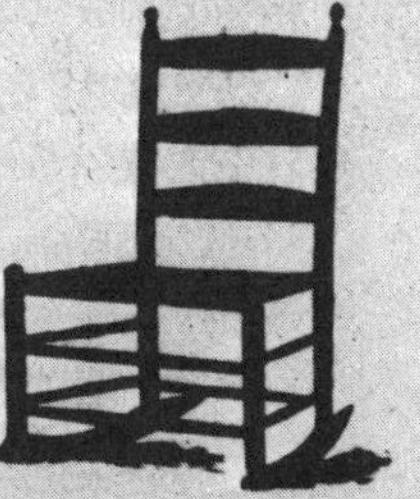

THIS chair is a great favorite with the ladies. It is broad on the seat, and very easy. We do not make this size with arms, and the back is lower than the large arm chairs, but have them with or without rockers.

Many of our friends who see the Shakers' chairs for the first time may be led to suppose that the chair business is a new thing for the Shakers to engage in. This is not the fact, however, and may surprise even some of the oldest manufacturers to learn that the Shakers were pioneers in the business, and perhaps the very first to engage in the business after the establishment of the independence of the country.

We have in our possession specimens of chairs made by our people more than half a century ago, which, judging from their appearance, would indicate that they were made in revolutionary times, and would adorn any cabinet of antiquities. The contrast between those and our present production is quite amusing.

The material with which we cushion our chairs is a specialty peculiarly our own. It is made of the best stock, and woven in hand looms with much labor, and forms a heavy and durable article, much more so than any thing which we are acquainted with. We have all

8 Catalogue and Price List of the

No. 3.

THIS is a favorite sewing chair, and for all general purposes about the chamber and sitting room. We have this size with arms, rockers, or without either.

of the most desirable and pretty colors represented in our cushions, and they can be all one color, or have a different colored border, or with different colored stripes running across the cushion.

We cushion the foot benches to match the cushioned chairs. They are twelve inches square on the top, with an incline to favor one's feet while sitting in the chairs, and they are nicely adapted for the purpose of kneeling stools.

When any of our friends wish some of our chairs they can order them of us by mail, addressed to R. M. WAGAN, Mt. Lebanon, Columbia County, N.Y. Our chairs are all nicely wrapped in paper before shipping, and the cushioned chairs are sacked with a cloth wrapper, for which an additional charge of fifty cents will be made. It is advisable to ship the chairs by express when there are only a few of them; the expense will be more, but the risk will be less than by freight. We do not ship any goods at our own risk, but deliver

Shakers' Chairs, Foot Benches, Etc. 11

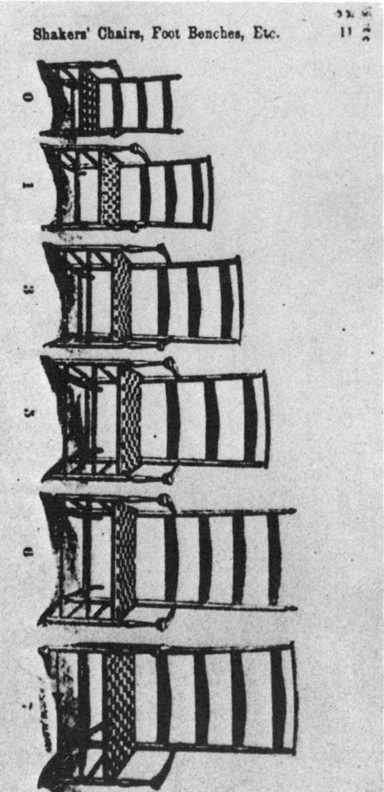

PRICE LIST OF SHAKERS' CHAIRS.

With Arms & Rockers		With Rockers.	
No. 7, per piece	$8 00	No. 7, per piece,	$7 50
" 6, " "	7 50	" 6, " "	7 00
" 5, " "	6 50	" 4, " "	6 50
" 3, " "	4 50	" 3, " "	4 00
" 1, " "	3 50	" 2, " "	3 50
" 0, " "	3 25	" 1, " "	3 25
		" 0, " "	3 00

PRICE LIST of SHAKERS' CHAIR CUSHIONS.

Back Cushions.		Seat Cushions.	
No. 7, per piece,	$4 00	No. 7, per piece,	$4 50
" 6, " "	3 50	" 6, " "	4 00
" 5, " "	3 00	" 5, " "	3 50
" 4, " "	3 00	" 4, " "	3 50
" 3, " "	2 37	" 3, " "	2 88
" 2, " "	2 13	" 2, " "	2 62
" 1, " "	2 00	" 1, " "	2 25
" 0, " "	1 75	" 0, " "	1 75

Back and Seat Cushions.

No. 7, per set	$8 50	No. 3, per set	$5 25
" 6, "	7 50	" 2, "	4 75
" 5, "	6 50	" 1, "	4 00
" 4, "	6 50	" 0, "	3 75

Foot Benches, $1.00; Cushioned, $2.75.

Two-step Benches, $1.50; Cushioned, $2.25.

Floor Rugs and Mats made to order, per sq. foot, 75c.

Fifty cents extra for Sacking Cushioned Chairs.

Manufactured by the Society of Shakers.

Address, R. M. WAGAN,

Mount Lebanon, N. Y.

THE

Shakers' Chairs

Are Exhibited at the

CENTENNIAL EXHIBITION,

In Philadelphia,

Location, P 52, MAIN BUILDING.

They also have a very ingenious Machine in the Agricultural Hall for

CUTTING GREEN CORN FROM THE COB.

Location, Column Letter L, Column Number 8.

CENTENNIAL

Illustrated Catalogue

AND

PRICE LIST

OF THE

Shakers' Chairs,

FOOT BENCHES,

Floor Mats, etc.,

Manufactured and sold by the Shakers, at Mt. Lebanon, Columbia Co., N. Y.

ALSO

CONTAINING SEVERAL PIECES OF SHAKER MUSIC.

ALBANY:
WEED, PARSONS & CO., PRINTERS.
1876.

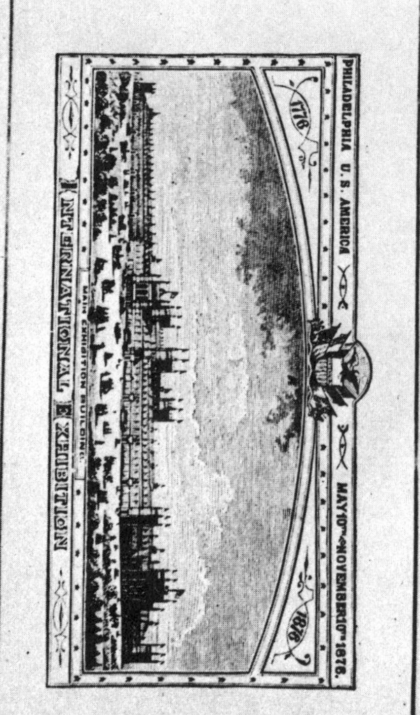

PRICE LIST OF SHAKERS' CHAIRS.

WEB SEATS.

With Arms and Rockers.		With Rockers.	
No. 7, per piece	$8 00	No. 7, per piece	$7 50
" 6, " "	7 50	" 6, " "	7 00
" 5, " "	6 50	" 4, " "	6 50
" 3, " "	4 50	" 3, " "	4 00
" 1, " "	3 50	" 2, " "	3 50
" 0, " "	3 25	" 1, " "	3 25
		" 0, " "	3 00

PRICE LIST OF SHAKERS' CHAIRS,

With Web Seat and Back.

With Arms and Rockers.		With Rockers.	
No. 7, per piece	$10 00	No. 7, per piece	$9 50
" 6, " "	9 50	" 6, " "	9 00
" 5, " "	8 00	" 4, " "	8 00
" 3, " "	5 50	" 3, " "	5 25
" 1, " "	4 50	" 2, " "	4 75
" 0, " "	4 25	" 1, " "	4 25
		" 0, " "	4 00

☞ All Chairs of our make will have a Gold Transfer Trade Mark attached to them, and none others are Shakers' Chairs.

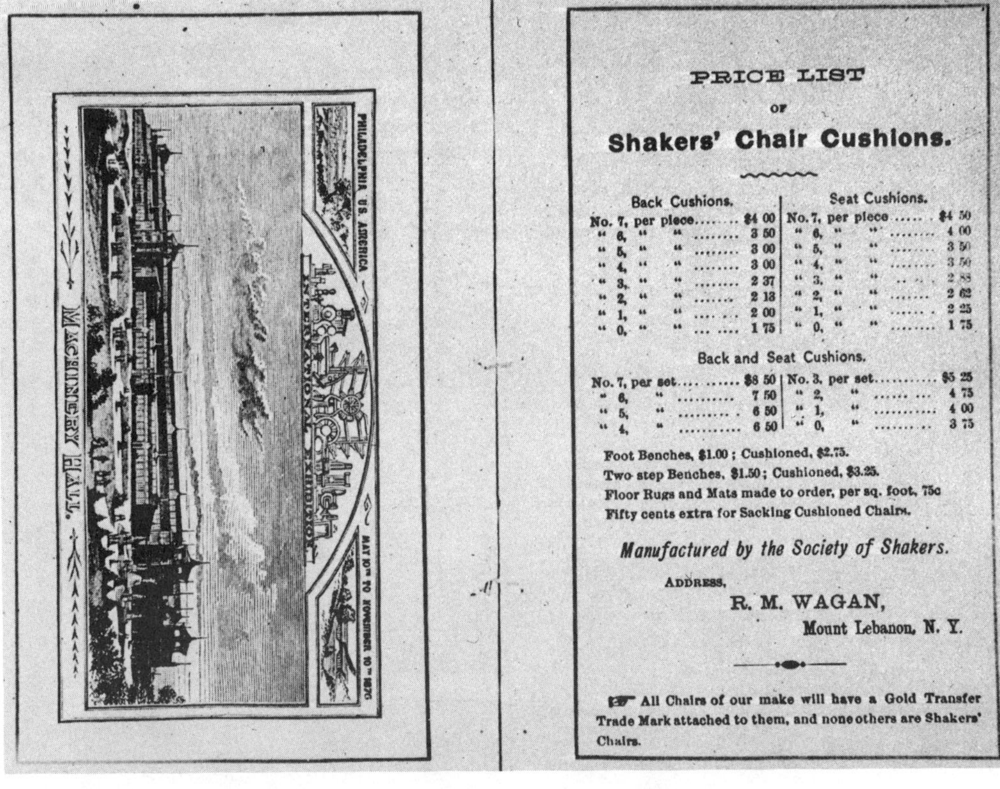

PRICE LIST

OF

Shakers' Chair Cushions.

Back Cushions.		Seat Cushions.	
No. 7, per piece	$4 00	No. 7, per piece	$4 50
" 6, " "	3 50	" 6, " "	4 00
" 5, " "	3 00	" 5, " "	3 50
" 4, " "	3 00	" 4, " "	3 50
" 3, " "	2 37	" 3, " "	2 88
" 2, " "	2 13	" 2, " "	2 62
" 1, " "	2 00	" 1, " "	2 25
" 0, " "	1 75	" 0, " "	1 75

Back and Seat Cushions.

No. 7, per set	$8 50	No. 3, per set	$5 25
" 6, "	7 50	" 2, "	4 75
" 5, "	6 50	" 1, "	4 00
" 4, "	6 50	" 0, "	3 75

Foot Benches, $1.00 ; Cushioned, $2.75.

Two-step Benches, $1.50; Cushioned, $3.25.

Floor Rugs and Mats made to order, per sq. foot, 75c

Fifty cents extra for Sacking Cushioned Chairs.

Manufactured by the Society of Shakers.

ADDRESS,

R. M. WAGAN,

Mount Lebanon, N. Y.

☞ All Chairs of our make will have a Gold Transfer Trade Mark attached to them, and none others are Shakers' Chairs.

ied by other manufacturers and by the time of the American centennial the Shakers used a trademark for identification and protection of their products and markets. The trademark was a gold stamp that was printed on sheets of paper and then cut and pasted on the backs of their chairs. Customers were warned in the advertising literature to "beware of substitutes."

Armchairs with rockers as well as rockers without arms and the simple ladder-back chairs were produced in quantity. The most expensive of these chairs, which were made in different sizes, cost eight dollars in 1875. The cheapest, probably a child-sized rocker without arms, was three dollars. Chairs at this time were generally finished in a dark stain. The seats were made of tape woven by the Shaker sisters on their specially designed hand looms. Back and seat cushions were sold separately and

BOTH PAGES: *Pages from Centennial chair catalogue in 1876. Note that Shakers also took opportunity to advertise another product on back page.* OLD CHATHAM.

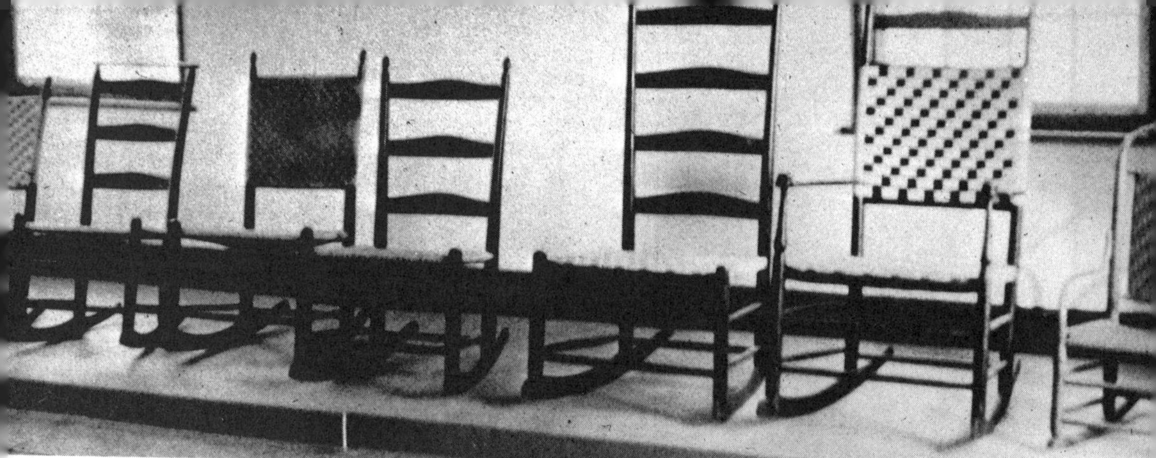

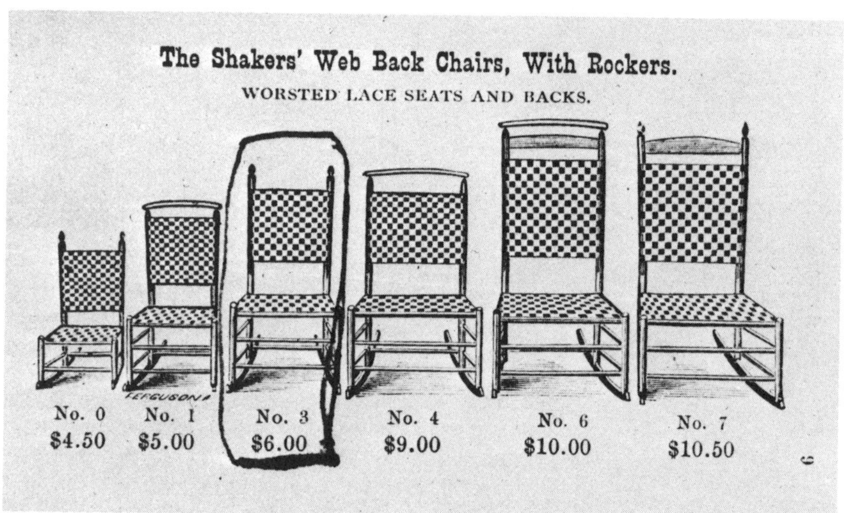
The Shakers' Web Back Chairs, With Rockers.

WORSTED LACE SEATS AND BACKS.

No. 0	No. 1	No. 3	No. 4	No. 6	No. 7
$4.50	$5.00	$6.00	$9.00	$10.00	$10.50

9

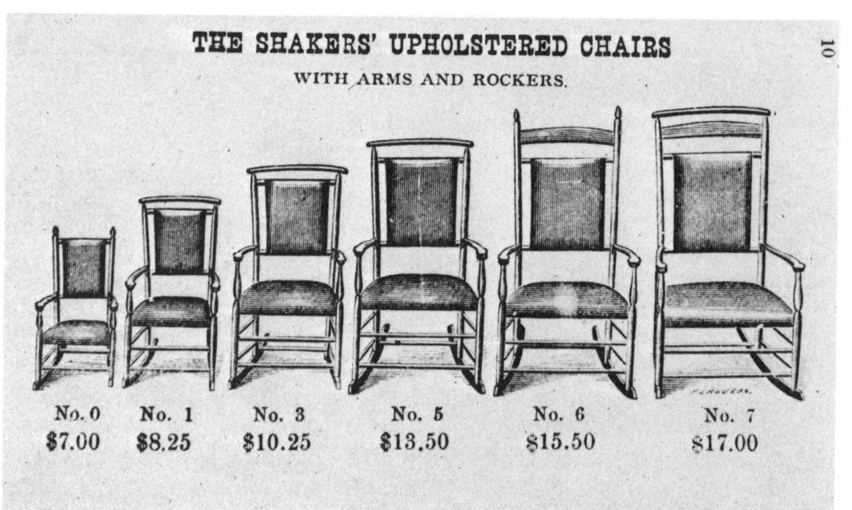
THE SHAKERS' UPHOLSTERED CHAIRS

WITH ARMS AND ROCKERS.

No. 0	No. 1	No. 3	No. 5	No. 6	No. 7
$7.00	$8.25	$10.25	$13.50	$15.50	$17.00

10

OPPOSITE TOP: *Assortment of Shaker chairs, some as illustrated in 1875 catalogue. Note bentwood child's chair on right, which was made at a later date.* HANCOCK.

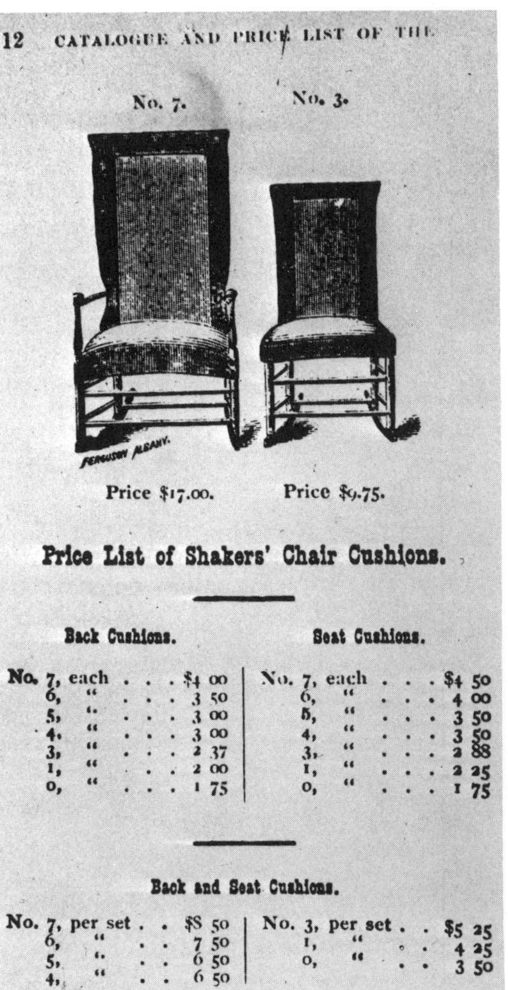

12 CATALOGUE AND PRICE LIST OF THE

No. 7.	No. 3.
Price $17.00.	Price $9.75.

Price List of Shakers' Chair Cushions.

Back Cushions.		Seat Cushions.	
No. 7, each	$4 00	No. 7, each	$4 50
6, "	3 50	6, "	4 00
5, "	3 00	5, "	3 50
4, "	3 00	4, "	3 50
3, "	2 37	3, "	2 88
1, "	2 00	1, "	2 25
0, "	1 75	0, "	1 75

Back and Seat Cushions.

No. 7, per set	$8 50	No. 3, per set	$5 25
6, "	7 50	1, "	4 25
5, "	6 50	0, "	3 50
4, "	6 50		

SHAKERS' CHAIRS, FOOT BENCHES, ETC. 13

We cushion this Foot Bench to match the Cushioned Chairs, in which manner the most of them are sold.

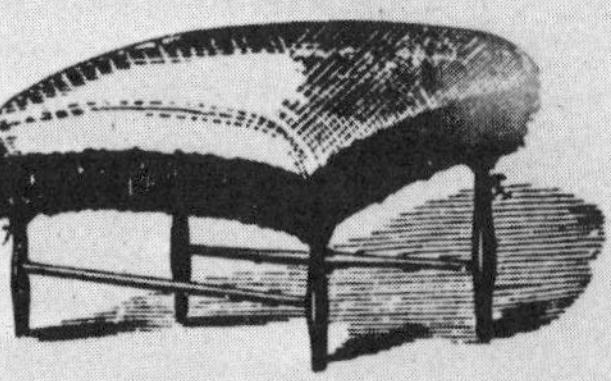

PRICE LIST OF SHAKERS' FOOT BENCHES.

Foot Benches, $1.00; Cushioned, $2.75.
Two-step Benches, $1.50; Cushioned, $3.25.

FLOOR RUGS.

Our Floor Rugs are made of the same material and colors as the cushions. When ordering the Floor Rugs be particular to state the dimensions in length and width; also describe the color of the center and border, if any border is desirable. Our Plush Floor Rugs are sold at the rate of seventy-five cents per square foot.

We also make Wool Rugs and Foot Cushions in the following colors: White, Yellow, Maroon, Blue, Black and Old Gold. Our foot stools are also covered with the above colors of Wool, at same price as with Plush.

☞We were awarded a Diploma and Medal at the Centennial Exhibition for combining in our chairs, Strength, Sprightliness and Modest Beauty.

LEFT BOTTOM AND THIS PAGE: *Pages from Shaker catalogue issued after the Philadelphia Centennial, giving prices and descriptions of latest styles in chairs and benches.* OLD CHATHAM.

cost as little as a dollar and seventy-five cents.

The man most responsible for creating a profitable and long-lasting business in chair manufacture at Mount Lebanon was Robert Wagan. Following Wagan's death in 1883, Elder William Anderson carried on. Anderson's successor was Eldress Sarah Collins, who was still running the business with outside help in 1933. Eldress Collins terminated the chair manufacturing business in 1947.

Although the Shaker chair industry was centered at Mount Lebanon, and by far the majority of the chairs still in existence came from that community, this did not preclude other Shaker families from making chairs for their own use and to sell. Each society had skilled woodworkers and mechanics who were capable of building chairs, and probably many were produced elsewhere. However, there is little difference in the styles of chairs from different communities, although western chairs had variations in the slat shapes and often the turnings on posts and legs were slightly different. There is evidence that chairs were made by a Gilbert Avery in Canaan, New York, and by Elder Philip Burlingame for the Enfield, Connecticut, community before the Civil War. Richard Wilcox is credited with having produced a quantity at the Hancock, Massachusetts, community.

The chair industry was carried on in the Ohio and Kentucky communities as well as in the eastern Shaker colonies. The style was similar to the early chairs produced by the eastern Shakers. However, later examples show a definite departure in style, and the traditional forms were somewhat modified. More turnings were used on the stretchers and turned legs were used rather than the plain tapered legs. The western Shakers, in their later chair patterns, became influenced somewhat by "worldly" designs and in the mid-nineteenth century were not averse to using details that were decorative rather than totally functional. There were many departures in furni-

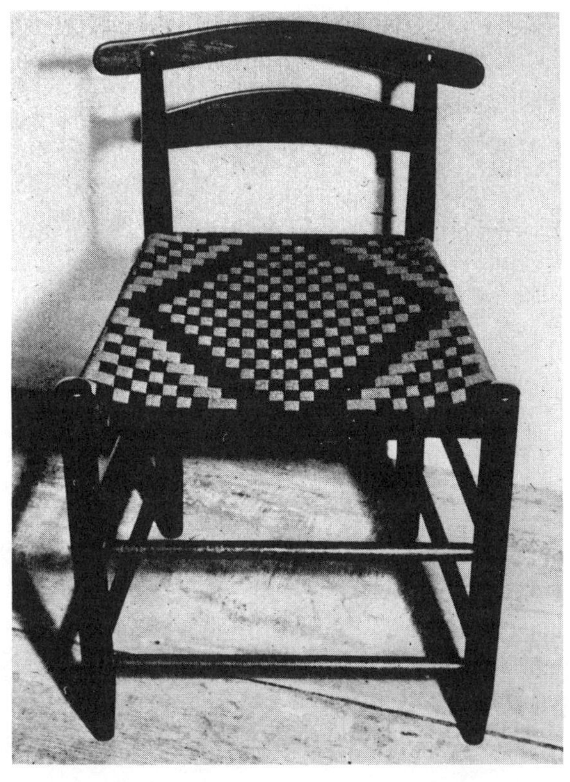

LEFT: *Low-back chair with unusual yoke-shaped slat. Seat tapes are red and black.* OLD CHATHAM.

BELOW: *Close-up view of Shaker tilting chair-foot. This device allowed one to lean back in chair without damaging floor or carpet.* BELFIT

ture styles by the Kentucky and Ohio Shaker craftsmen, giving many of the western items a distinctive appearance.

Some of the earliest Shaker chairs, made for their own use, were painted yellow or red, although many were left in the natural wood. The woven tape for seats was made in a variety of colors and color combinations. Woven slat seats were also used.

The combination of their being delicate and light in appearance and weight and yet extremely sturdy accounts for Shaker chairs having become an instantaneous success on the open market. A Shaker catalogue stipulates that Shaker chairs combined "all the advantages of durability, simplicity and lightness." The largest chairs did not weigh over ten pounds and the smallest weighed less

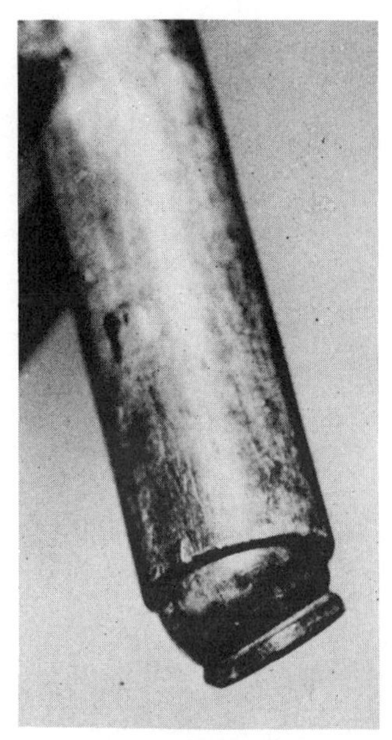

than five. The catalogue further states that "the largest person can feel safe sitting down in them without fear of going through them."

The frames of Shaker chairs were generally made of well-seasoned maple. Many of the earlier chairs were constructed entirely of this wood, while later chairs have slats of birch, cherry, or butternut. The finials on the posts are of various shapes and are always gracefully tapered. An ingenious method for making the straight-backed chairs more comfortable was the previously mentioned tilting device used under the back legs of many of the Shaker chairs. A wooden ball is inserted in a socket carved out of the back posts and is held with a leather thong. The thong is knotted at one end and fixed to the foot of the chair with a small wooden dowel. This simple arrangement enabled one to tilt back comfortably without slipping or marking the floor or tearing the carpet. Chairs equipped with a tilting back have stood hard wear for many years despite the simplicity of the invention.

Although the Shakers distributed their chairs widely for many years, they also sold them in their own shops along with cushions and mats made by the Shaker sisters. The various methods of cushioning the chairs to make them more comfortable were devised by the sisters, and seat cushions became a profitable business in conjunction with the sale of the chairs, themselves. Often the cushions would be as expensive as the chairs, particularly at a later date when the chair business became somewhat mechanized, but the cushions were handmade. The material for the cushions required a good deal of hand-looming and hand-sewing and were, therefore, comparatively high-priced. For instance, a two-step bench listed in a Shaker catalogue could be purchased for $1.50, but cost $3.25 when equipped with cushions.

Late nineteenth-century Shaker chair manufacturers

COLORS OF

BRAID AND PLUSH,

Used in our Chairs and Cushions.

Colors of Braid.		Colors of Plush.	
No.		Letter.	
1	Black.	A	Scarlet and Bl'k Stripe.
2	Navy Blue	B	Blue and Black Stripe.
3	Peacock Blue.	C	Orange and Bl'k Stripe.
4	Light Blue	D	Blue.
5	Maroon.	E	Black.
6	Pomegranate.	F	Scarlet.
7	Brown.,	G	Maroon.
8	Grass Green.	H	Orange.
9	Dark Olive.	I	Peacock Blue.
10	Light Olive.	J	Pomegranate.
11	Old Gold.	K	Olive.
12	Drab.	L	Old Gold.
13	Scarlet.	M	Drab.
14	Orange.	N	Ecrue.

Any two of above colors can be used in combination in Seats and Backs, or in solid colors.

Any two of above colors of Plush can be used in combination or solid colors in cushions.

N. B.—Please use numbers and letters when ordering the colors of braid and plush, and mention which you want for center and border of cushions. The plush cannot be used in combination of colors on the *upholstered* chairs: only one color, except the *A*, *B* and *C*, which are two colors combined in narrow stripe.

Advertisement for materials used on chairs and chair cushions. All was woven in sisters' workshops. OLD CHATHAM.

did become influenced by outside styles. The bentwood chair was made at Mount Lebanon around 1880 and shows direct influence from the outside "worldly" styles. It was made of wood that was steamed and bent. This technique was first used with success by the Austrian,

LEFT: *Shaker footstool covered in hand-loomed plush.* OLD CHATHAM.

BOTTOM: *Shaker bentwood chair fashioned after Thonet Austrian chairs shown at Centennial in Philadelphia.* OLD CHATHAM.

Thonet, and was shown at the centennial exhibition. It is obvious that the Shakers, who were also presented with medals for some of their wares shown in Philadelphia, were not unaware of the marketing possiblities of manufacturing more stylish chairs. While the Shaker bentwood chair is not as elaborate as those made by other manufacturers, it is obvious that the advantage of producing strong, handsome furniture by Thonet's method was not lost to Shaker craftsmen, who were beginning to have more contact with outside influences by this time.

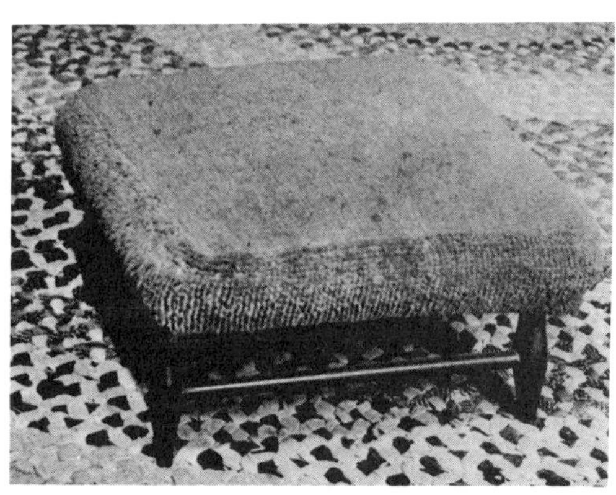

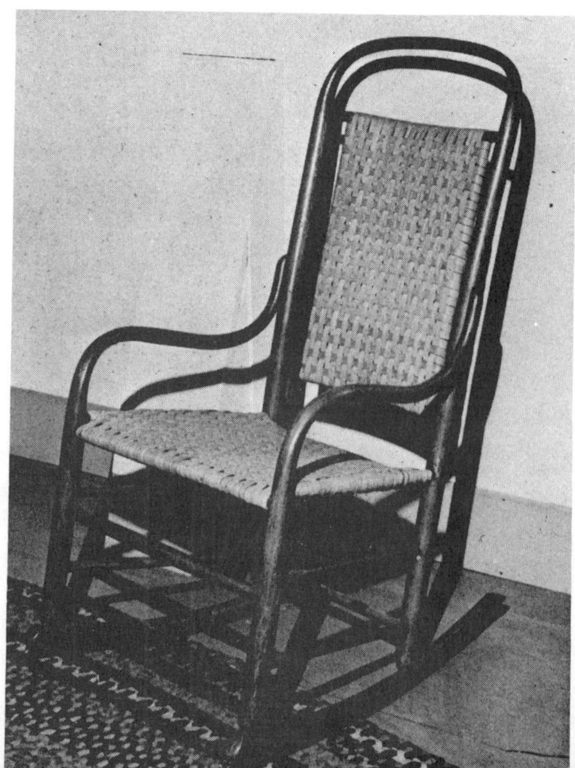

CHAPTER 15

SHAKER BOXES, SIEVES, AND COOPER'S WARE

Varnish, if used in dwelling houses, may be applied only to the moveables therein, as the following, viz., Tables, stands, bureaus, cases of drawers, writing desks, or boxes, drawer faces, chests, chairs, etc. etc. Carriages kept exclusively for riding or nice use may be varnished. No ceilings, casings or mouldings, may be varnished. Oval or nice boxes may be stained reddish or yellow, but not varnished. Bannisters or hand rails in dwelling houses may be varnished. Millenial Laws, 1821. Revised, 1845.

The most familiar Shaker product, and the one that was manufactured for a longer period than any other, is the familiar oval wooden box. Oval boxes were made for sale by the Shakers throughout the nineteenth century, and production continued until 1961. A Shaker brother, Delmar Wilson, of Sabbathday Lake, Maine, was the last to manufacture the boxes. The Second Family at Mount Lebanon was still producing boxes in the 1930s. Although many thousands were made throughout Shaker history, both for sale and for the Shakers' own use, the oval boxes are still the one Shaker item most

TOP: *Three Shaker oval boxes. Box at top of pile is somewhat atypical in joining.* OLD CHATHAM.

BOTTOM: *Shaker decorated box is somewhat atypical. It is varnished and stenciled in brown paint.* OLD CHATHAM.

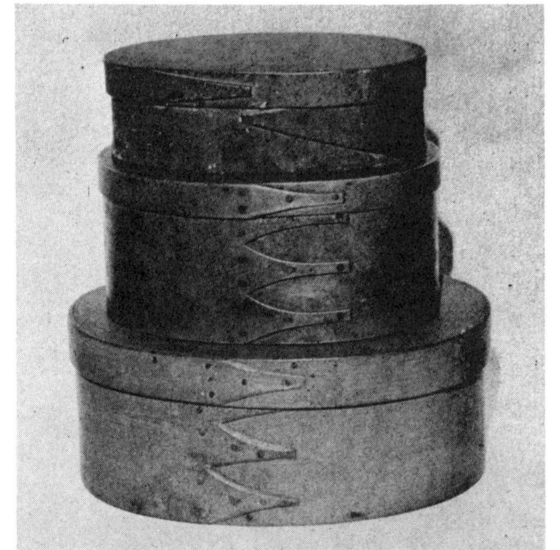

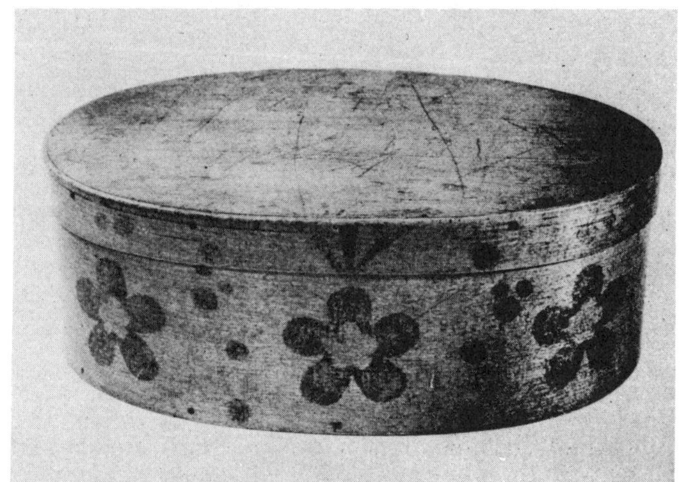

in demand by collectors and the one that is most popularly associated with the Shaker sect.

As with many of the successful industries of the Shakers, oval boxes were at first made by hand, and as time went on, improvements in methods were adapted. The earliest rims were cut from logs in a common saw mill. In 1830 a buzz saw was used. At first planed by hand, the rims were planed by machinery by 1832. At no time, however, in the history of Shaker oval boxes, was the element of handcrafting absent.

The oval boxes made and sold by the Shakers were a refinement of the wooden boxes made elsewhere in New England at a very early date. The greatest improvement was the use of "fingers" or "lappers" in the joinery. These lappers were fastened with copper rivets, and while the majority of the boxes were varnished, many were painted.

The tops and bottoms of the boxes were made of pine, and the rims were usually of maple. The boxes were sold in graduated nests of twelve, nine, seven, or five. Molds and "shapers" were made of wood, and wood patterns for the tops and bottoms were formed so that sizes were standardized around 1833. Each size was given a number. The price for the smallest box in 1900 was three dollars a dozen.

Shaker oval boxes, as with many other products adapted by the Shakers, were better made and more carefully finished than those produced elsewhere. The wood was properly seasoned and the covers fit perfectly.

By the first quarter of the nineteenth century, Shaker oval boxes were being made in woodworking shops of every community. The bentwood rims were steamed or

Three Shaker boxes. Medium-sized box has fingers (or lappers) that are left-handed. It is probably earlier than others. Small box is painted yellow. BELFIT.

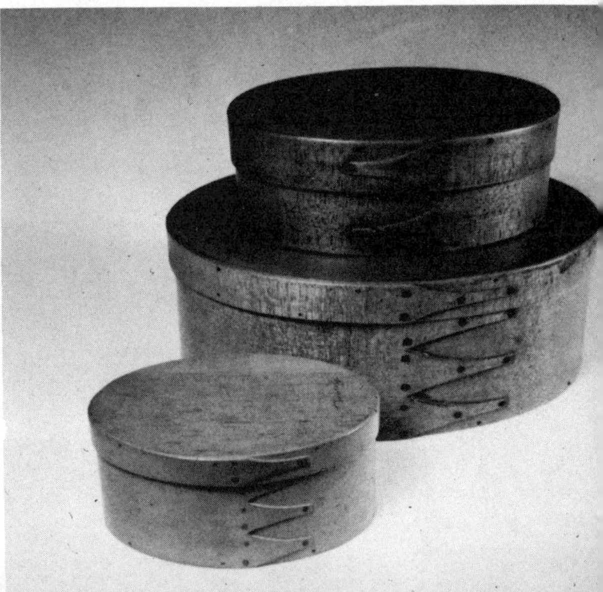

Workbench showing oval form for shaping box lids and tools used. HANCOCK.

soaked and then wrapped around the molds, which were held onto the workbenches with a vise. The rivets were pounded in against metal strips attached to the molds. Red, green, blue, and yellow are the colors most often found on the painted boxes.

Besides the familiar oval shape, round boxes were also made. Handled carriers were designed with or without covers. The oval boxes, fitted with handles and lids, were often converted into fancy sewing baskets by the Shaker sisters of the early part of this century and were an extremely popular shop item. The interiors of these boxes were padded and lined, often with beautiful silk damask fabrics. Suitable fittings, made of the same matching fabric, were added. Pincushions, emeries, beeswax, and

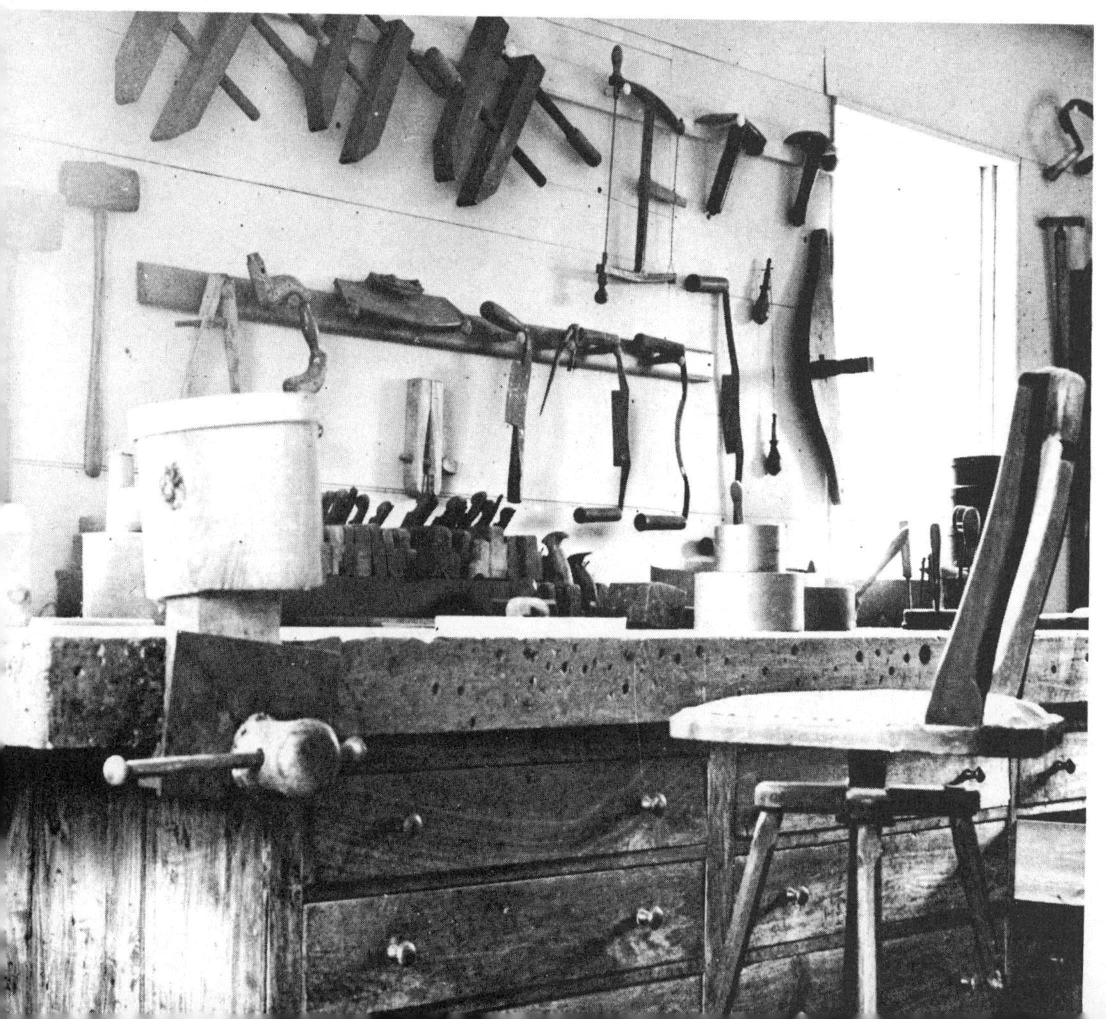

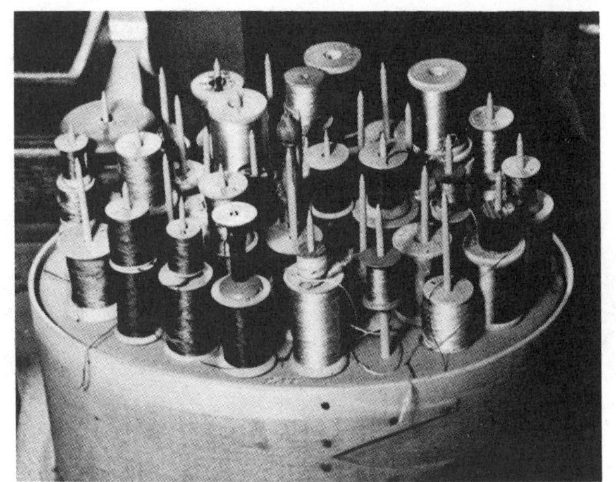

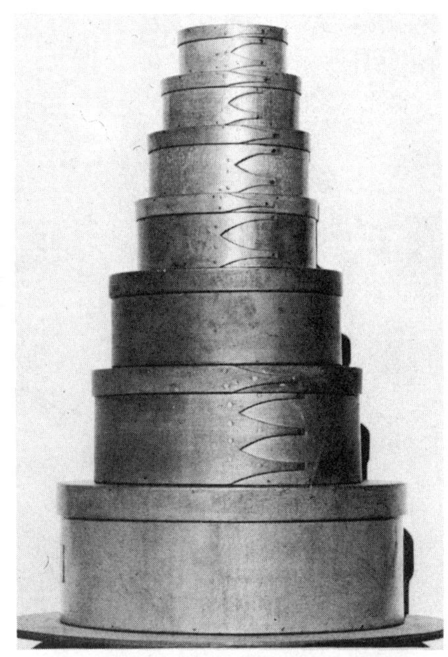

needlecases were attached to the box interiors with ribbons. The boxes were sold by the Shaker sisters at vacation resorts in Maine, New York, and New Hampshire, as well as in their own shops. At times these boxes were made to order for special customers and were lined with fabrics supplied by them.

The fittings of Shaker sewing boxes and baskets were rather standardized as to shapes and types of materials used. The poplar straw baskets or boxes were fitted with small envelope-style needlecases bound in the same material. A special tool with serrated edges, probably the forerunner of pinking shears, was designed to facilitate the cutting of the flannel "leaves" for the needlecases. The emeries were strawberry shaped and often leaves were appliquéd and embroidered on them to make them look more realistic. The pincushions were tomato or melon shaped.

While the oval, lidded boxes were an outside industry

LEFT: *Large Shaker oval box is fitted with rack to hold spools of thread.* OLD CHATHAM.

RIGHT: *Stack of seven Shaker boxes graduated in size so that they nest one inside the other.* OLD CHATHAM.

TOP: *Oval box fitted with sewing equipment and lined with green silk. These boxes were sold in sisters' shops.* BELFIT.

BOTTOM: *Wood carriers were also fitted out for sewing by sisters.* OLD CHATHAM.

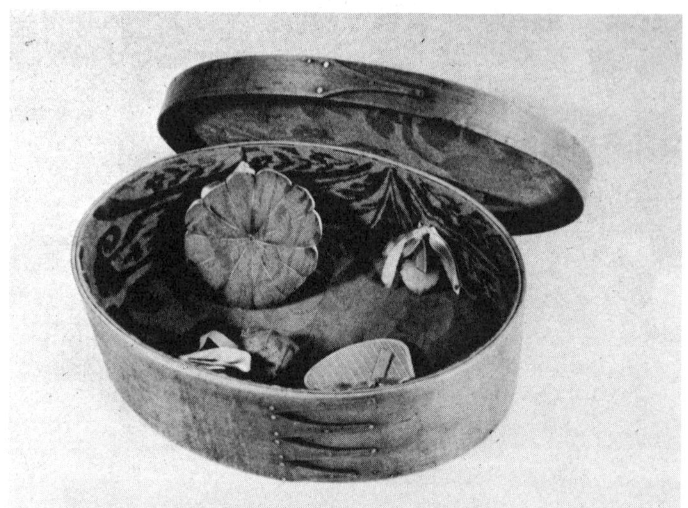

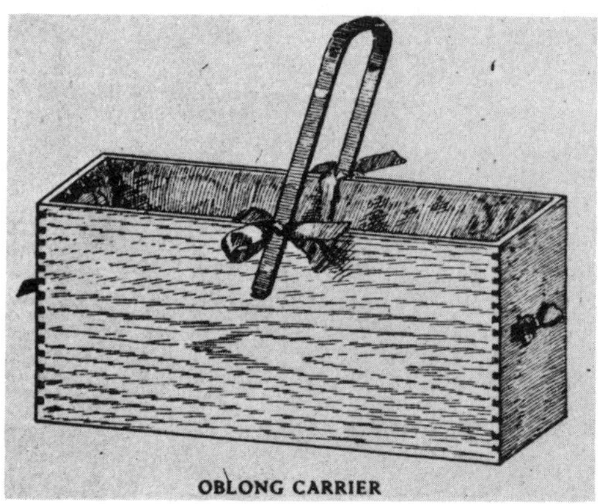

OBLONG CARRIER

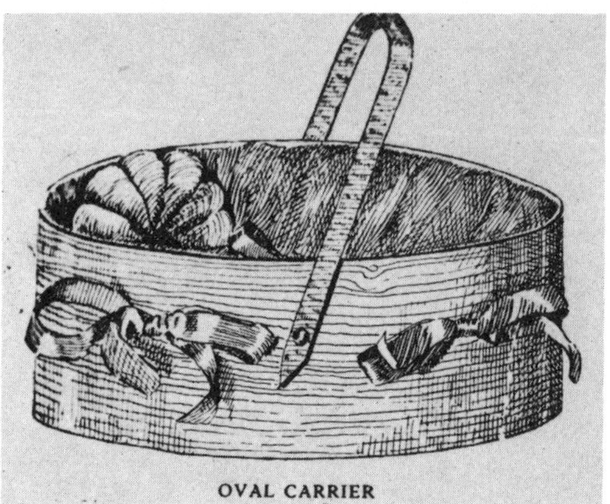

OVAL CARRIER

that provided a steady income to Shaker communities, a great many boxes were made solely for the Shakers' own use. Strawberry boxes, made in a truncated pyramid shape, with holes drilled into the sides for ventilation, were made in quantity. These boxes were made to fit into a larger wooden box, which held a dozen of the pint- or quart-size berry boxes. Many compartmented boxes were made for the packing and shipping of seeds and herbs. Many cylindrical pasteboard boxes were made for herbs and medicines as well.

Boxes were made to fit every need of the Shakers as it arose, and everything had its place in the Shaker dwellings. In the era of fancy Victorian spittoons, the Shakers used a round wooden box filled with wood shavings to serve the same purpose. Boxes to hold shavings or kindling were placed near the Shaker stoves, as were larger metal boxes for holding the ashes. Each room was equipped with a "tin, earthen, or other safe vessel, to keep friction matches in."

A variety of boxes was made for kitchen and shop use. There were cheese boxes and wooden buckets for

TOP: *Shaker berry box was made in truncated pyramid shape to allow for ventilation when dozen boxes were packed into larger storage box.* BELFIT.

BOTTOM: *Paper-covered box in bright blue and orange. One of many boxes made by Shakers.* BELFIT.

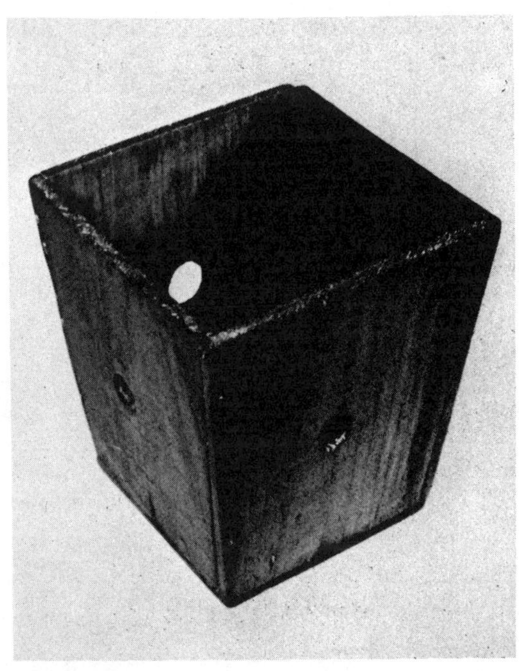

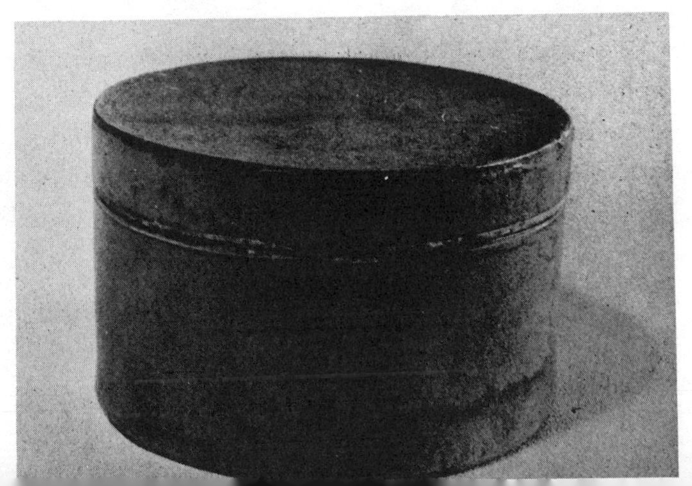

RIGHT: *Small Shaker sieve made of woven silk. Diameter, 2 inches.* BELFIT.

BELOW LEFT: *Woven-hair sieve with Shaker tape and copper rivets. Sieve has handle for carrying.* OLD CHATHAM.

BELOW RIGHT: *Three-legged Shaker sieve made of woven hair.* OLD CHATHAM.

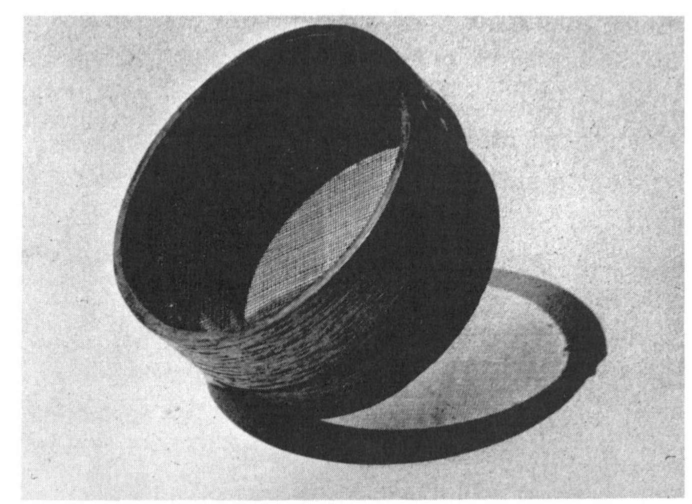

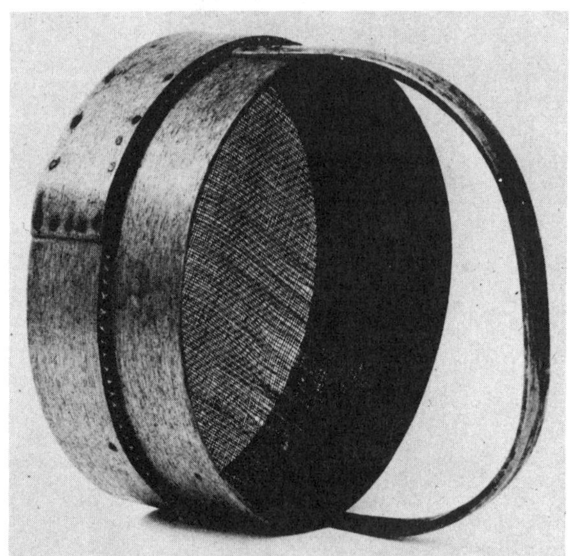

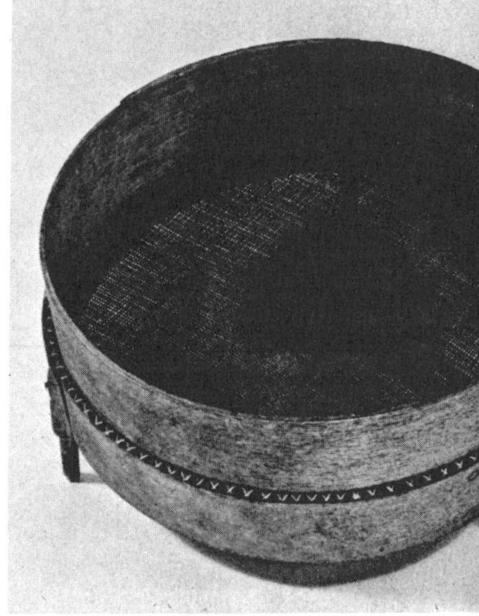

applesauce as well. Carriers for gathering fruit and vegetables appeared in a variety of shapes and sizes. Although "superfluous paper boxes" were forbidden, there are examples of hat boxes that were covered in attractive papers and small, brightly painted paper boxes were made for sale by twentieth-century Shakers. From early days, specially made boxes for storing Shaker men's hats were used. Just as the carpenters and joiners designed special tools for certain jobs, they designed containers to hold many of the Shaker household objects.

A type of Shaker-made sewing box that is unique in design and materials is the poplar-wood-covered box. However, since this category of holder for sewing equipment resembles woven baskets more closely, they will be discussed in the chapter devoted to that subject.

Another Shaker industry closely associated with the manufacture of wooden boxes was the making of sieves in a variety of sizes. Shaker sieves were created for many different household purposes and a smaller amount was sold to chemists and pharmacists. From fine sieves for sifting flour to great "riddles" for sorting seeds, many of these objects were made principally by the South and Second families at New Lebanon. The manufacture of sieves was not as widespread as the box industry.

Sieves were made of silk thread, and hair from horses' manes or cows' tails. These were woven by the sisters on special looms. The mesh was stretched between two hoops and tightened or sewed on the outside, on a specially designed "sieve-binder." A special braid made by the Shakers often held the mesh taut between the two wooden hoops. There are records that indicate that sieves were sold as early as 1810, and by 1830 they were being produced for sale in some quantity. Records also indicate that brass wire was used along with silk and hair in the making of the mesh.

Pails, tubs, firkins, casks, and barrels were also manufactured by the Shakers at an early date. The industry did not last as long as some others, nor were as many of these items made for the Shakers' own use. Perhaps one of the reasons for this is that a supply would suit the needs of a community for rather a long time, and

TOP LEFT: *Shallow sieves were made in many sizes for a variety of purposes around kitchen and farm.* OLD CHATHAM.

after the Civil War, when the number of Believers began to dwindle, fewer pieces of cooper's ware were needed and the Shakers concentrated on those industries which were more lucrative. Small pails were made for storing

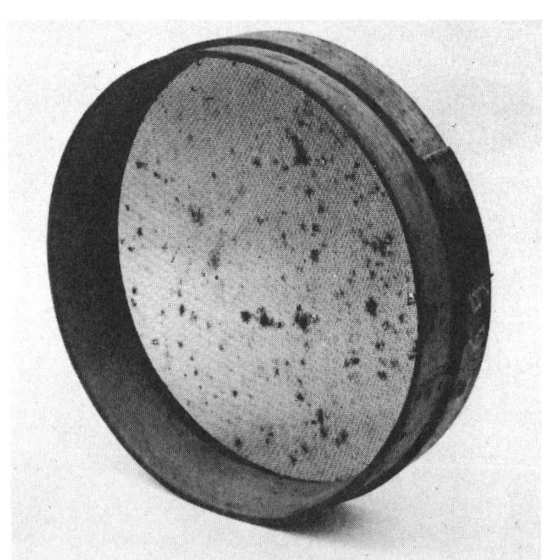

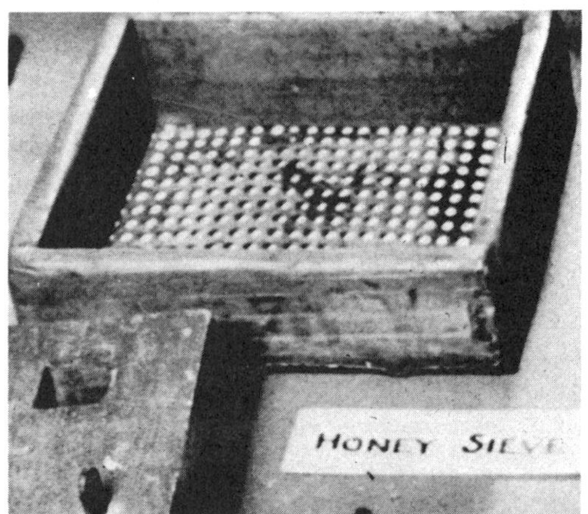

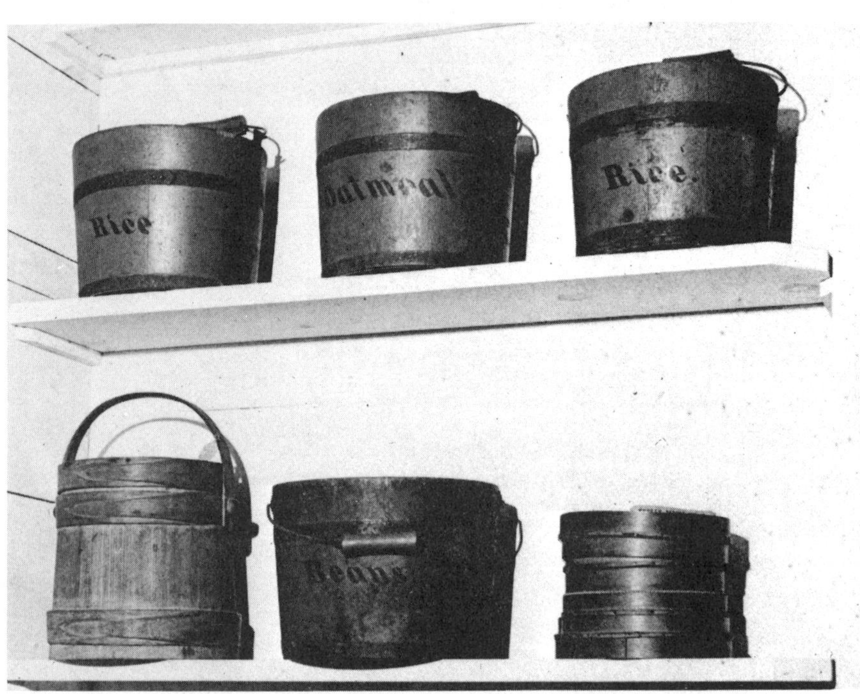

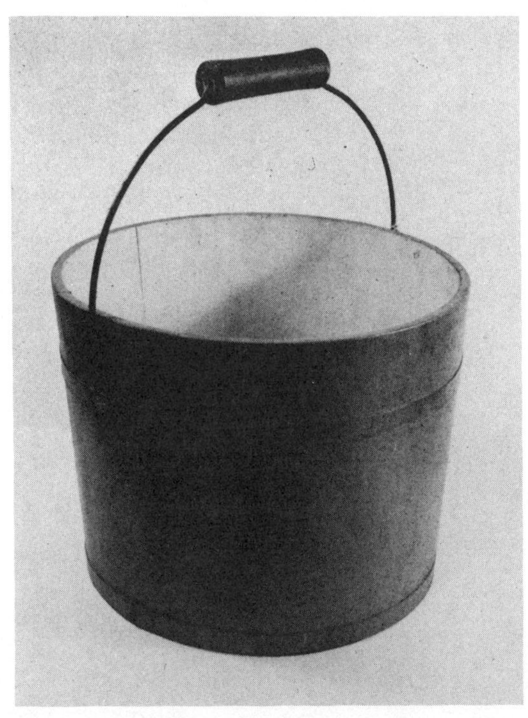

and selling certain Shaker products throughout the nineteenth century, however. These tubs were also made to sell empty, usually in nests of three. The earliest were bound with wood hoops, while later tubs were banded with iron.

The coopers' shop at New Lebanon listed a large variety of products as early as 1789, and this list indicates that tubs were made to hold beer, sugar, cheese, and meat. Washtubs and flour barrels were also constructed. Firkins and tubs to hold applesauce, seeds, sugar, salt, flour, meal, and grain were turned out in the Shaker shops. Wooden buckets for washing clothes and dishes, and milk pails, were all necessities for early Shaker housekeeping. It is probable that, as special needs arose in Shaker households, pails and barrels of many sizes were made, but cooper's ware was not produced in quantity for sale in the latter half of the nineteenth century.

OPPOSITE TOP RIGHT: *Many types of sieves were made by Shakers. This honey sieve has perforated tin strainer in bottom.* OLD CHATHAM.

OPPOSITE BOTTOM: *Buckets, barrels, and other cooper's ware were made by Shakers from early days.* OLD CHATHAM.

ABOVE: *Paint was used judiciously on some wood items. This bucket, painted blue on outside and yellow on interior, is somewhat atypical.* OLD CHATHAM.

CHAPTER
16
WOODENWARE

It is disorderly for brethren and sisters to spend much time in making conveniences or articles of manufacture for each other, save such as come within the regular line of business, done by brethren and sisters in general, except by the direction of the Deacons and Deaconesses, each sex in their own order. Millenial Laws, 1821. Revised, 1845.

Shaker carpenter shops turned out so many small objects made of wood that a complete list would be almost endless. While a great many of these products were made for sale to the world, many other items were devised to be used only in Shaker communities. Wooden hangers in a variety of shapes were made in quantity. Multiple hangers for three or more garments became the models for our modern space-saving hangers that hold a half-dozen skirts or several blouses in the same space as one.

Thousands of wooden boxes were constructed by the Shakers, and the manufacture of these became such an important industry that they have been treated in a

OPPOSITE TOP LEFT: *Shakers made many mortars and pestles to use in preparing herbal medicines.* OLD CHATHAM.

OPPOSITE TOP RIGHT: *A variety of wood hangers as made for many purposes.* BELFIT.

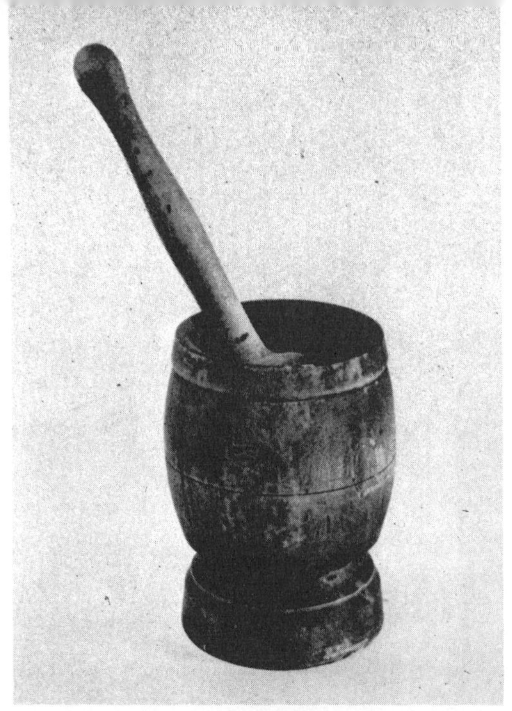

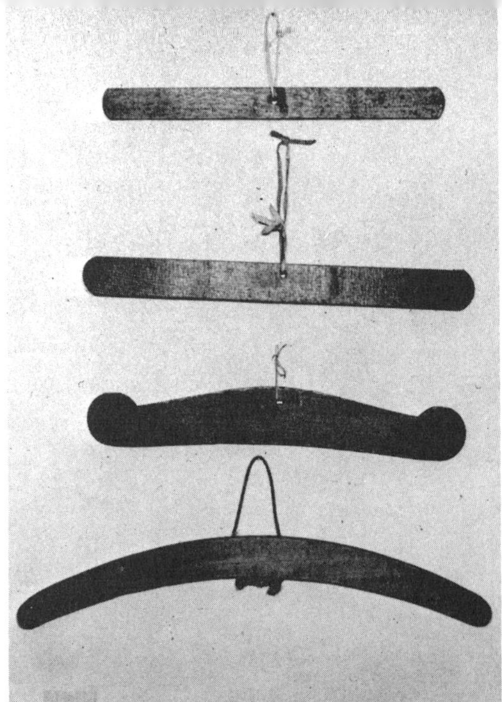

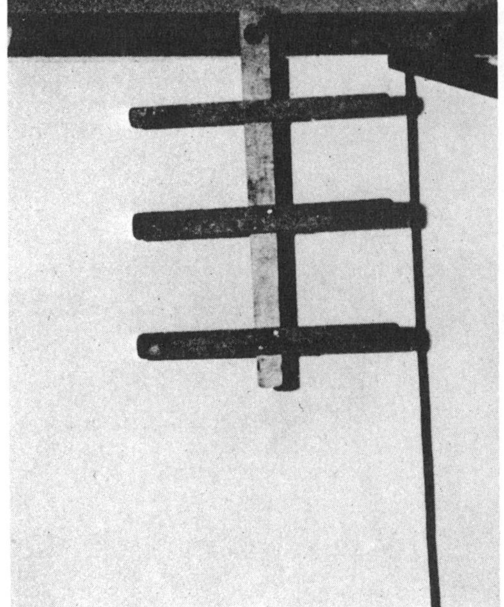

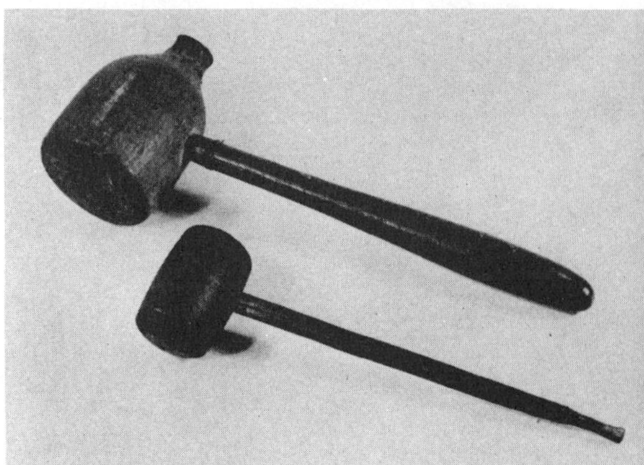

BOTTOM LEFT: *A multiple hanger for hanging three garments in the space of one.* OLD CHATHAM.

BOTTOM RIGHT: *Many different sizes and types of mallets were made by the Shakers. Small end at top of upper mallet was used for corking bottles.* OLD CHATHAM.

separate chapter. Besides the familiar oval boxes, Shaker craftsmen also produced the many boxes in which the herbs and medicines were shipped. Berry boxes of wood with ventilating holes were made in pint and quart sizes

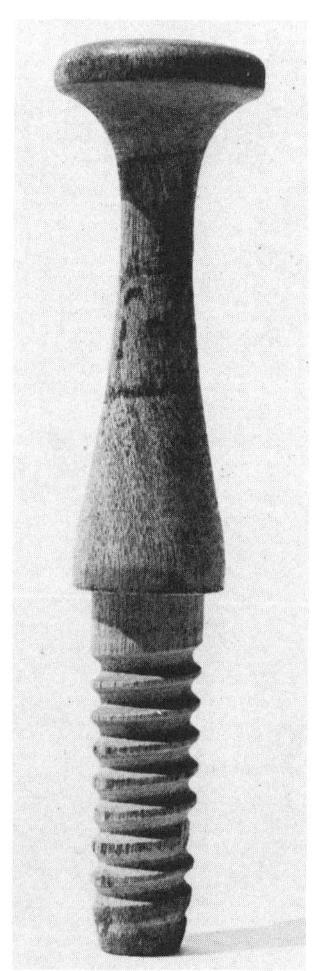

and these were fitted into larger boxes that held a dozen of the smaller boxes.

Pegs and pegboards were also an important Shaker wood product. Thousands of the screw pegs were needed, since they surrounded the walls of every Shaker room. Small mirrors, backs for the enormous variety of brushes made and sold by the Shakers, mallets, mortars and pestles for the herb industry and for kitchen use, and handles for tools were also needed in quantity.

Spools for thread and yarn exhibit the Shakers' feeling for, and understanding of, wood and wood grains, as clearly as does the important Shaker furniture. Letter openers of bird's-eye maple, darning eggs for stockings, and children's tops of beautifully turned wood were made by the Shakers.

Implements for kitchen use were made of wood in the

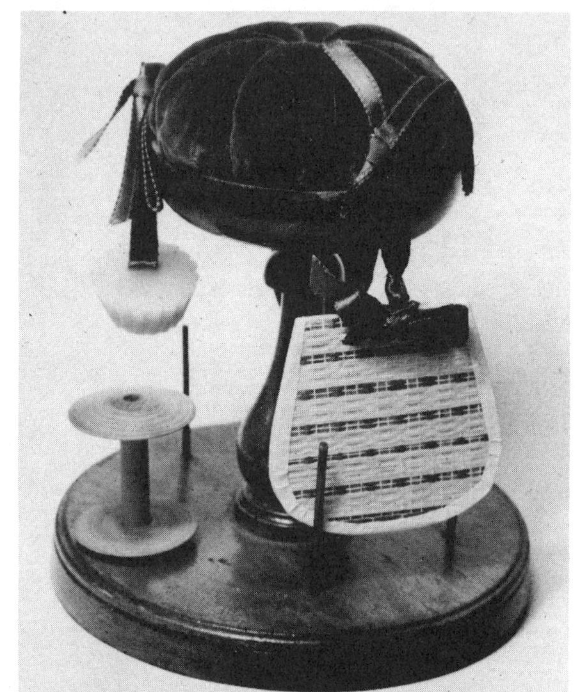

ABOVE: *The Shaker wooden screw peg is a symbol of the sect's neatness. Over five thousand were used at Hancock alone.* BELFIT.

RIGHT: *Making and outfitting sewing stands were a combined effort of the brethrens' shop and the sisters' workrooms.* BELFIT.

brethren's shops, also. Wooden dippers in nests of three or more were made for sale. Scoops, spoons, spatulas, rolling pins in a variety of shapes and sizes, wooden bowls, cutting boards, and chopping blocks were built to last.

The manufacture of table swifts, a Shaker innovation, was an important industry at Hancock until around 1865. The thin wood ribs of the table swifts were made by a machine developed at Hancock in 1835. Most of the

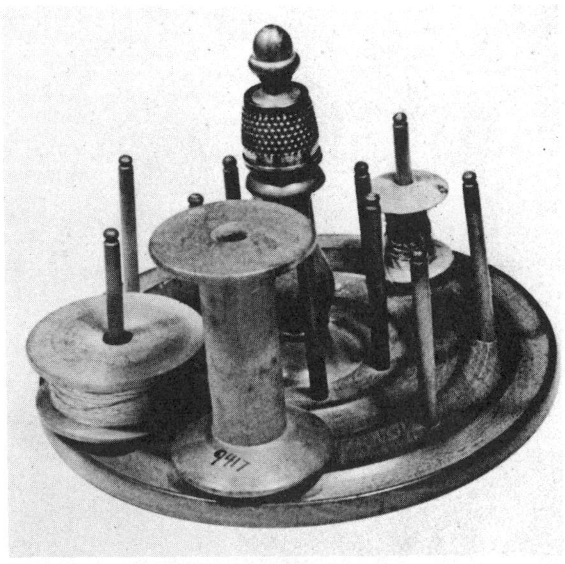

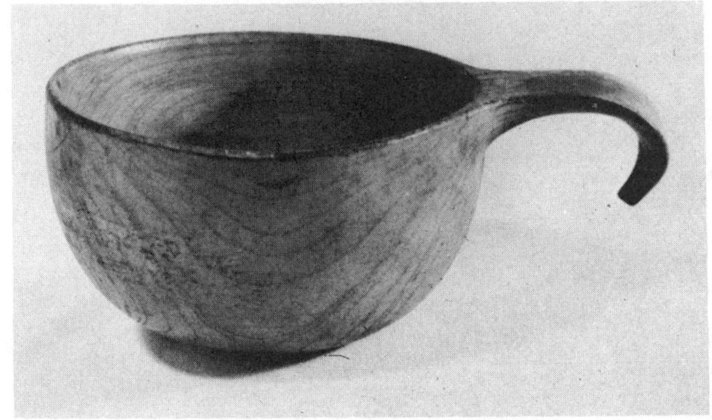

ABOVE: *Wooden thread rack was popular gift item that could be purchased in Shaker shops.* OLD CHATHAM.

LEFT: *One of the most satisfying forms to have come out of brethrens' woodworking shops, dippers were made in nests of three for sale to the world. This one is stained yellow.* BELFIT.

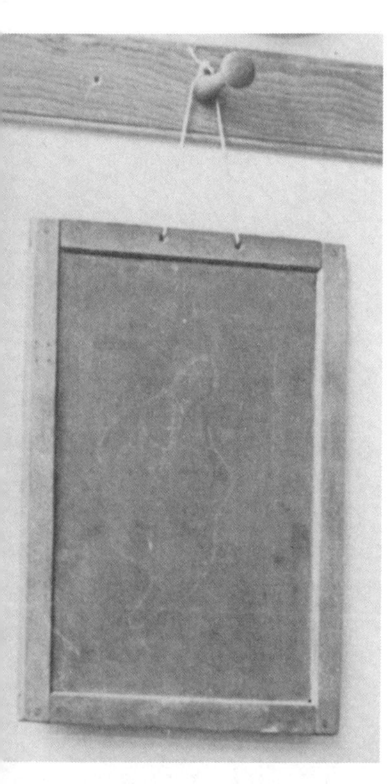

existing table swifts, used for holding yarn while it is being wound into balls, are stained yellow, although a few have been found in natural wood grains. The swifts folded up when not in use.

The manufacture of clock cases, hanging shelves, and racks for a variety of purposes are just a few of the endless variety of small wooden objects that were made in the Shakers' shops.

Spinning wheels and wheel parts formed an early Shaker industry and were probably manufactured and sold in the late eighteenth century. Most certainly the

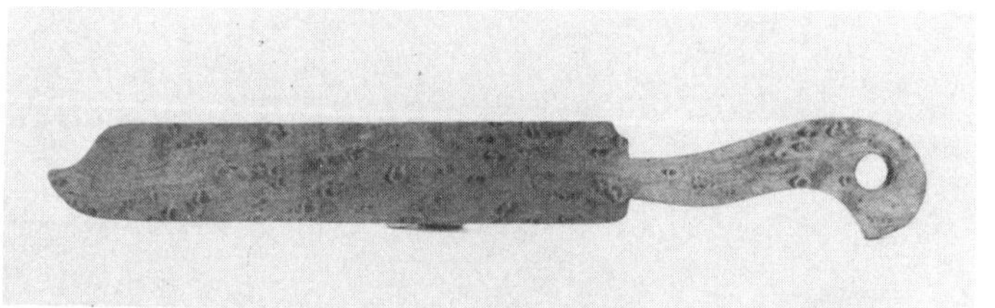

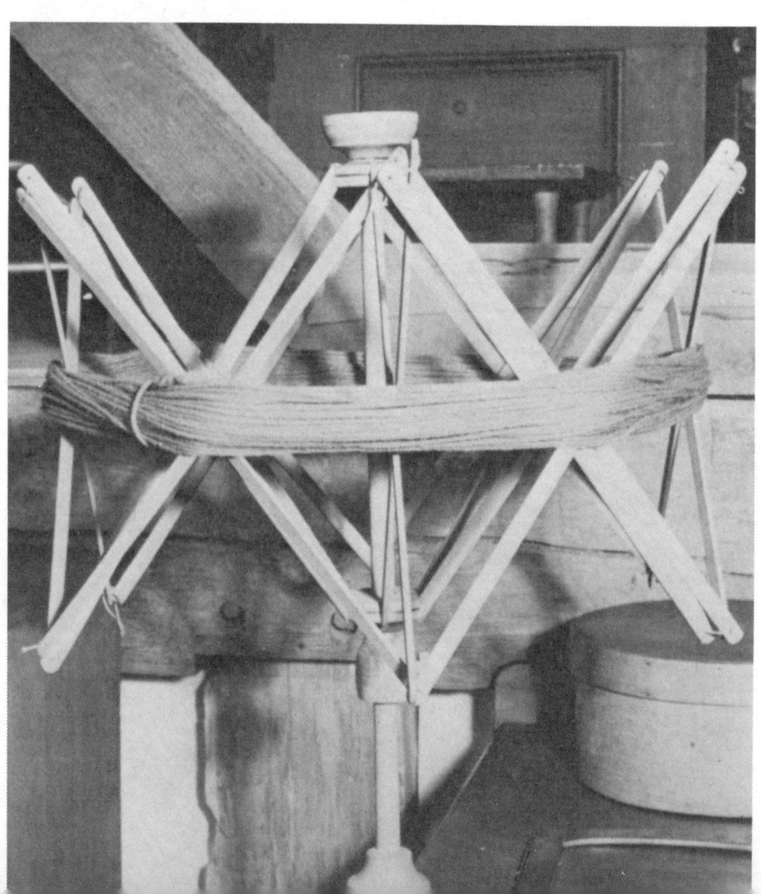

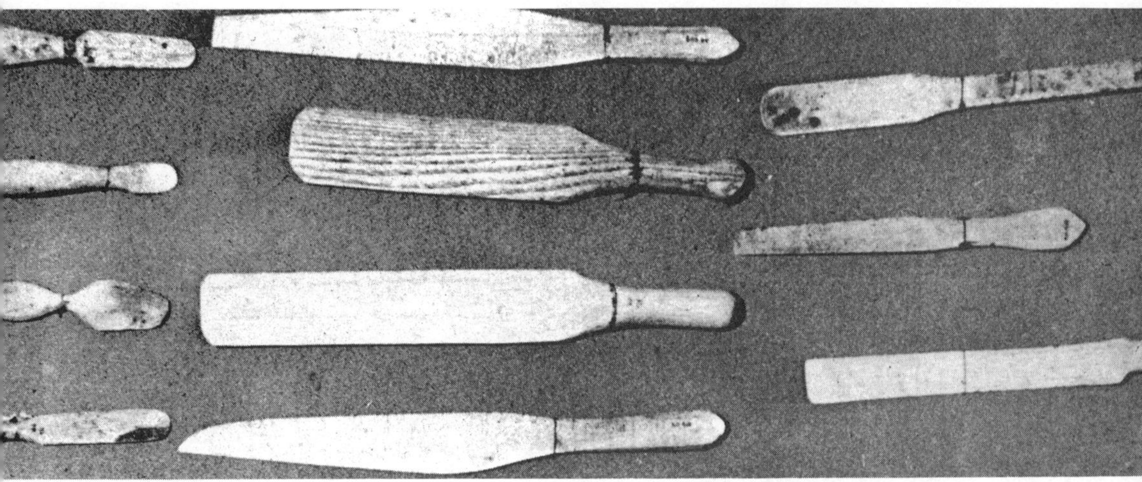

business of selling spinning wheels was well established by the beginning of the nineteenth century, during which they were made for the first thirty years in quantity at New Lebanon and probably other Shaker communities as well.

Wooden pails in many shapes and sizes were manufactured, as well as barrel staves and finished barrels bound with iron strips, which constituted a lucrative business. Wooden shingles became a Shaker industry, and handles for brooms, brushes, and mops required a great deal of the Shaker craftsman's time and effort.

Besides all the small items made of wood at Shaker villages, much of the machinery for producing these products was devised or improved by the Shakers. Broom vises, a variety of looms and molding planes in many sizes, label presses and herb presses all had to be built to order and maintained. Cheese presses were also Shaker made.

When one considers the variety of small wooden goods made by the Shakers throughout the nineteenth century for their own use, it is even more impressive when we understand that enormous amounts of them were also

ABOVE: *A variety of spatulas, paper knives, etc., made in Shaker woodworking shops.* OLD CHATHAM.

OPPOSITE TOP LEFT: *Shaker slate, probably for listing duties in kitchen or shop.* HANCOCK.

OPPOSITE TOP RIGHT: *Bird's-eye maple letter opener is graceful shape and shows Shakers' understanding of beautiful wood grain.* BELFIT.

OPPOSITE BOTTOM: *The manufacture of table swifts such as this one was a successful Shaker business. They were marketed in England as well as in this country.* OLD CHATHAM.

RIGHT: *Chalk line safe made of turned wood. Probably sold in Shaker shops.* BELFIT.

MIDDLE: *Wood mold for shaping beeswax used in sewing boxes.* OLD CHATHAM.

BOTTOM: *Wooden kitchen implements made by Shakers.* HANCOCK.

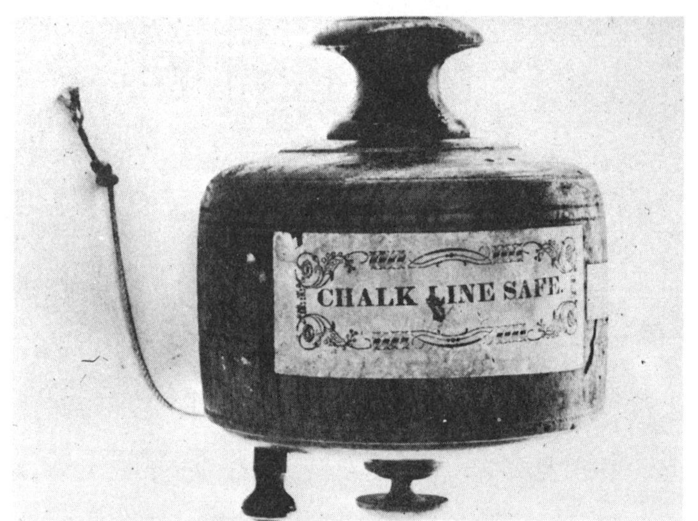

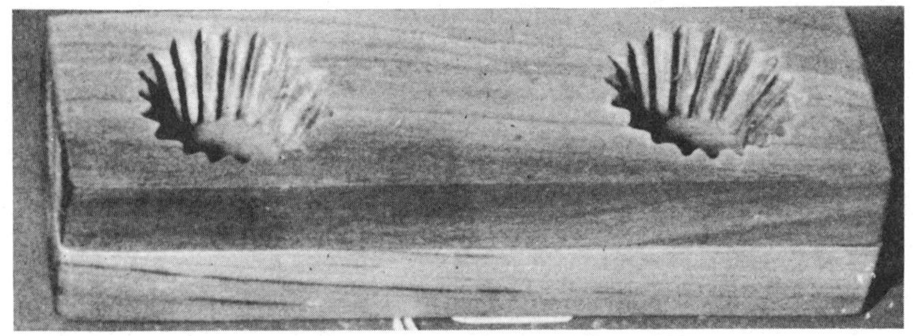

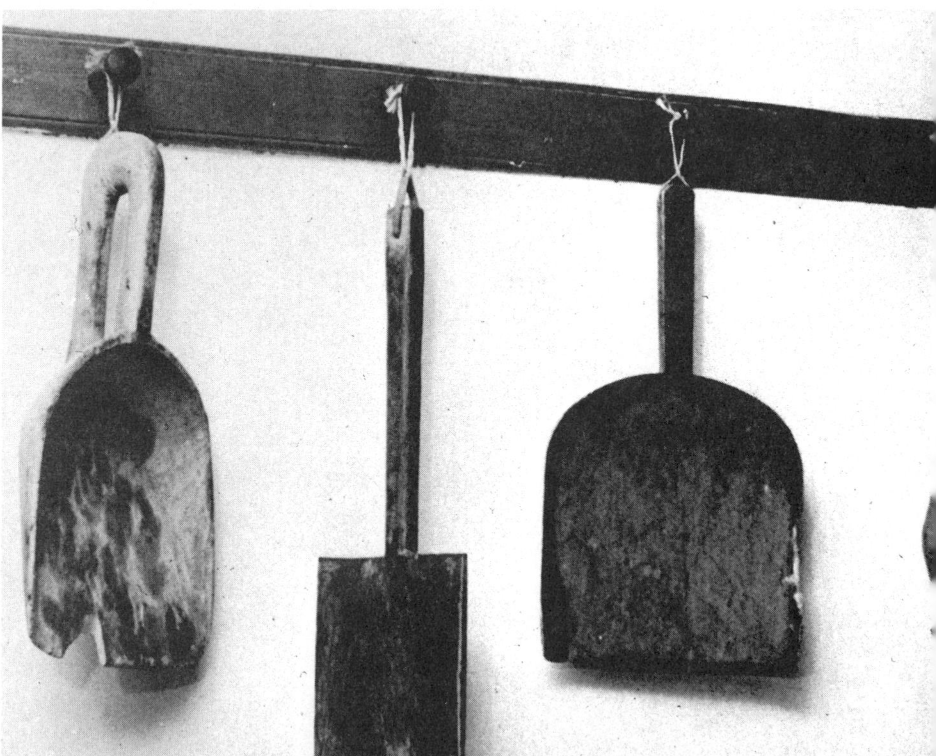

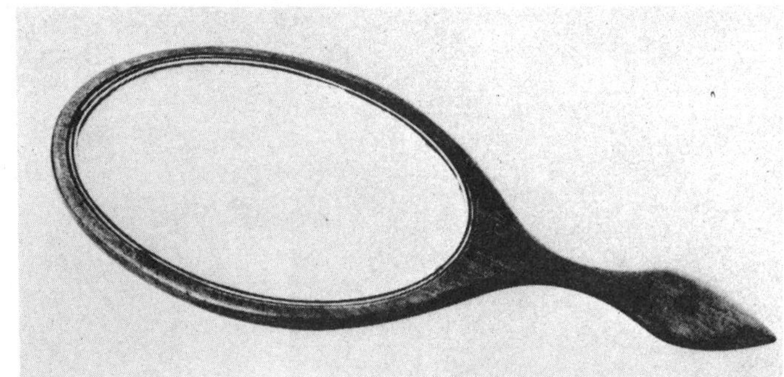

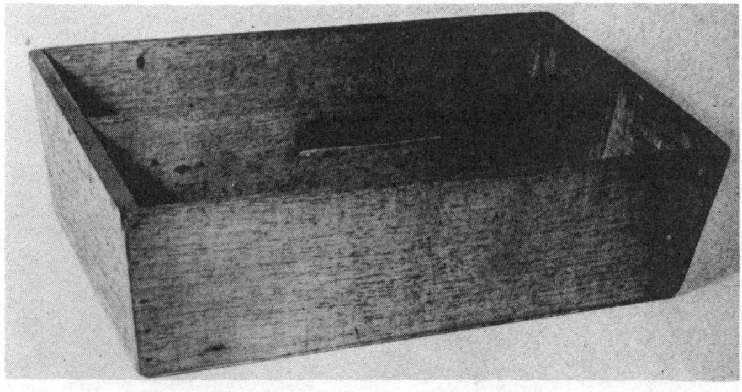

made for sale. Because they were made with the usual Shaker understanding of, and reverence for, wood, many small objects still exist today. Except for the oval boxes, which are easy to identify as Shakermade, other products which were sold are not as well known nor is their origin always easy to prove.

Only through the study of museum collections such as that found at Old Chatham, New York, can we learn which of these heretofore anonymous objects are truly Shaker. It is unlikely, for instance, that most American craftsmen working in the first half of the nineteenth century would lavish as much care and attention in the manufacture of a simple spool for thread as is obvious in the spool illustrated in this chapter. The wood grain conforms to the shape of the spool, and the wood is carefully finished.

TOP: *Shakers could use only small mirrors. This hand mirror is perfectly balanced and gracefully shaped.* BELFIT.

BOTTOM: *Double-compartment knife box.* OLD CHATHAM.

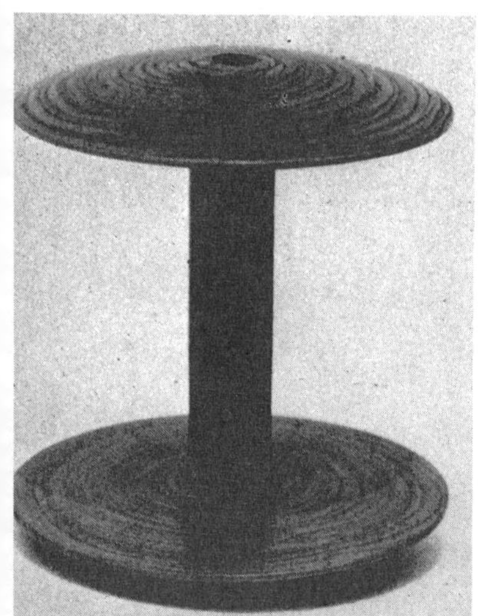

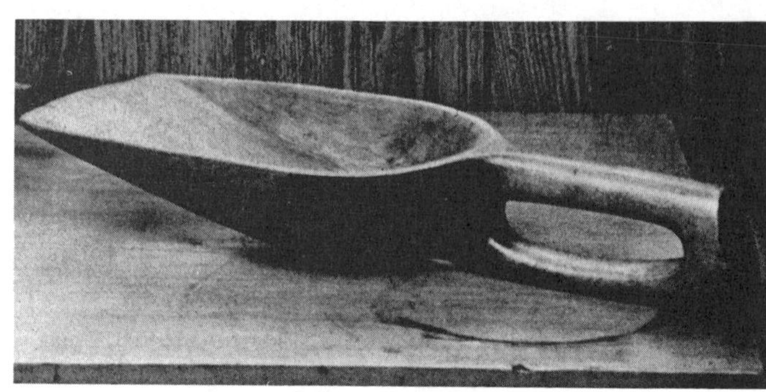

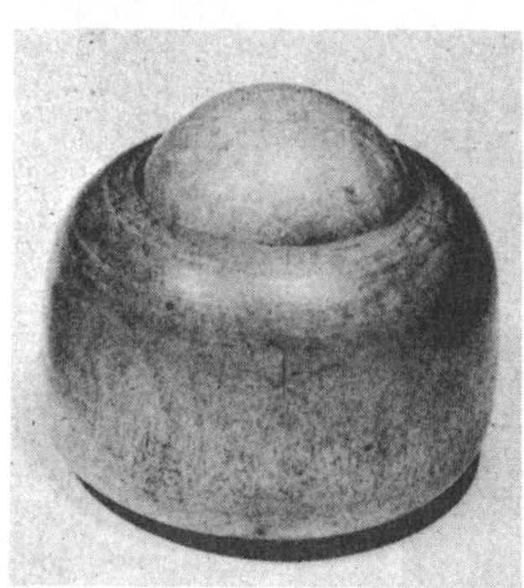

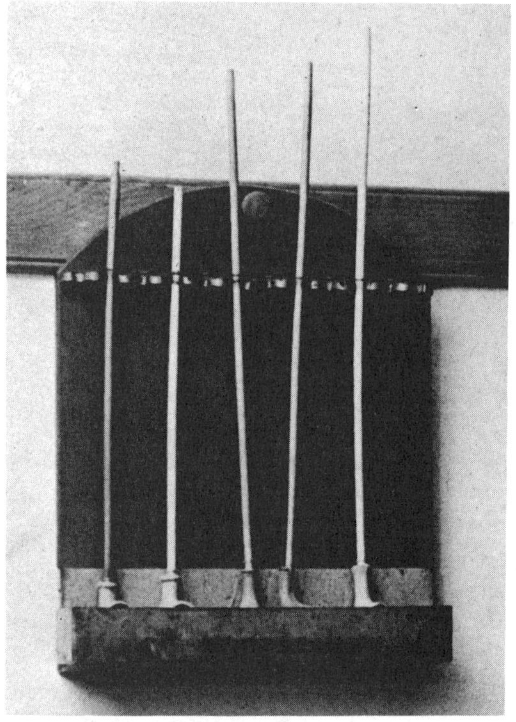

TOP LEFT: *Wood spool for thread illustrates Shaker reverence for wood grain.* BELFIT.

TOP RIGHT: *An apple-butter scoop carved out of a single block of maple.* HANCOCK.

BOTTOM LEFT: *Darning egg made of revolving wooden ball inside wooden case.* OLD CHATHAM.

The apple-butter scoop from Hancock illustrated here, carved from a single block of maple wood, is also a magnificent design used for a practical object. The darning egg shown in this chapter, which has a movable ball encased in a circle of beautifully grained and polished wood, had to have been a labor of love. The joinery on the outside case is impossible to detect.

When we consider that the Shaker craftsmen made the majority of the tools used in their woodworking shops, and in many cases designed the tools themselves, we can only be amazed at the enormous amount of work that was done. One important invention credited to the Shaker brethren is the common clothespin. The wired snap-type clothespin is also claimed to have been invented by the Shakers.

Of all the small objects made of woodenware for sale to the world, the dippers are, perhaps, the most graceful. They were made in a variety of sizes and shapes for many different purposes. Quantities of the dippers were sold to outsiders. Dippers were undoubtedly produced almost from the beginning of the earliest Shaker communities, and one is recorded as having been sold in June 1789 at New Lebanon for one shilling, fourpence.

Usually made from one solid piece of wood, dippers and scoops were sanded, polished, and stained. Maple and ash were the woods most commonly used. The dippers were usually sold in nests of three graduated sizes and were made with holes in the handles so that they could be hung on the wall.

OPPOSITE BOTTOM RIGHT: *Pipe rack with tin bottom to protect against fire also hung on pegs. Pipes and pipe stems were Shaker products.* HANCOCK.

BELOW: *The common clothespin was another Shaker invention and many were made for sale by the brethren.* OLD CHATHAM.

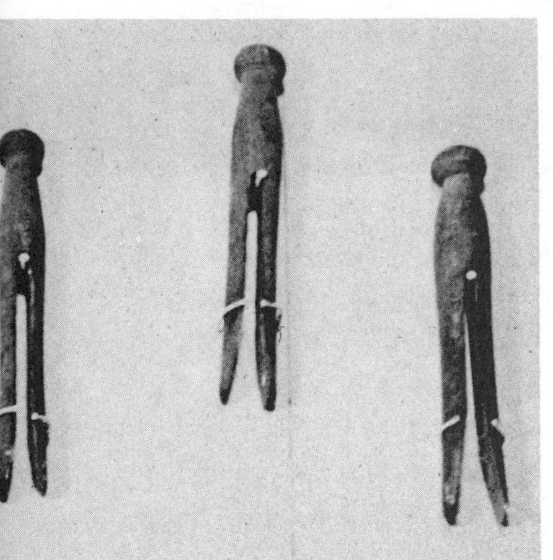

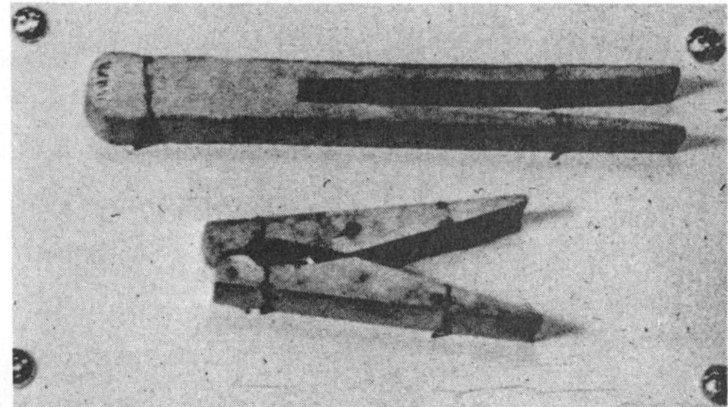

CHAPTER 17

BASKETS

No lighted lamps or candles may be held over chests, drawers, shaving baskets, or wood boxes. Millenial Laws, 1821. Revised, 1845.

As opposed to the oval boxes which were somewhat standardized in shape and size at a fairly early date, Shaker baskets were made in an almost infinite variety of weaves, shapes, and sizes, according to the many purposes for which they were to be used. The need for many different types of baskets in a basically agricultural community led to the weaving of literally hundreds of different types, many of which today cannot be absolutely identified as having been made by the Shakers. Baskets for the gathering and storing of garden seeds, for gathering and drying as well as sorting herbs and herb bark and roots for medicines, and for use in the weave rooms, washrooms, shops, and kitchens were woven by the Shakers. Specially made baskets for strawberry, grape, cherry, and plum gathering and larger baskets for apples can be found today. Cheese baskets with large open weaves were used in Shaker dairies.

Basketmaking was primarily an occupation of the Shaker women, and it is probable that they learned the art from the groups of Indian basketmakers who lived near the first Shaker communities. Poplar wood and split black ash were the two most commonly used materials for Shaker baskets. Palm leaf, imported from Cuba, was also used.

Shaker baskets were extremely cheap before the Civil War, with small ones selling for as little as ten cents. The industry did not continue to any large extent (with one exception) following the Civil War, although basketmaking for the Shakers' own use went on at Mount Lebanon and other communities.

The one type of commercially oriented basketmaking that continued through the end of the nineteenth century and even into the twentieth was the woven poplar boxes and baskets made by the Shaker sisters and sold in quantity in their shops. These baskets were first made around 1850. The native poplar trees were cut, when frozen, into twenty-four-inch lengths, put through a Shaker-invented plane, which took off very thin strips of the wood. These wood strips were then shredded into fine strips,

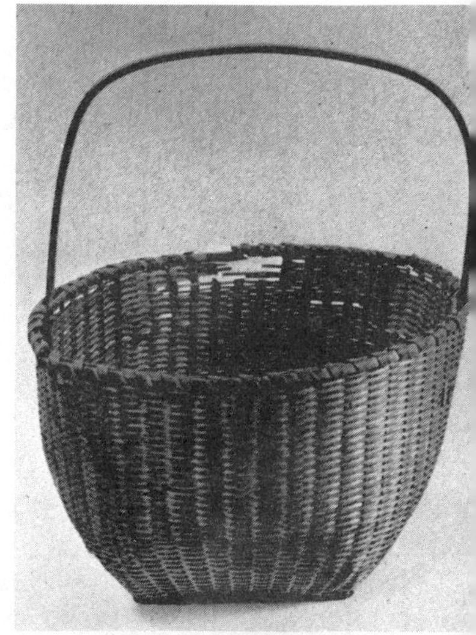

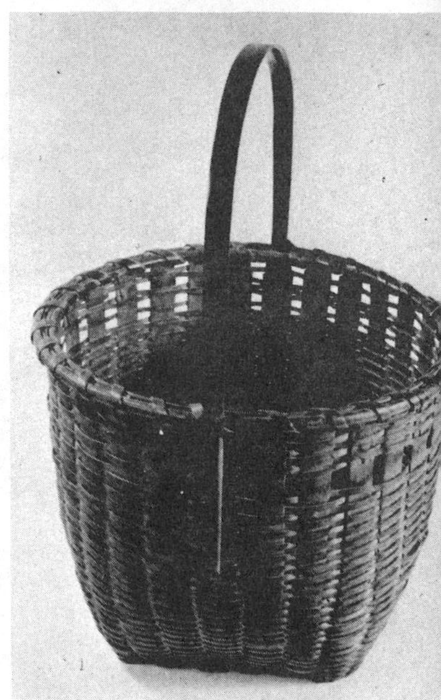

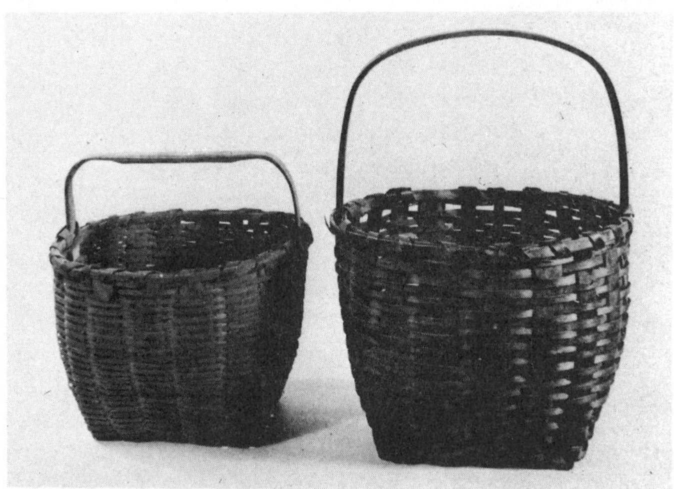

Group of four Shaker baskets with handles. OLD CHATHAM.

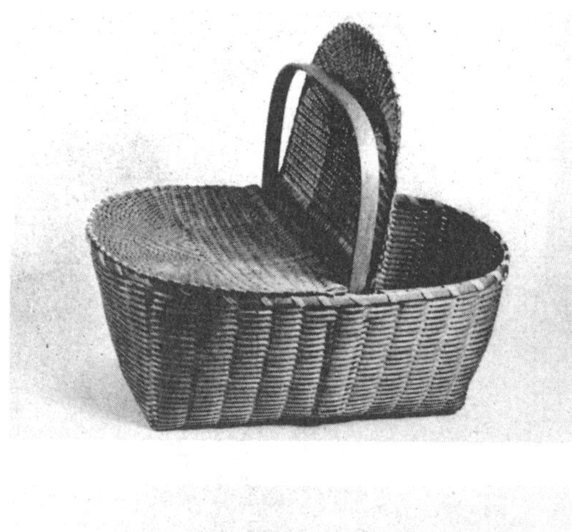

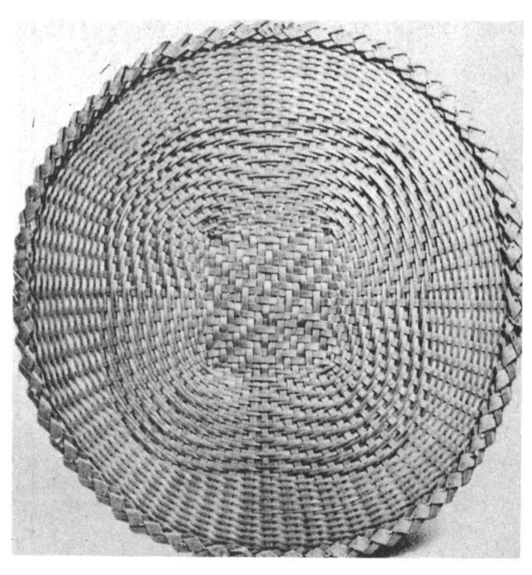

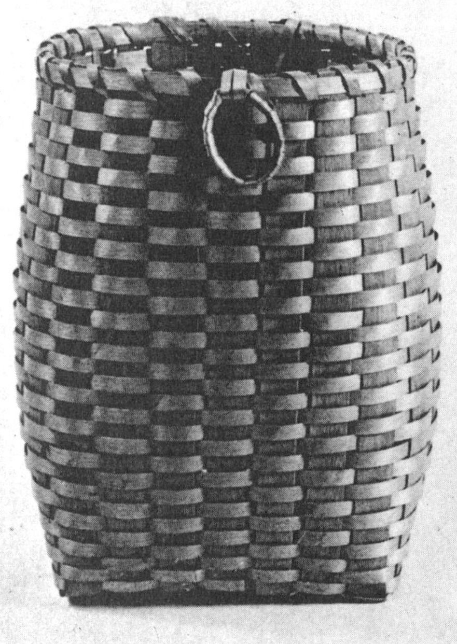

TOP LEFT: *Shaker basket with double-hinged lid.* OLD CHATHAM.

ABOVE: *Woven straw table mat. Although many of these were made, few have survived.* OLD CHATHAM.

LEFT: *Deep Shaker basket made to hang on wooden peg.* OLD CHATHAM.

BELOW: *Two small Shaker woven straw baskets, one with double-hinged lid.* OLD CHATHAM.

OPPOSITE TOP LEFT: *Large round basket used in making cheese.* HANCOCK.

OPPOSITE TOP RIGHT: *Woven straw cover for whisk broom.* OLD CHATHAM.

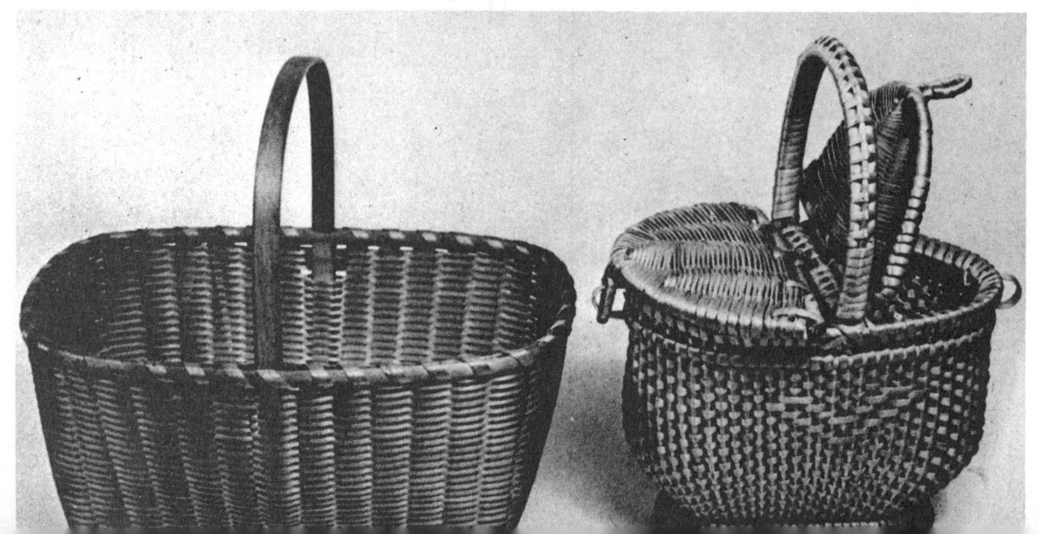

MIDDLE LEFT: *Tool for splitting poplar woo hand for making straw cloth for boxes and items. A machine was later developed for this u* BELFIT.

BOTTOM LEFT AND RIGHT: *Sewing basket of poplar straw.* BELFIT.

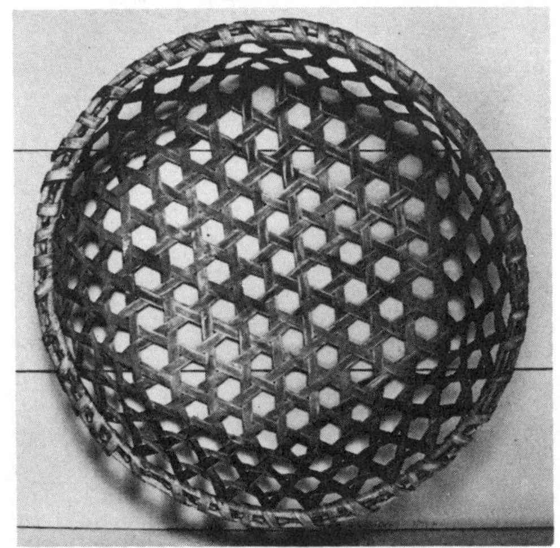

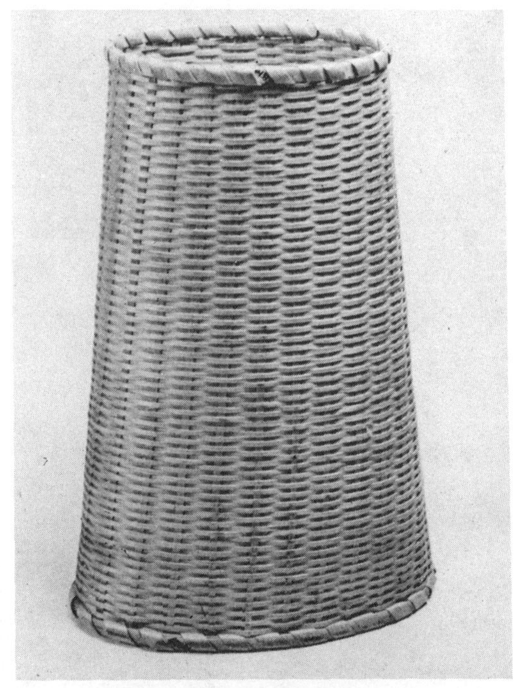

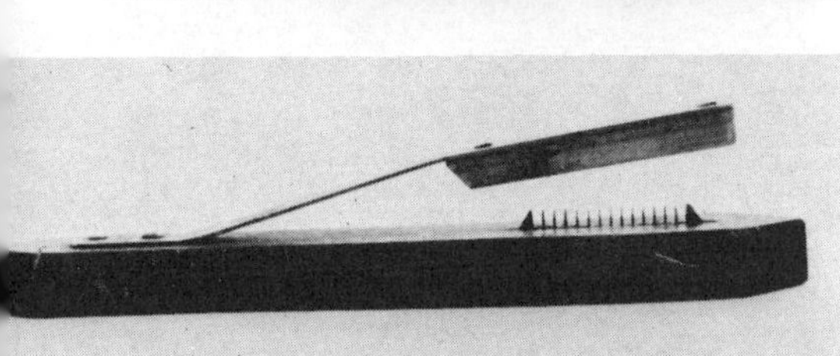

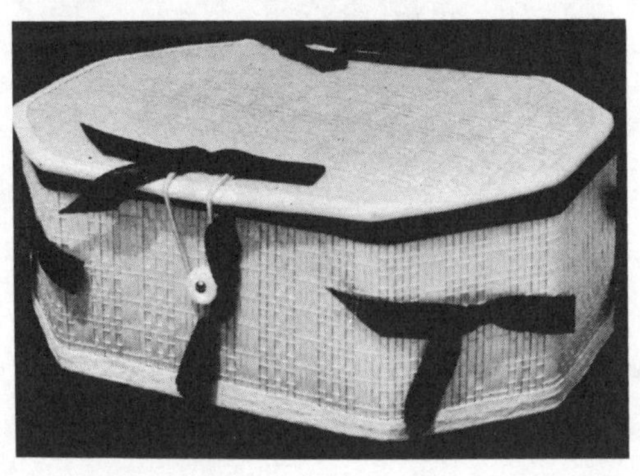

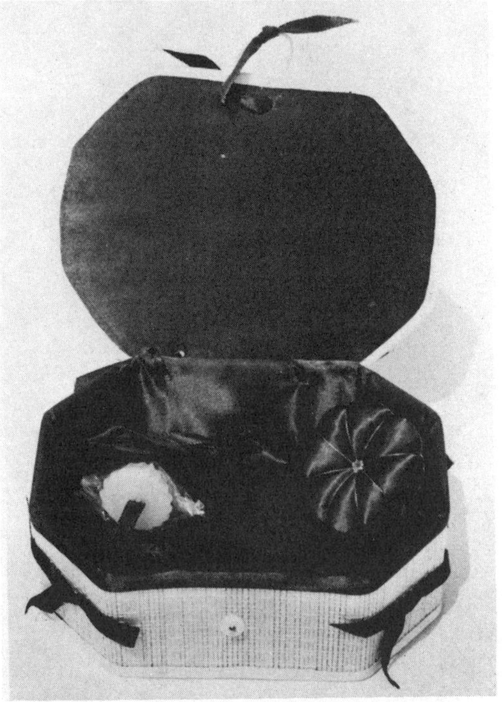

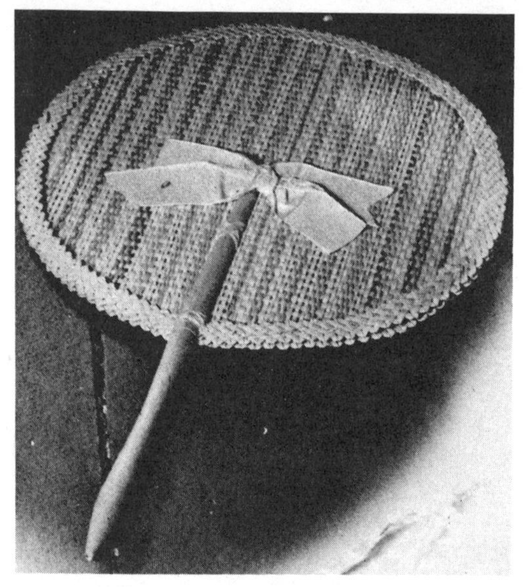

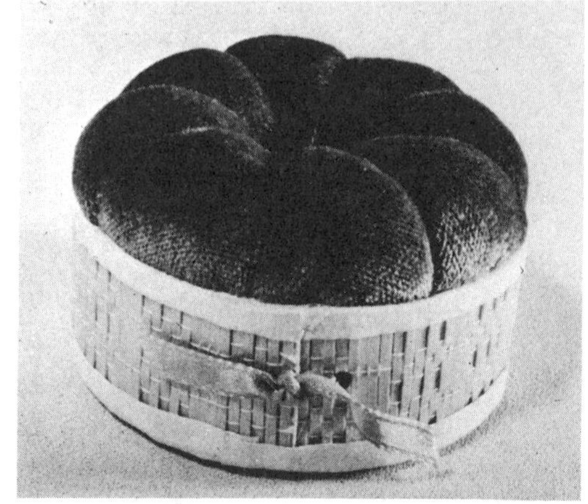

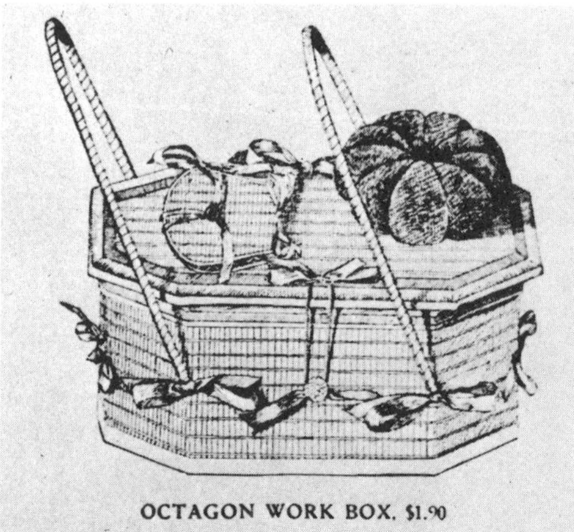

OCTAGON WORK BOX, $1.90

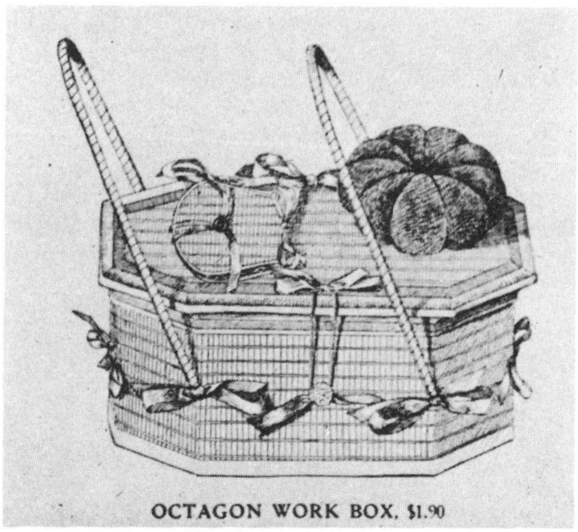

OCTAGON WORK BOX, $1.90

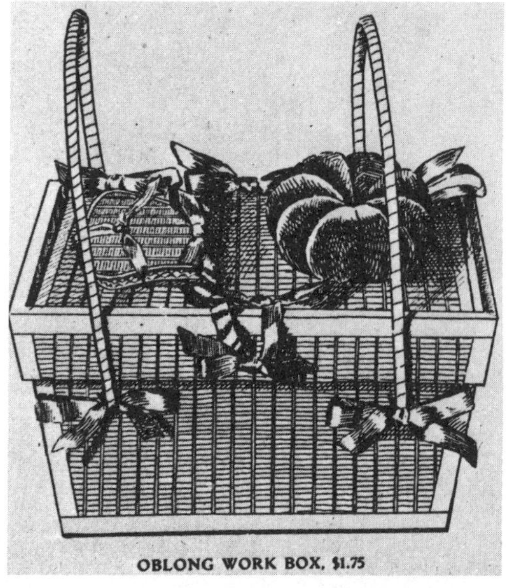

OBLONG WORK BOX, $1.75

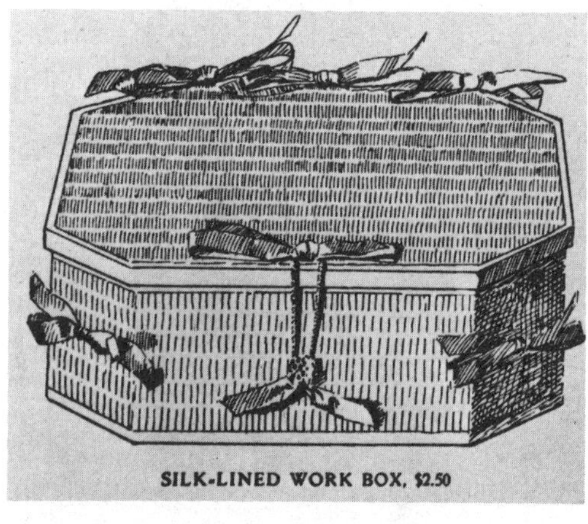

SILK-LINED WORK BOX, $2.50

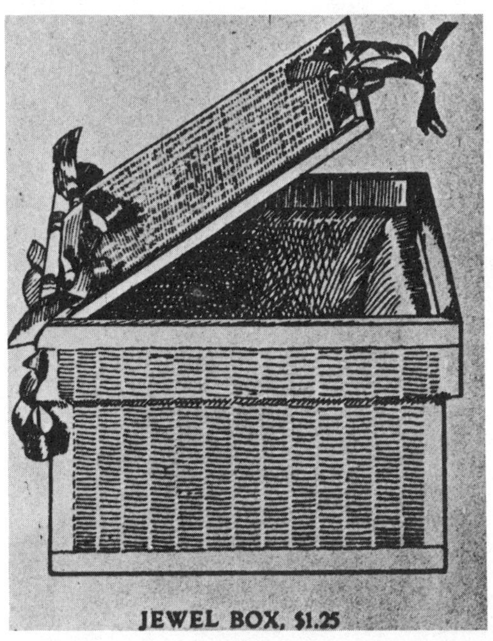

OPPOSITE TOP LEFT: *Woven straw fans and paper fans were an early shop item for the Shaker sisters. They remained popular throughout the nineteenth century.* OLD CHATHAM.

OPPOSITE TOP RIGHT: *Pincushion made of velvet and poplar wood fabric. Although this material gave the same effect as woven straw, it was actually shredded wood that was woven on a loom.* BELFIT.

OPPOSITE BOTTOM FOUR AND LEFT: *Shaker boxes made to sell in sisters' shops. Toward end of nineteenth century Shakers were apt to use "superfluous decoration" to make salable objects. These boxes were all made of woven poplar straw.* OLD CHATHAM.

at first by hand and later by an electric-powered machine invented by Brother Irving Greenwood. The strips were then woven on hand looms by the sisters. A paper pasted to the reverse side of the straw cloth made it firmer and less susceptible to breakage. The straw cloth was then made into many types of baskets edged with tape and lined with satin. Small accessories such as needlecases and pincushions were also made of poplar straw.

A wide variety of items were made from the strawlike poplar fabric woven by hand on Shaker looms. Handkerchief boxes, doll bonnets, sewing baskets in a variety of sizes and styles, bottoms for workbags, and even jewel boxes were made to sell in the sisters' shops. These were adorned with small hand-tied ribbon bows. Accessories were also made for the sewing boxes out of poplar straw fabric. The Shakers used their inventiveness and creativity in devising a great variety of products out of this versatile material, that seems to have been exclusively theirs.

CHAPTER
18
SHAKER ART

No maps, Charts, and no pictures or paintings, shall ever be hung up in your dwelling-rooms, shops, or Office. And no pictures or paintings set in frames, with glass before them shall ever be among you. But modest advertisements may be put up in the Trustees Office when necessary. Millenial Laws, 1821. Revised, 1845.

Although it is not our purpose here to discuss the Shaker religion except as it manifested itself in Shaker goods and products, a religious phenomenon took place among the Shakers in 1837 that prompted a decade of change in Shakerdom. It also led to a legacy of Shaker religious folk art that would not have existed without it.

"The new era" in Shaker history began in August 1837, when a group of adolescent girls, gathered together at Niskayuna for instruction, were overcome with a sudden fit of dancing, whirling, and shaking. They sang of a journey they were making to "heavenly places." Following this strange experience, other groups of girls and finally adult members of the family were overcome with the same kind of actions and claimed that they had "visions." Within a year these "gifts" passed through the entire world of Shakerdom.

The next ten years of Shaker religion were called

TOP: *Spirit drawing,* An Emblem of Heavenly Sphere, *1854. Hancock. Ink and watercolor. Height, 23¾ inches; width, 18⅝ inches.* HANCOCK.

BOTTOM: *Spirit drawing,* A Type of Mother Hannah's Pocket Handkerchief. *New Lebanon, 1851. Ink and watercolor. Height, 14 3/32 inches; Width, 17 1/16 inches.* HANCOCK.

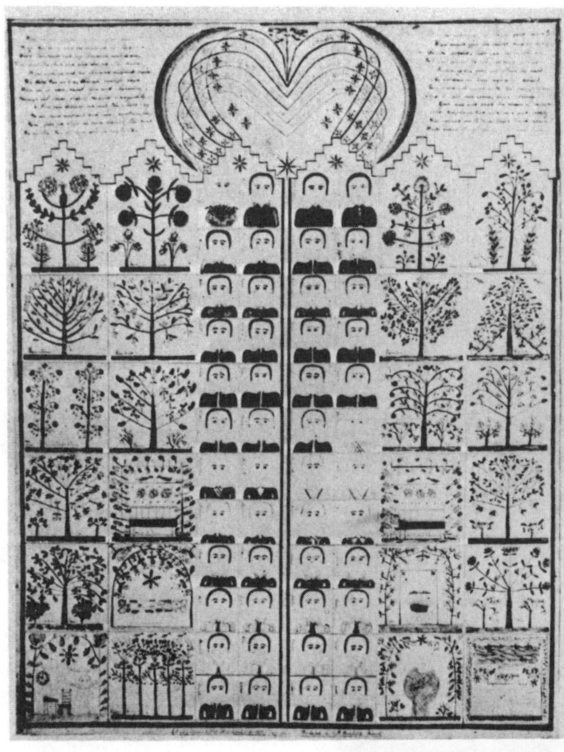

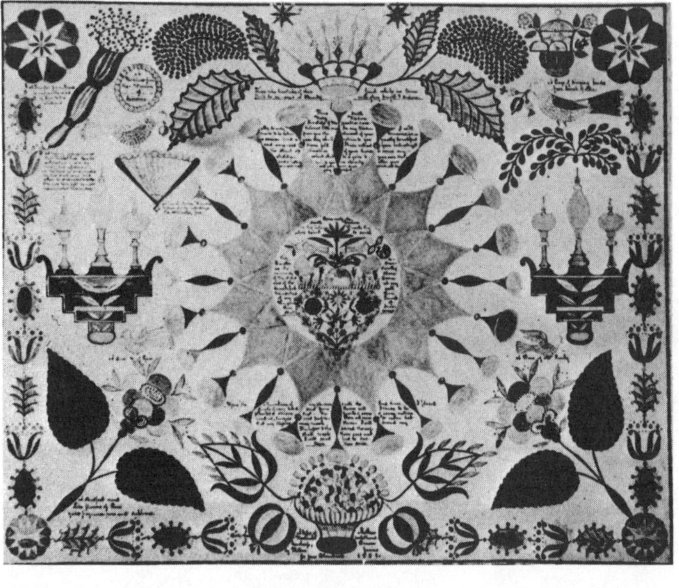

"Mother Ann's Second Appearing" and the "new era." Certain "chosen" members of the various communities became "instruments" through whom messages were sent by Christ, as well as by Mother Ann, Father Joseph Meacham, and other leaders of the Shakers who had long departed this world. Often there would be an intermediary appearing under such names as "Angel of Love" or "Angel Gabriel." These messengers brought scrolls on which the heavenly thoughts were written. Not only departed Shaker leaders, but other secular leaders of note such as Washington, Lafayette, and even Alexander the Great sent word from heaven to the Shakers on earth.

The messages were designed to bring the Shakers back to the fold. By this period in Shaker history the first

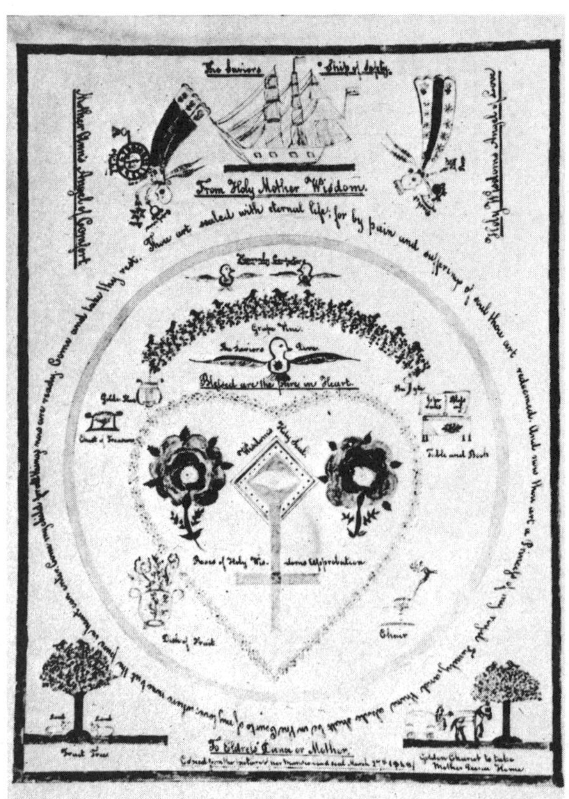

Spirit drawing, From Holy Mother Wisdom to Eldress Dana or Mother. *Hancock, 1848. Ink and watercolor. Height, 9 25/32 inches; width, 7 23/32 inches.* HANCOCK.

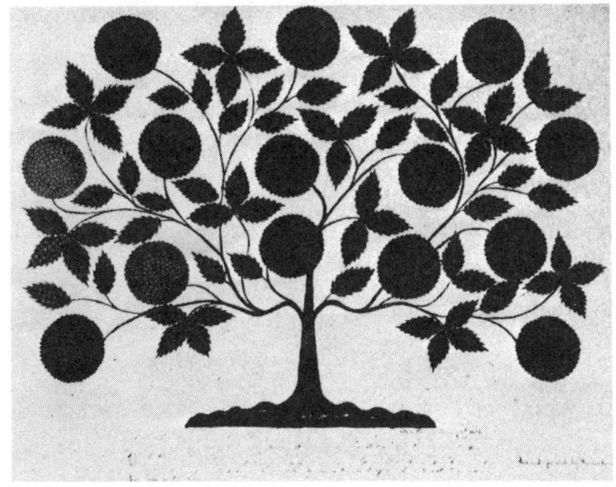

Spirit drawing, The Tree of Life. *Hancock, 1854. Ink and watercolor. Height, 18 ⅛ inches; width, 23 5/16 inches.* HANCOCK.

generation of organized Shakers had begun to die off. The Shaker population was reaching its zenith, and there were a great many young people who had been brought into the sect by their parents or who had been taken in as orphans. The Shaker communities, after the early years of deprivation, had become economically sound, and the younger generation became impatient with old laws that did not seem to pertain to them. The comforts of the outside world beckoned, and many of the elders feared that the young would be too much influenced by "worldly" ways.

Far from disillusioning or discouraging the visitations, the ministry saw them as an opportunity to renew the spiritual values that might otherwise be changed or lost. They encouraged the "instruments" through whom Mother Ann warned of her displeasure with backsliders and dissenters. Mother Ann, speaking through her intermediaries, admonished that, rather than deviate from the orders, the sect should return to the old and true ways of its religion. They should labor harder, dress more plainly, remove superfluities of furnishings, and confess and repent.

Smoking and drinking, both of which had been allowed by the sect to a limited extent previously, were forbidden. The revival led to the writing down of the Holy Laws of Zion of 1840 which called for the return to the old Shaker beliefs and set down a stricter and more detailed way of life. The Millenial Laws that were revised in 1845 further detailed the many "do's and don't's" of Shakerdom.

The Shaker revivals eventually took many strange and unusual forms. Those "possessed" of the gifts of Heaven sang in unknown languages, went into deep trances, whirled like tops for long periods, and received "notices of love" in the form of paintings and spiritual messages. While the gifts were imaginary and ranged anywhere from "precious jewels" to "cakes of love", the messages were written down by the intermediaries in the form of inscribed papers and small books.

Eventually, the "notices" from Heaven took the real form of cards, cutouts, drawings, and paintings. Most of these were made toward the end of the decade of the renewal of the Shaker faith, and took the form of complicated folk pictures in bright colors. The drawings are symmetrical and many contain as a central motif the "tree of life and light."

The divinely inspired and meticulously drawn "spirit paintings" were symmetrical and painstakingly detailed as to the gifts that were being bestowed and were obviously made with less of the high excitement and emotions than showed up in the early days of the renewal of the faith. It is probably significant that the majority of spirit drawings that survive today were executed by young girls and women of the sect, who seemed to have been "overcome" more often than the men.

The drawings are precise and symmetrical, and the many written messages are carefully placed in beautiful calligraphy. While "art for art's sake" was completely outside the Shaker beliefs at the time, these spirit draw-

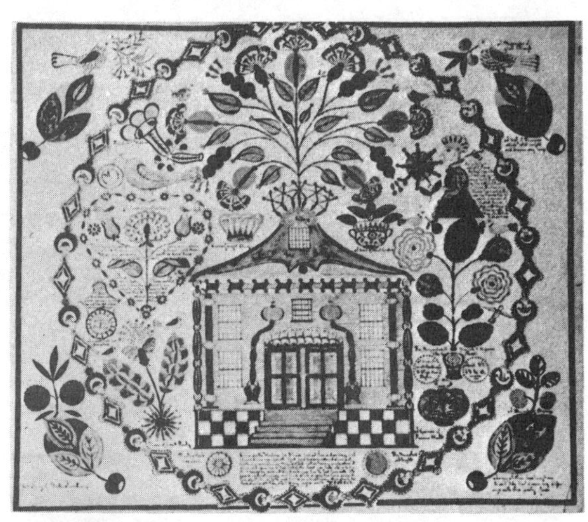

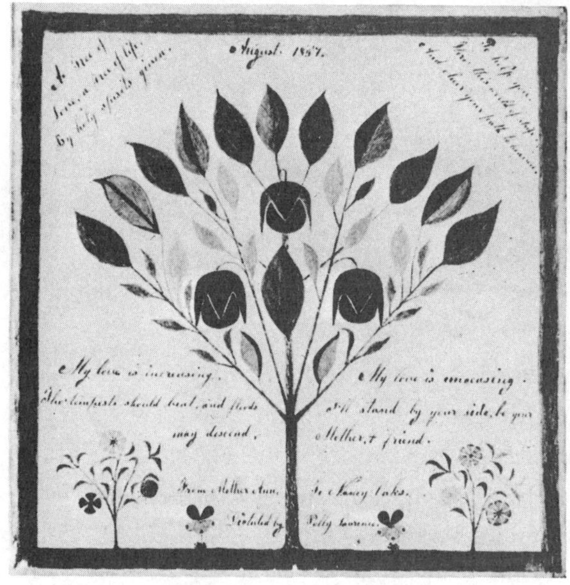

TOP: A Present From Mother Lucy to Eliza Ann Taylor. *Blue ink and watercolor on blue paper. Height, 14 inches; width, 16⅜ inches.* HANCOCK.

BOTTOM: From Mother Ann to Nancy Oaks. *Ink and watercolor. August, 1857.* HANCOCK.

ings were totally acceptable, since they were believed to be real messages from the beyond. Highly personal in nature, they were never meant to be displayed to the "world" or thought of as examples of Shaker art. Those who executed the paintings and drawings were not responsible for the forms that they took. Rather, the hand

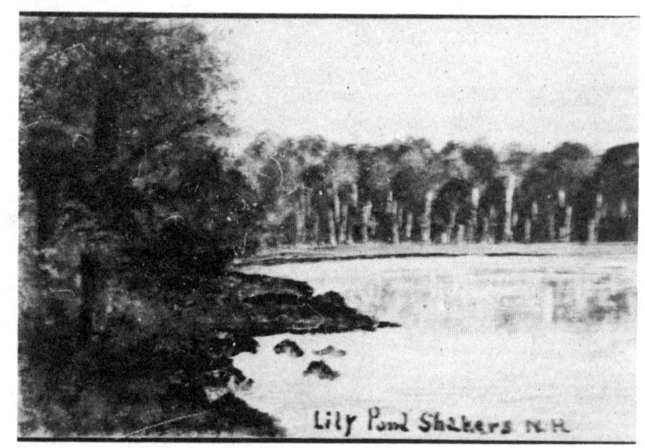

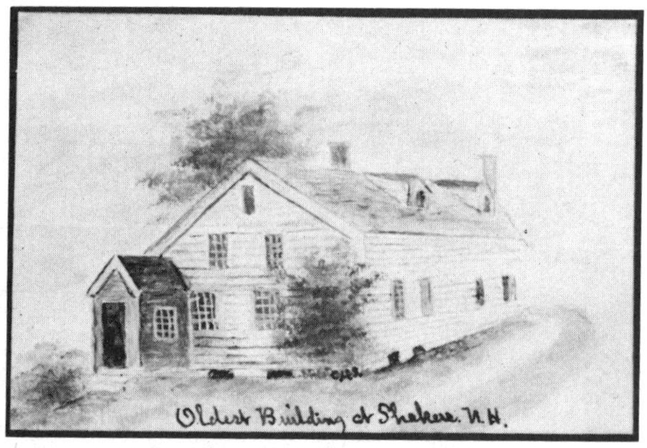

TOP: *Postcard hand painted in oils by Sister C. H. Sarle.* View of Lily Pond at Canterbury. OLD CHATHAM.

BOTTOM: *Sister Sarle painting on postcard,* Oldest Building at Shakers, N.H. OLD CHATHAM.

was directed by the divine spirits who spoke to them.

One charming spirit drawing "from Holy Mother Wisdom to Eldress Dana or Mother" shows "The Saviour's Ship of Safety," "Mother Ann's Angel of Comfort," "a golden watch" [with the time set at 11:30], "Holy Wisdom's Angel of Love," a "grape vine," "Wisdom's Holy Seal," a "golden harp," a "chest of treasures," a "dish of fruit," a "chair," "Roses of Holy Wisdom's Approbation," a "golden chariot to take Mother Dana home," "fruit trees," "lambs", and other "gifts."

"Flowers of Love and Purity" and "a sprig of understanding" were gifts given through another intermediary, Eliza Ann Taylor, from Mother Lucy (Wright). Still another drawing, "A Type of Mother Hannah's Pocket

Handkerchief," includes in its symbolism many gifts and "a cage of singing birds from Sarah of old."

That these spirit drawings were not meant to be displayed, but had deep religious and mystical significance to the revivalist Shakers, is apparent. There is no way of knowing how many of these highly personal declarations of faith were drawn, but it is probable that a great many of the "messages" were sent along with departed members of the faith, since they were "heavenly gifts" and would be needed only in the next world. Less than sixty spirit drawings have survived, but it is a certainty that a great many more were drawn during the frenzy of revivalism.

The few spirit drawings that are left, however, are, with one exception, the only paintings and drawings the Shakers have bequeathed to us. Unable to express themselves artistically in any manner except by practical handicrafts, because of Shaker laws that ruled out the use of any pictures on the walls or superfluous decorations of any kind, the Shakers were able, in the decade of spiritual revival, to express their deep religious convictions in these colorful and meticulously drawn "messages."

The Millenial Laws of 1845, while not exactly broken by twentieth-century Shakers, have been bent a little from time to time. By this time there were indications that the sect would continue to decrease in this world. The Millenial Law that stated that "Believers may not in any case or circumstances, manufacture for sale, any article or articles, which are superfluously wrought, and which would have a tendency to feed the pride and vanity of man, or such as would not be admissable to use among themselves, on account of their superfluity," probably seemed somewhat outdated.

The sisters, always aware that their shops must carry goods that would find a market, added ribbons to their sewing boxes and did embroidery and other needlework to order for their customers. Eventually, the solid color dresses that the sisters wore were replaced with bright prints. Fortunately, one elderly Shakeress, with a distinct talent for painting, was allowed to indulge in her art.

Sister C. H. Sarle painted on postcards many miniature scenes of her home in the Shaker village at Canterbury, New Hampshire, and these postcards evidently found a ready market with the souvenir seekers who visited the sisters' shops. Woodland scenes of the surrounding New Hampshire hills with which Sister Sarle was familiar

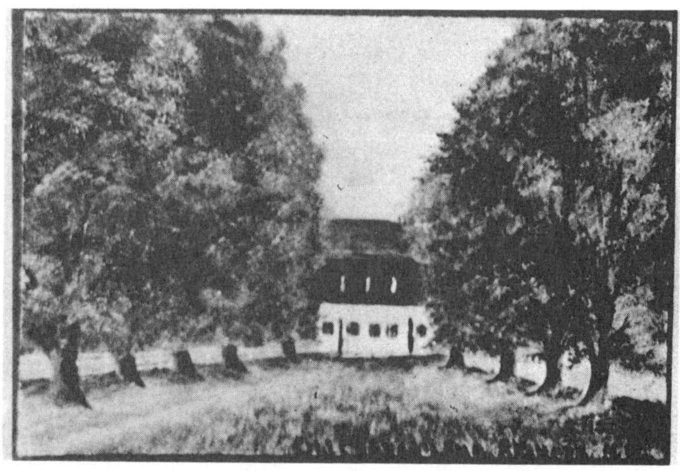

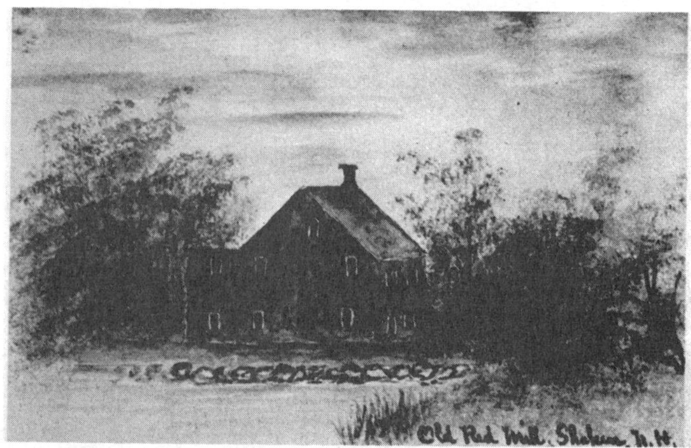

TOP: Old Church Lane, Shakers, N.H. *Oil painting on postcard by Sister C. H. Sarle.* OLD CHATHAM.

BOTTOM: *This miniature painting, although unsigned, is obviously the work of Sister Sarle of Canterbury.* BELFIT.

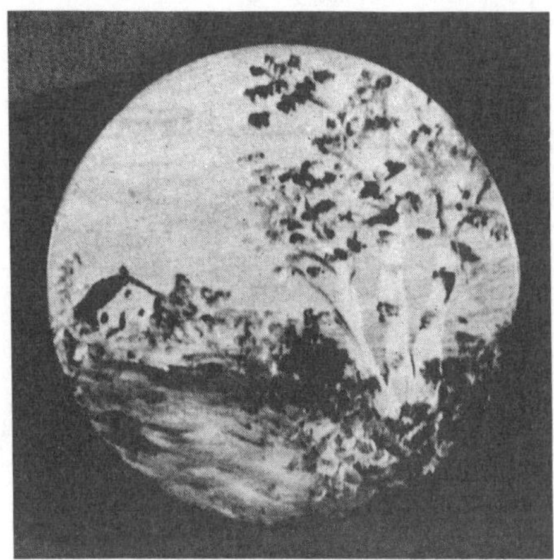

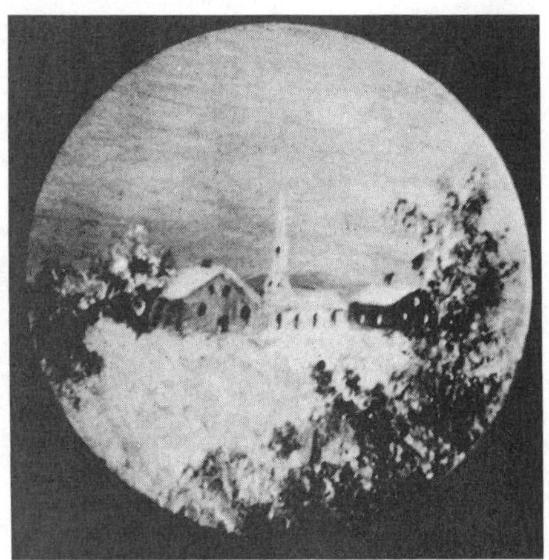

were recorded in charming miniature-size oil paintings. Small, round Shaker boxes were also decorated with Shaker buildings and country scenes.

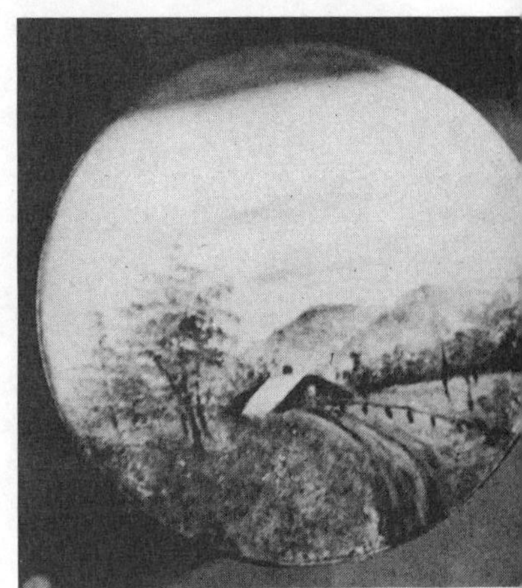

Sister Sarle was old when she began to paint the various miniature Shaker scenes. Too feeble to do her regular labor, she stayed in her room and supplied the shops with a great many of her cards, paintings, and boxes. The majority of these paintings were signed, which was another indication that the letter of the Millenial Laws was no longer followed. It was obvious that the surviving Shakers felt that it was more important for the elderly Shakeress to feel useful and keep busy than to adhere strictly to law. Sister Sarle, the only Shaker artist to have left any kind of pictorial record as to what her Shaker surroundings meant to her, displayed a distinct talent for painting in her many miniature New Hampshire scenes. Although she died as recently as 1955, when in her eighties, few examples of her work have been saved. It is to be hoped that more will come to light with this recognition of her work. She is unique in that within the limitation of surfaces only a few inches in size, she is the only Shaker artist to have left a pictorial record of the Shakers' love for their buildings and surrounding countryside.

Three Canterbury scenes painted by Sister Sarle on box lids. All approximately 3 inches in diameter. OLD CHATHAM.

CHAPTER

19

SHAKER CLOCKS

Fancy articles of any kind, or articles which are superfluously finished, trimmed or ornamented, are not suitable for Believers, and may not be used or purchased; among which are the following; also some other articles which are deemed improper, to be in the Church, and may not be brought in, except by special liberty of the Ministry.

Silver pencils, silver tooth picks, gold pencils, or pens, silver spoons, silver thimbles, (but thimbles may be lined with silver,) gold or silver watches, brass knobs or handles of any size or kind. Millenial Laws, 1821. Revised, 1845.

Watches were considered an unnecessary luxury by the early Shakers, and probably since they were also thought of as a personal adornment, only the elders were allowed to own them. However, time was of great importance in keeping the communes running smoothly and therefore clocks were a necessity in the Shaker sect. Very early the Shakers relied on bells to tell them when it was time for various community activities. As the sect gathered more members, many clocks were installed in the shops and dwellings. The earliest, used in quantity and installed around 1830, were probably purchased and were portable.

Both tall case clocks and wall clocks were made in the first part of the nineteenth century by Shaker craftsmen, and these were built in the manner of Connecticut clockmakers. It is probable that the earliest Shaker-made clocks had wooden works. According to Robert F. W. Meader, director of the Shaker Museum at Old Chath-

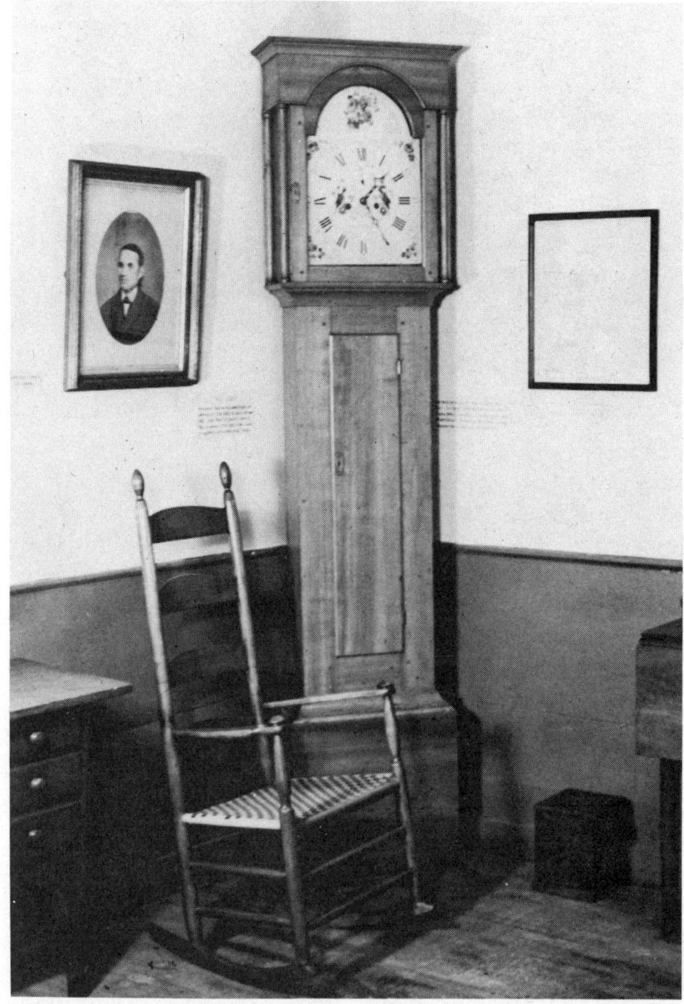

Tall case clock. Works made by Benjamin Youngs, of South Family, Watervliet, New York. Decorated clock face was made and painted in England. Case was made by Erastus Rude in 1811. Works were made between 1790 and 1805. Clock was repaired by Youngs' nephew in 1848. OLD CHATHAM.

LEFT: *Wall clock made to hang on peg. Dated 1840. Made by Isaac Youngs, it has weight-driven movement and wooden gears.* HANCOCK.

RIGHT: *Shaker-made hanging clock dated 1840. Front of case has glass panels. Made by Isaac Youngs, chief clockmaker at New Lebanon.* HANCOCK.

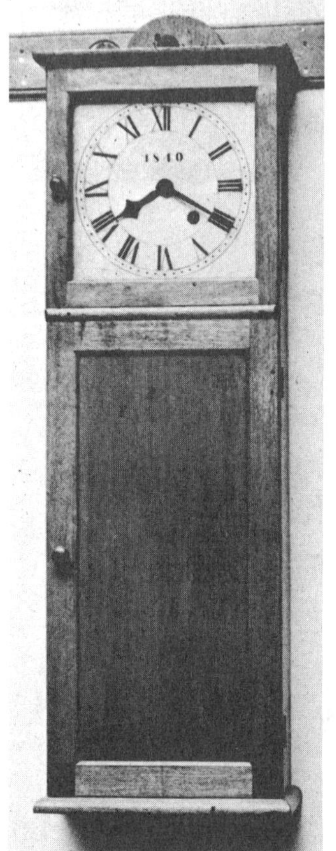

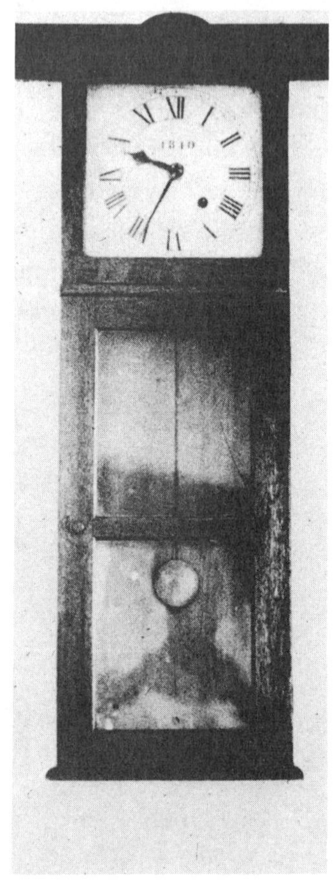

am, the first documented Shaker clockmaker was Amos Jewett (1753–1834), who was one of the earliest Believers at New Lebanon. Other Shaker clockmakers were Benjamin Youngs (1753–1818) of Watervliet, New York, and his two nephews, Benjamin S. Youngs (1774–1855), also of Watervliet, and Isaac N. Youngs (1793–1865), of New Lebanon. This family included a long line of Connecticut clockmakers, and Benjamin was the first of the three to become a member of the Shaker sect. He turned over to the Shakers his farm property at Watervliet when he entered the Society of Believers. The older Youngs specialized in the making of grandfather clocks with brass movements and strikes. However, he did not make the cases for his clocks. One of Youngs' clock movements, now at Old Chatham, is dated 1811. A tall case clock made by Benjamin Youngs, in the same museum, is undated, but the case was made by Erastus Rude in 1811. A note pasted inside the clock tells us that Youngs' nephew Benjamin repaired the clock in 1846. This clock has an English painted face.

Isaac Newton Youngs, the elder Benjamin's other nephew, made coffin-case clocks, in which the back board of the case was also the back plate of the movement. Handwritten instructions were often pasted inside the cases of Isaac's clocks. (Isaac also invented two instruments to aid in the learning and singing of Shaker music, in which he was vitally interested. The first invention is the "mode-ometer," a pendulumlike metronone, and a "tone-ometer" that set pitches.)

Two interesting clocks made by Benjamin S. Youngs, in the Henry Ford Museum, are called "dwarf tall case alarm clocks," and each is only slightly over a yard high. Two clocks of about the same height, dated 1840, can be seen at Hancock Shaker Village. One has a solid wood door covering the pendulum and the other has glass panels inserted. Both are made to hang from the ubiquitous Shaker pegs.

A clockface that was made by Amos Jewett is in the collection at Old Chatham. It is signed above the dial by the maker and dated 1789. This is Jewett's earliest known clockface and also the earliest Shaker clock on record. The face is drawn by hand on paper and pasted on a wood base. Numbered "12", it is obvious that Jewett made many other clocks, some of which are certain to be found someday.

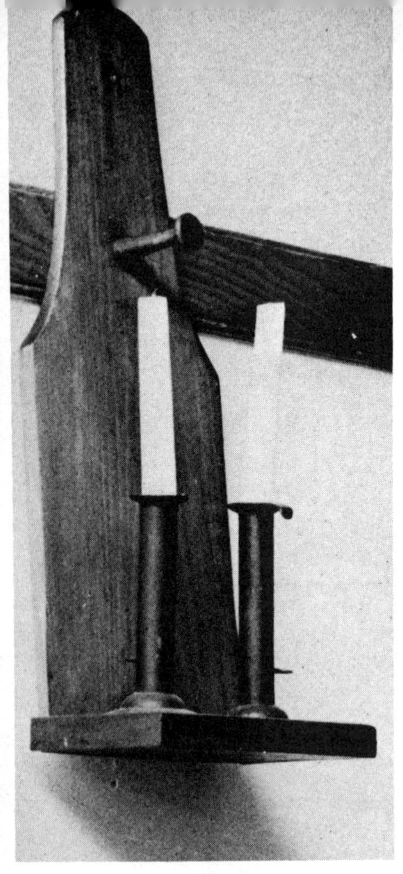

ABOVE: *Wooden hanging candle sconce holds two push-up iron candlesticks. Shakers made their own candles.* HANCOCK.

OPPOSITE TOP: *Adjustable double candle stand used in shoemaker's shop (1800).* HANCOCK.

BOTTOM LEFT: *Perforated tin candle lantern for outdoor and barn use.* OLD CHATHAM.

BOTTOM MIDDLE: *Tin lantern with glass panels and ring for hanging on peg.* OLD CHATHAM.

BOTTOM RIGHT: *Kerosene lamp is not Shaker made, but Shakers did make reflector and sconce.* OLD CHATHAM.

CHAPTER 20

SHAKER LIGHTING DEVICES

No one is allowed to carry fire about the dooryards, or among the buildings, unless safely secured in a lantern, fire-box, or other safe vessel.

No one may enter a closet, garret, or clothes room, or other places not frequented, with a lighted lamp or candle, unless it be enclosed in a lantern.

Lighted lamps or candles must not be carried to the barns, or out buildings unless inclosed in a lantern, and no lanterns are allowed to be carried into hay mows, nor to be opened in the barns, in any place, where sparks would be liable to set anything on fire. Millenial Laws, 1821. Revised, 1845.

The above and many other Millenial Laws, strictly adhered to, were part of "Shaker Orders to Prevent Loss by Fire." Shaker candlesticks, lanterns, and central lighting fixtures were devised by tinsmiths and ironworkers for safety and convenience. Sconces and candle stands were made in the woodworking shops and many candlesticks were devised that could be hung from pegs on the wall. These sconces could then be moved as needed.

The earliest form of lighting device used by the Shakers was a simple wrought-iron, push-up candlestick in which white Shaker-made candles were burned.

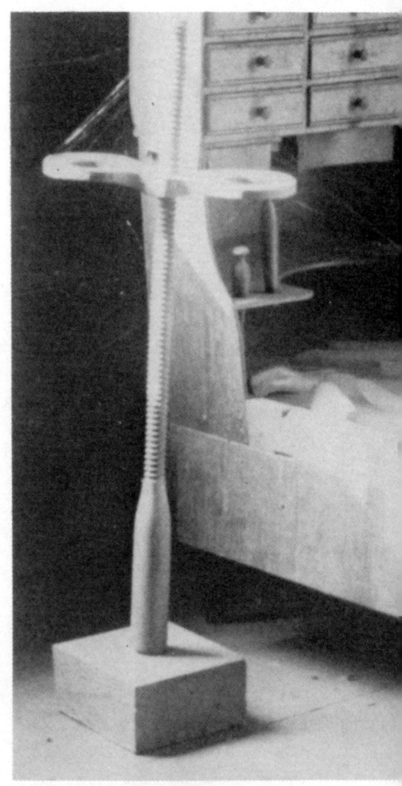

Punched tin lanterns in a variety of shapes and sizes can be found. It is obvious that the Shakers were, from the early times, particularly aware of the danger of fire, and many lanterns were made with glass panels. Few lanterns can be found with open sides. As with all Shaker furnishings, lamps, lanterns, and candlesticks were of the most simple utilitarian designs. In the period when painted and colored glass "gone-with-the-wind" lamps decorated overfurnished American parlors, the Shakers used simple clear glass kerosene lamps purchased from American glasshouses. However, the Shakers improved the efficiency of these purchased lamps by devising holders that attached the lamps to the wall and had tin funnellike shades with chimneys that vented the smoke and fumes out-of-doors or into a stove chimney. The

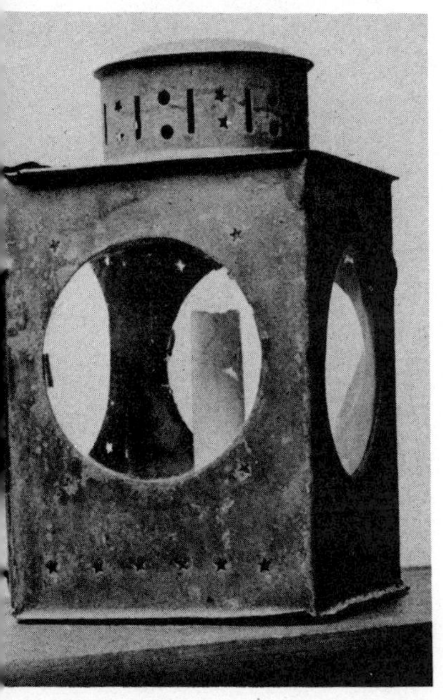

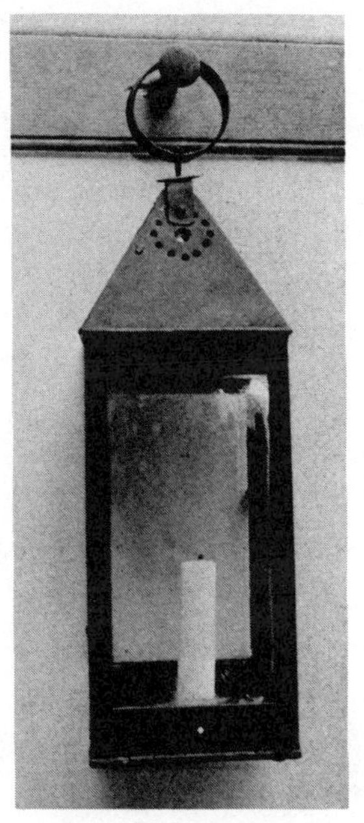

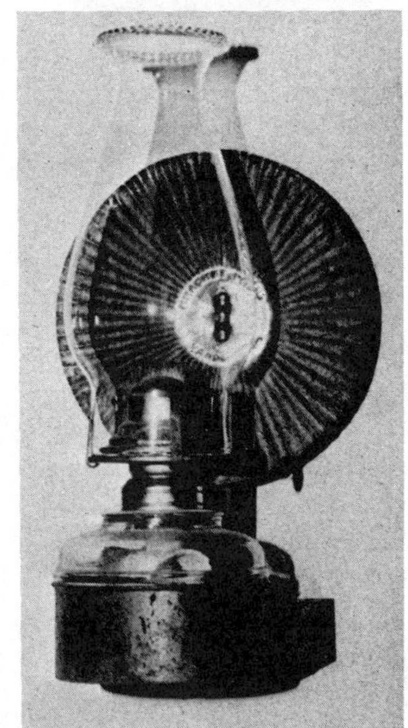

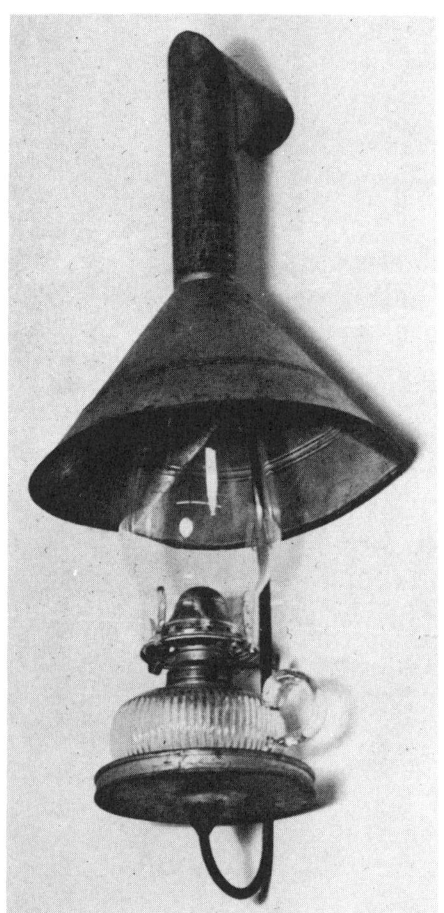

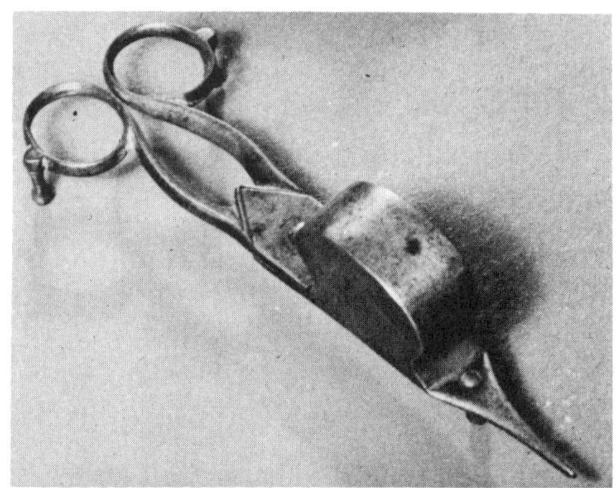

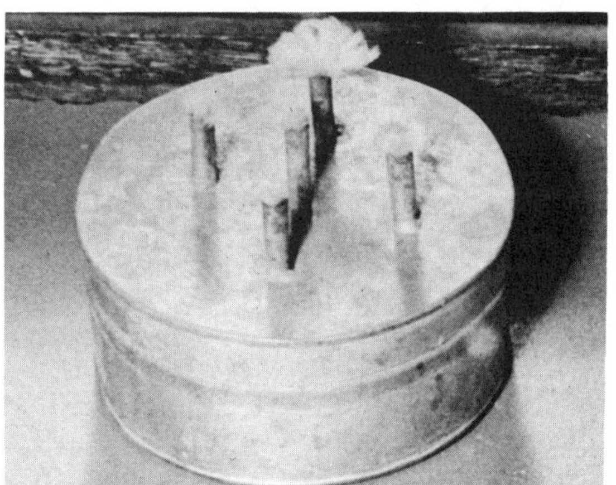

LEFT: *Wall sconce with chimney and flue to outside. Lamp is easily removed for cleaning.* OLD CHATHAM.

TOP RIGHT: *Wick trimmer, a necessity in caring for kerosene lamps.* OLD CHATHAM.

BOTTOM: *Five-wick tin shop light. Shakers were very careful about using fire around shops.* OLD CHATHAM.

holder and vent were fixed to the wall, but the lamps could be easily removed for refilling and cleaning.

A safe five-wick shop light was designed by Shaker tinsmiths. In this device the fuel was completely enclosed in the covered round can and small chimneys held the adjustable woven wicks. This light was probably as safe as any light with an open flame can be. The size of the flame could be controlled, and the lamp could not tip or spill.

Candlemaking was an early occupation of Shaker sisters. They produced many candles each year for their own use and in later times made them to sell in their shops.

There were some ceiling-hung candleholders made and these, too, were of simple utilitarian design. The one ceiling fixture illustrated in this chapter is made of a tin cylinder to which is attached six flat arms with scalloped trays under the candles to catch the dripping hot wax.

TOP: *Shaker push-up (or "hog-scraper") candlestick. Table, crotcheted antimacassar, and wood darning egg are also Shaker made.* OLD CHATHAM.

MIDDLE: *Tin and wrought-iron ceiling fixture.* HANCOCK.

BOTTOM: *Bundle of Shaker wick sticks for use in lighting stoves and lamps. These were probably made for sale, also.* OLD CHATHAM.

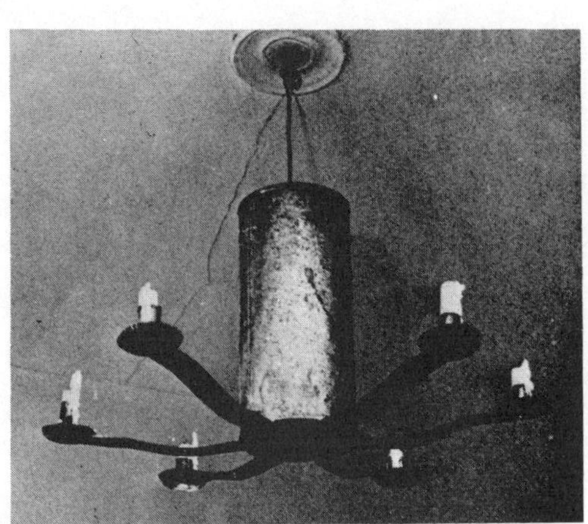

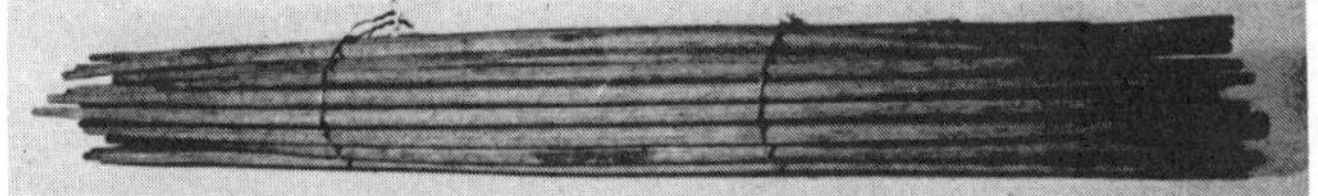

CHAPTER 21

TINWARE AND OTHER METALWORK

No one should take tools, belonging in charge of others, without obtaining liberty for the same, if the person can consistently be found who takes charge of them.

When anyone borrows a tool, it should be immediately returned, without injury, if possible, and if injured, should be made known by the borrower to the lender;—'The wicked borrow and never return.' Millenial Laws, 1821. Revised, 1845.

A great many metal products were made by the Shakers from a very early date. Tinsmithing was most certainly an early occupation. Patterns and matching finished products at the Old Chatham Shaker Museum that came from Canterbury attest to the fact that a great variety of tin products were made there. It is probable that many of the Shaker communities produced some tinware early in the nineteenth century.

Identifying early tinware as having been made by the Shakers is complicated by the fact that there is little difference between other tinware products of the period and their own.

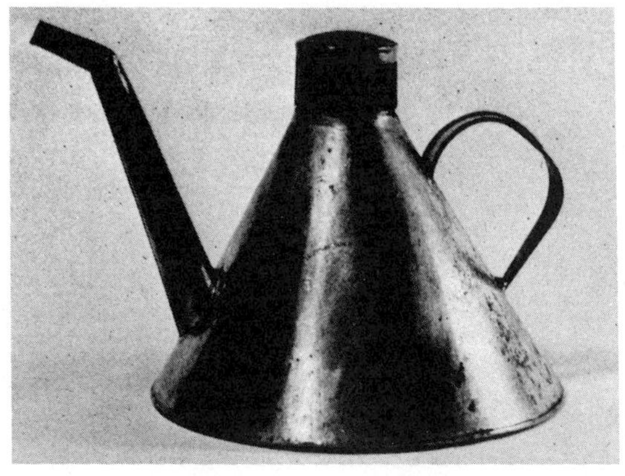

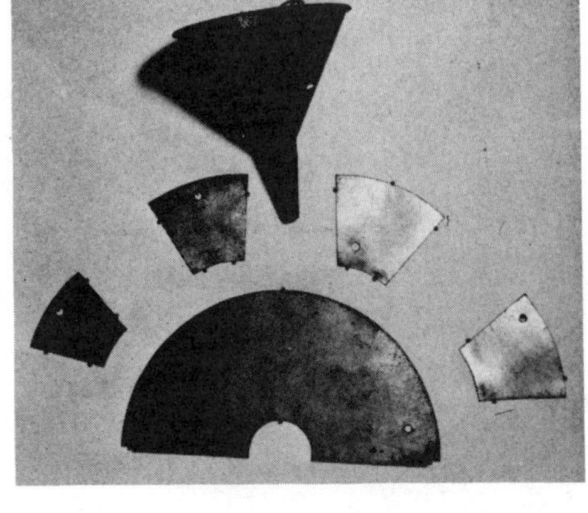

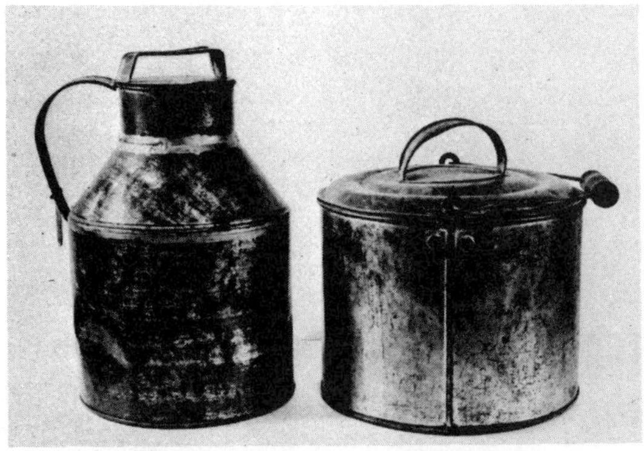

TOP LEFT: *Oilcan of simple straightforward design typical of Shaker tinware.* BELFIT.

TOP RIGHT: *Shaker funnel and pattern from Canterbury, N.H.* OLD CHATHAM.

LEFT: *Shaker milk pail and cooking pot with wire handle and turned wood grip.* OLD CHATHAM.

BELOW LEFT: *Tin pattern for matchsafe from Canterbury.* OLD CHATHAM.

RIGHT: *Assembled matchsafe made by Shakers.* OLD CHATHAM.

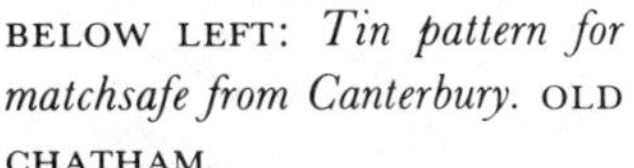

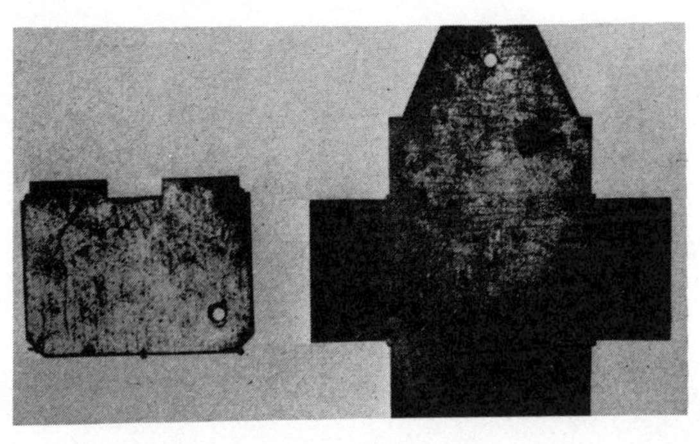

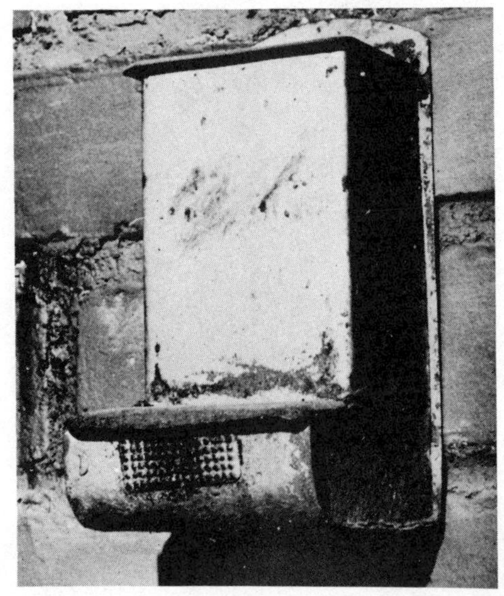

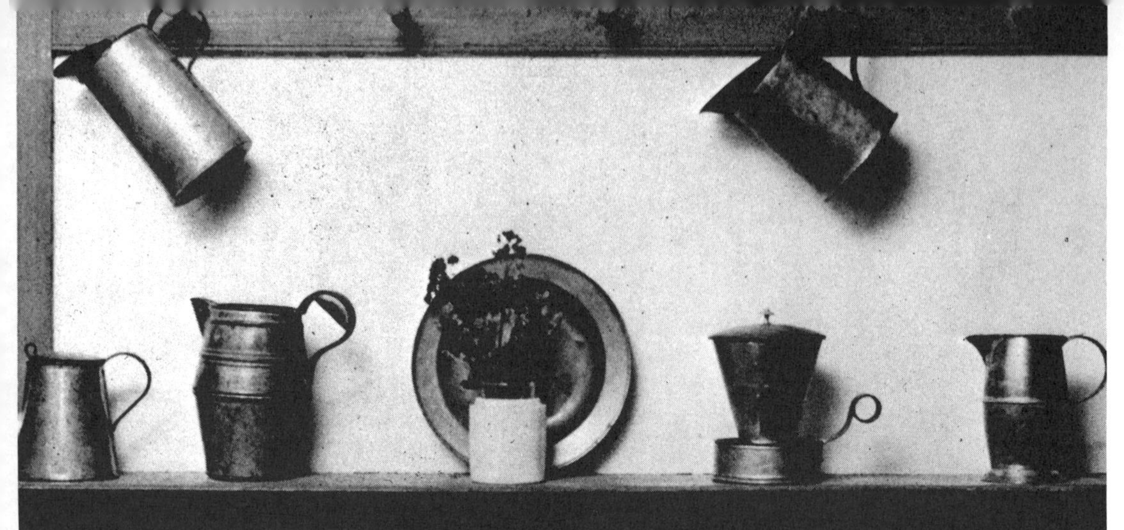

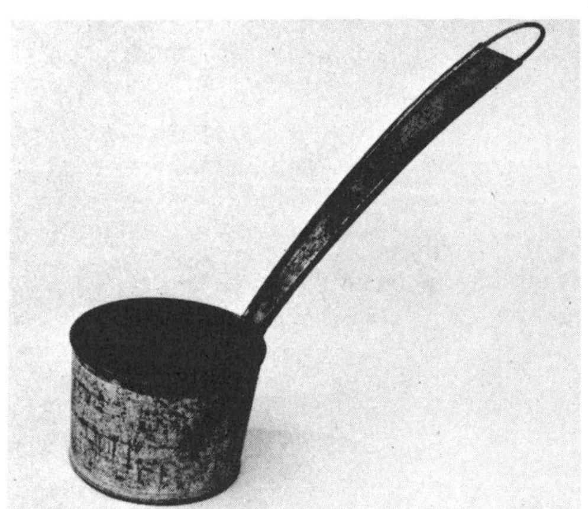

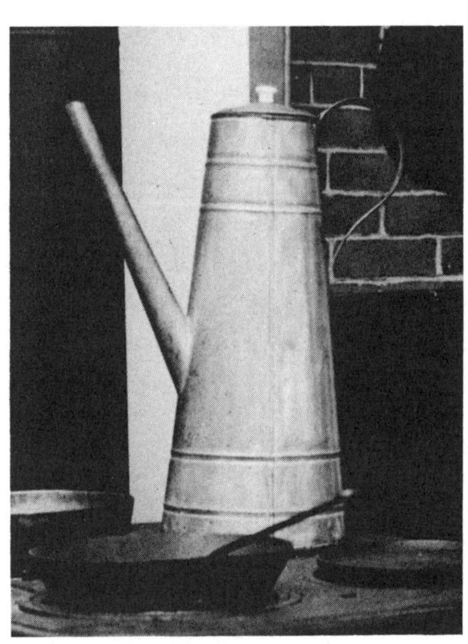

TOP: *Variety of tinware pitchers on display at Shaker Village.* HANCOCK.

BOTTOM LEFT: *Tin dipper with rolled edges on handle. Wire is run through rolled edge to form loop for hanging.* BELFIT.

RIGHT: *Tall coffeepot of superb design is undoubtedly Shaker.* HANCOCK.

Therefore, the documented tin objects at Old Chatham Shaker Museum have a great deal of significance. The existence of patterns and a roller press in the same display are both important documentation for identifying and dating Shaker-made tinware.

As with all early Shaker products, the designs of their tinware are simple and functional. Vessels for household and farm use were the major products made of tin. Designed in the traditional styles of the first half of the nineteenth century, Shaker pitchers, pans, pails, funnels, and various kinds of pots were in demand by outsiders, and the tinsmithing industry was an important segment of Shaker production, particularly at Hancock, whose

TOP LEFT: *Three perforated tin spatulas have pleasing sculptural forms when hung on wall.* HANCOCK.

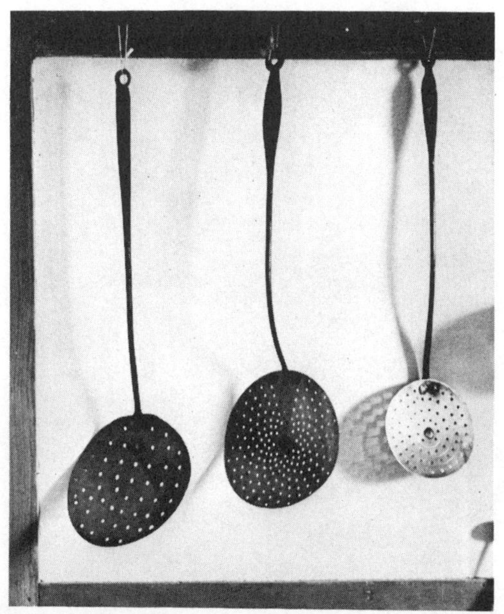

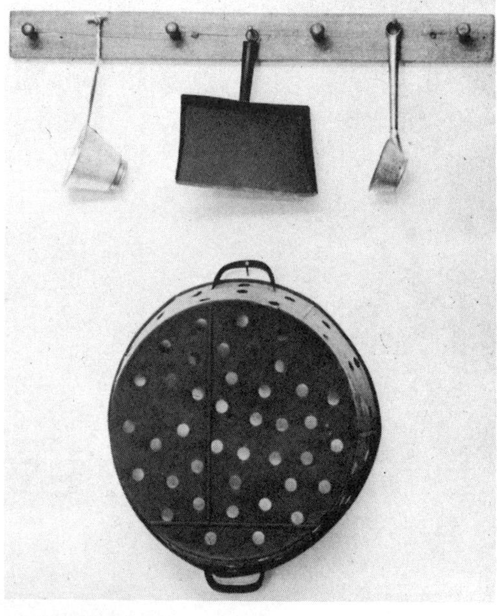

RIGHT: *Two tinware scoops, a dustpan, and a cheese sieve.* HANCOCK.

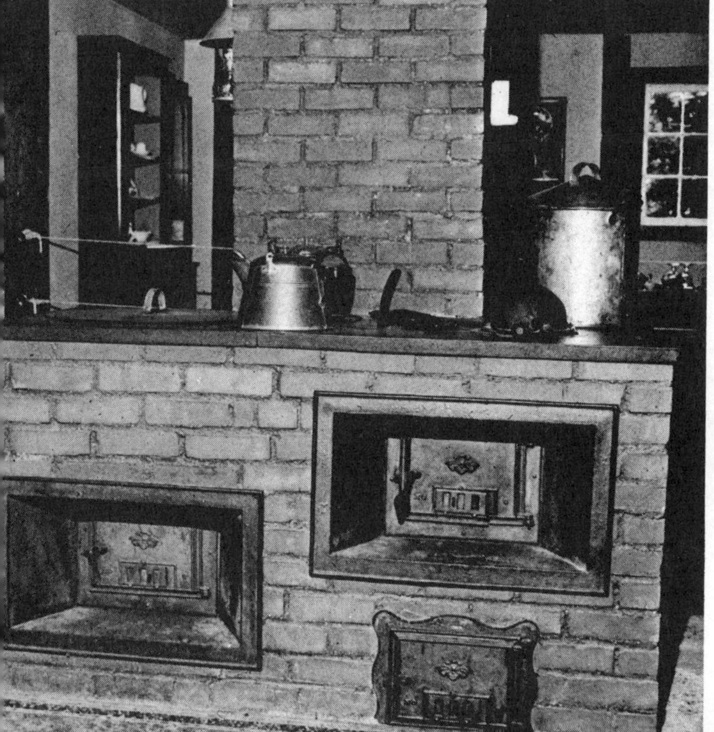

LEFT: *Stove from Canterbury, New Hampshire. Metal parts were cast in Concord, New Hampshire, in 1840. Although the stove has no ovens (ovens were built separately) it does have a built-in soup kettle (left). Shaker tin kettle and pot on top of stove.* OLD CHATHAM.

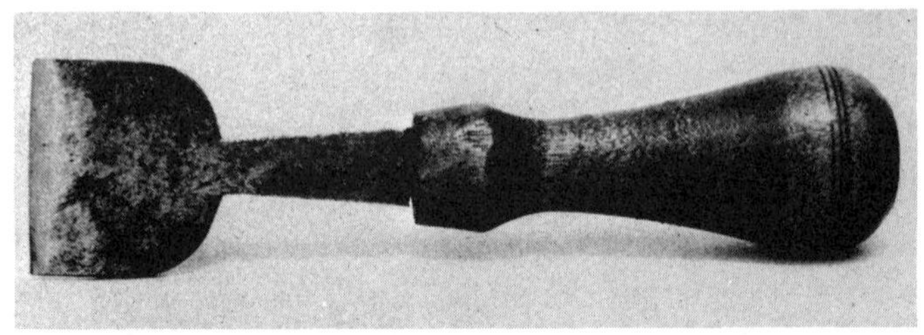

TOP: *Thousands of tools were made in Shaker shops. This is a small chisel.* BELFIT.

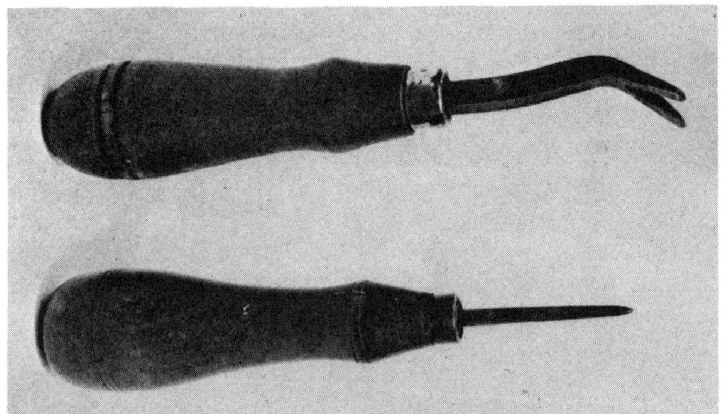

MIDDLE: *Shaker-made tack puller and awl. Shaker tools are comfortable in the hand and are carefully balanced.* BELFIT.

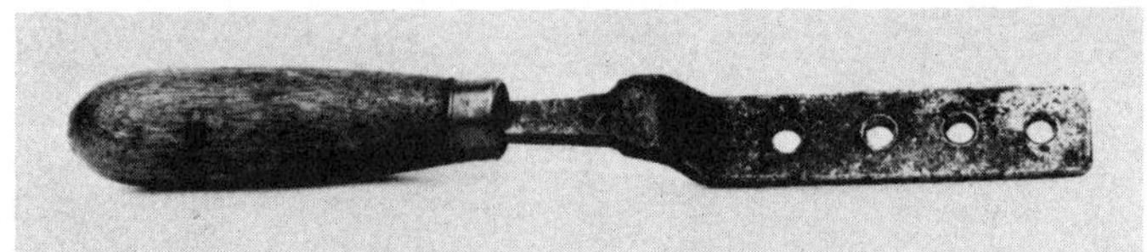

BOTTOM: *Shaker screw thread gauge and cutter.* BELFIT.

tinware was sold throughout western New England and eastern New York. Simplicity, quality, and good construction can be found in the many pieces of Shaker tinware that survive today.

Many other products were made of metal from the earliest Shaker times. Nails, at first wrought of copper or iron, were made for the Shakers' own use and produced for sale in the late eighteenth century. Later, cut nails replaced this product, and they were sold in quantity until 1830.

Tools by the hundreds were manufactured by the Shakers. Many of these were completely innovative and were designed to do special jobs required in the many areas of Shaker production. Millenial laws dictated that a supply of such tools and articles that brethren made to be used by sisters should be ordered by the deacons and delivered to the deaconesses, to whom the sisters then would apply for whatever they needed.

The Shakers were not averse to purchasing tools from outside manufacturers when it proved to be more expedient than making their own. If the quality could be proven to be as good or better than the Shaker-made product, tools were bought. Therefore, it is often difficult to identify as Shaker-made many of the tools that were found in their shops. However, it is known that certain common objects for the home workshop and farm, such as knives, tailor's shears, shovels, hoes, augers, and chisels were made in ample supply in Shaker shops for their own

LEFT: *Brethren designed and made tools for special purposes for the sisters' work. These tools were designed and made to punch out woven poplar cover and leaves for needlecases sold in shops.* BELFIT.

RIGHT: *Iron hardware on reconstructed door of the famous round barn at Hancock illustrates Shakers' simple but careful placement and balance of mundane objects in their architecture.* HANCOCK.

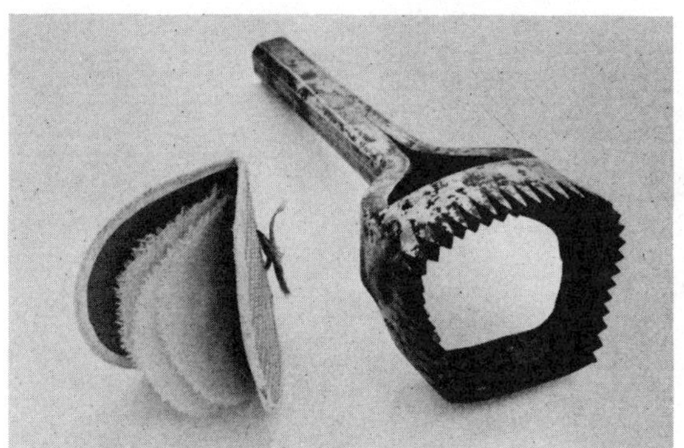

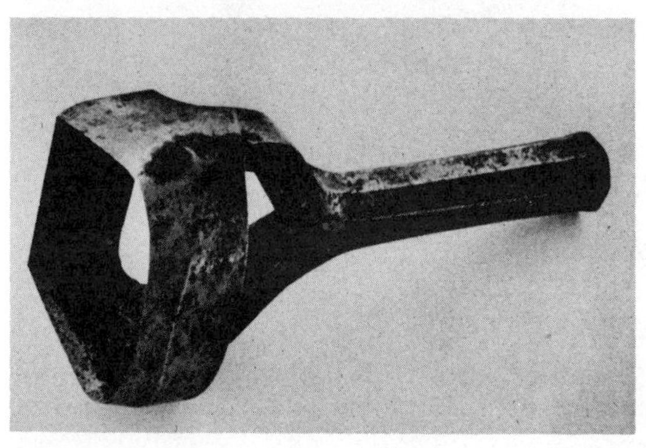

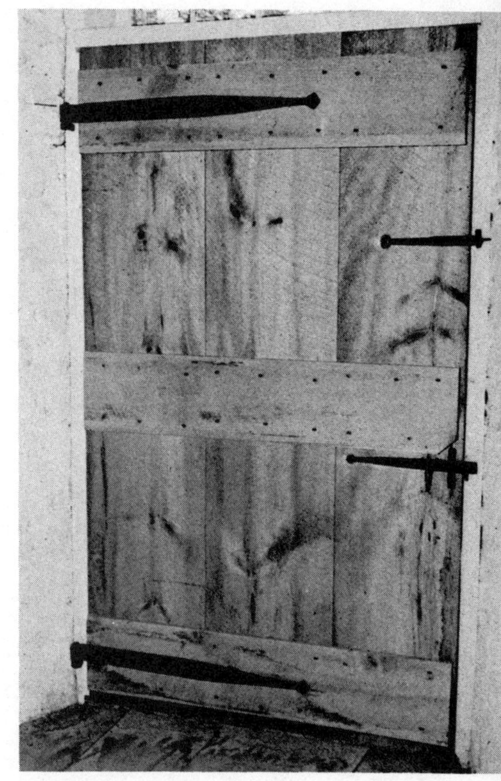

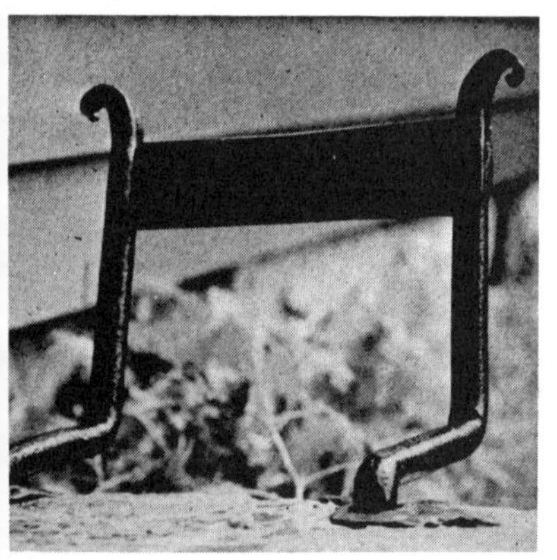

use and to be sold to outsiders in surrounding areas. Hinges and other door hardware, chains, wire, axes, and farm and shop machinery were Shaker products. In 1793 Benjamin Brude invented a machine for setting card teeth, and many other innovations were devised for making the products used in the manufacture of textiles. The metalworker and carpenter often worked together in devising improved machinery to be used in the herbal medicine and seed businesses. An herb press, for com-

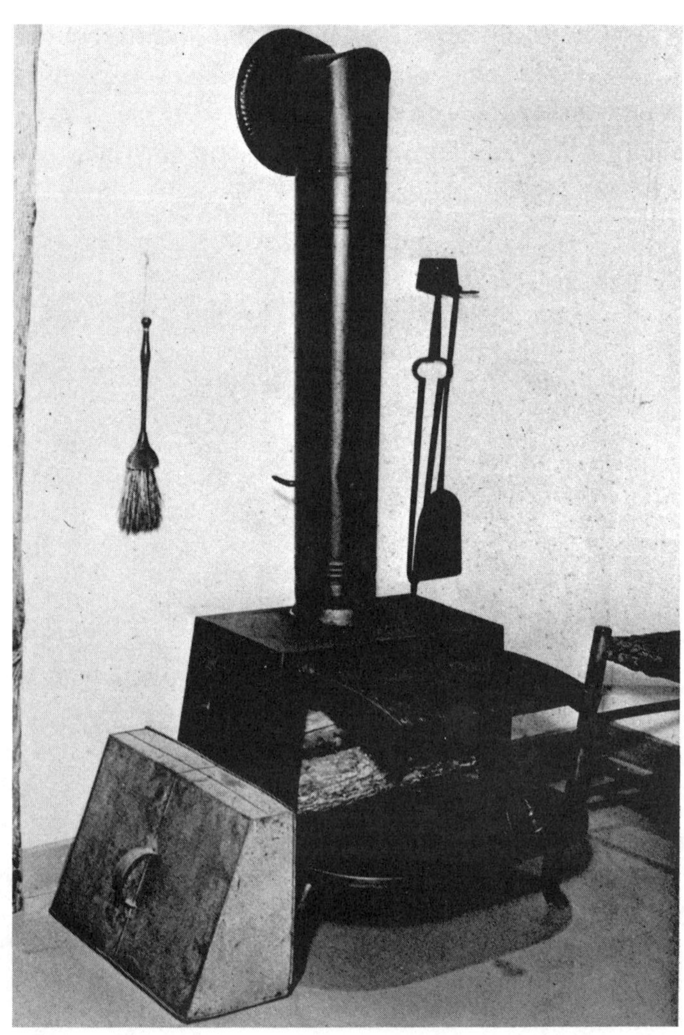

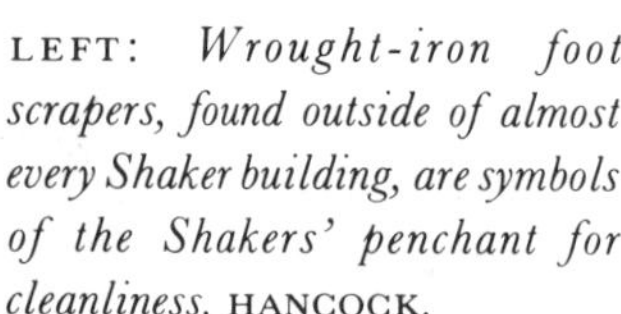

LEFT: *Wrought-iron foot scrapers, found outside of almost every Shaker building, are symbols of the Shakers' penchant for cleanliness.* HANCOCK.

RIGHT: *Earliest Shaker stove designed at Canterbury. Later stoves, where the firebox was turned around and the fueling door was placed on the narrow end, were far more efficient. Doors of other Shaker stoves open from left to right. Metal firebox was safety precaution.* OLD CHATHAM.

pressing herbs into blocks, was an important aid to the Shakers involved in that industry.

Because the Shakers had such complete workshops for producing metal products and also for repairing metal objects, they did work for outsiders in these areas. They forged iron railings for their own doorsteps. Boot scrapers, door locks, fasteners and hinges, locks and keys were all made by the brethren. Few locks were needed by the Shakers themselves. They believed that "it is desirable to have all so trustworthy that locks and keys will be needless."

A metal product of Shaker foundries that was infinitely important to the Shakers' own comfort was the iron stove that efficiently heated all Shaker rooms. Designed and made to be strictly functional, the black box-shaped stoves that dominate all Shaker interiors are an excellent example of "form following function." The Shakers considered fireplaces dirty and inefficient. There were many Millenial Laws governing the use of fire, and it is obvious that the Shakers were aware of the care that one must exert to avoid that catastrophe in their dwellings. The stoves, therefore, were built on legs, well up from the floor. Shelves, ample in size although varied in shape, protected the floor from sparks and ashes. While few of these stoves are identical in design, all appear similar. Shapes of legs vary from straight to curved to cabriole. Most of the eastern Shaker communities had their own foundries where the stoves were made. Western Shakers had stoves made by outside foundries to their specifications.

Stoves designed for community cooking were also innovative and efficient. Built-in kettles were not unusual. Built-in ovens were models of efficiency. Large-scale cooking required special designs and structure in the stoves used, and many innovations can be found. One built-in kettle, at the Cook Room of Hancock Shaker

Shaker wrought-iron stove with five-sided apron and small pad feet. Spitbox full of shavings is in foreground. OLD CHATHAM.

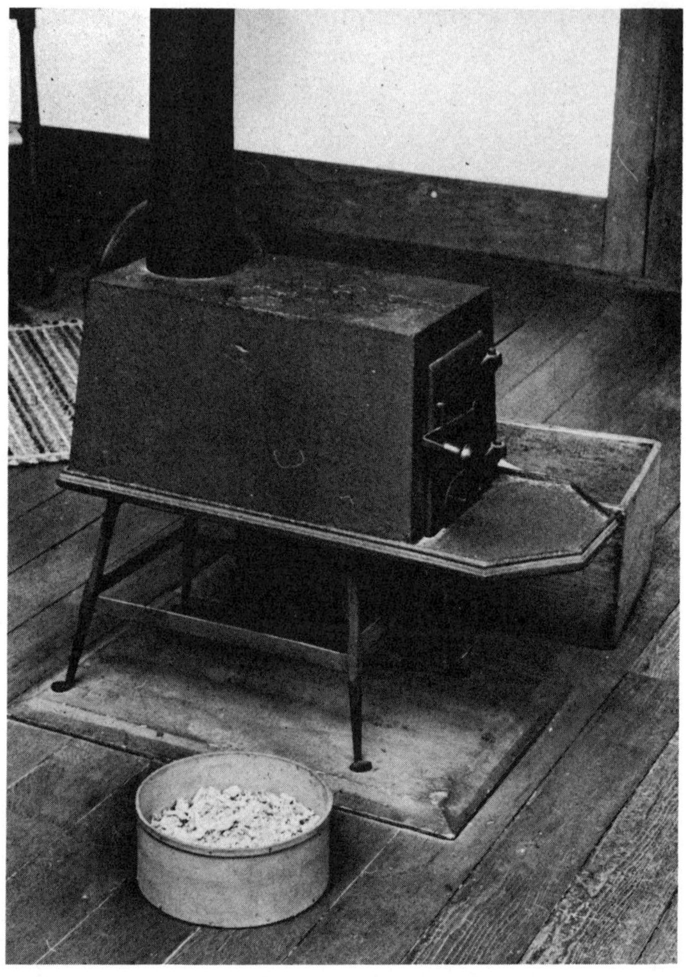

village, was piped directly to the village's water supply and was used for steaming. The cookstove from Canterbury, New Hampshire (now at Old Chatham Shaker Museum), has a built-in soup or stewing kettle.

One rather important Shaker invention made of metal is the pen nib invented at the New Lebanon, New York, Shaker Society around 1817. Previous to this, quill pens were in use, and the metal pen was an enormous improvement. The first pen nibs were made of brass, but by 1819 silver was being used with more success. A plate-rolling machine at New Lebanon was used for rolling the metal for the nibs. Special shears for cutting the slits in the nibs were also a Shaker invention. One Shaker inventor from New Lebanon wrote in 1819, "I now have my new shears with which I have cut 292 pens in 14 minutes! This is doing it with dispatch!"

A letter written by G. A. Lomas, Watervliet Shaker, to the editor of *Scientific American* in November 1878 was written with a Shaker silver pen made in Watervliet in 1819. "Some of our people," Brother Lomas wrote, "now living, sold these pens in the year 1820 for 25 cents, and disposed of all that could be made at that price ... "

Not only the nibs themselves, but the machinery and tools for making them, were Shaker inventions. Pen handles of tin or wood were also produced and sold. The handles closed telescopically for easy storage. Shaker silver pens were somewhat expensive for the time, and in 1825 one could be purchased for thirty-one cents. The price went down as production increased, and in 1828 a half gross of "cased silver pens" sold for fifteen dollars. Gradually steel nibs produced elsewhere crowded the Shaker-made nibs off the marketplace. Shaker pen nibs were still being used at the end of the nineteenth century and are, today, perhaps one of the rarest Shaker relics.

A list of all Shaker metal products would be endless. At New Lebanon, for instance, brass and steel shoe buckles were made in the eighteenth century. Knee buckles and jacket, coat, and sleeve buttons of brass and pewter were produced and sold around 1825. Harness brasses were also made by Shaker craftsmen.

The first metal pen nibs, invented by the Shakers, were made of brass, but two years after their invention it was found that silver was more efficient. OLD CHATHAM.

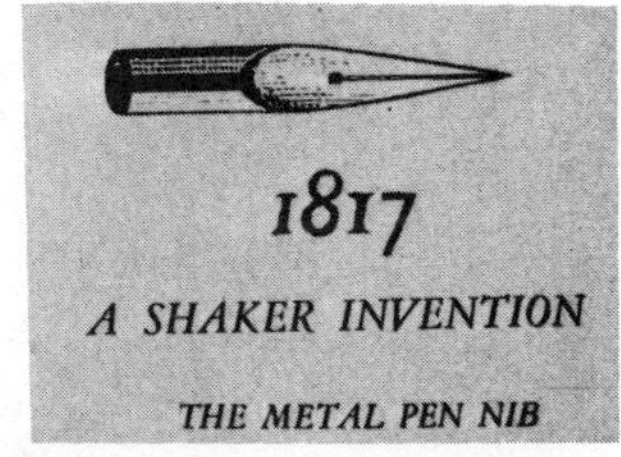

BOTTOM: *Sand cast-iron grave markers replaced stones in middle of nineteenth century.* OLD CHATHAM.

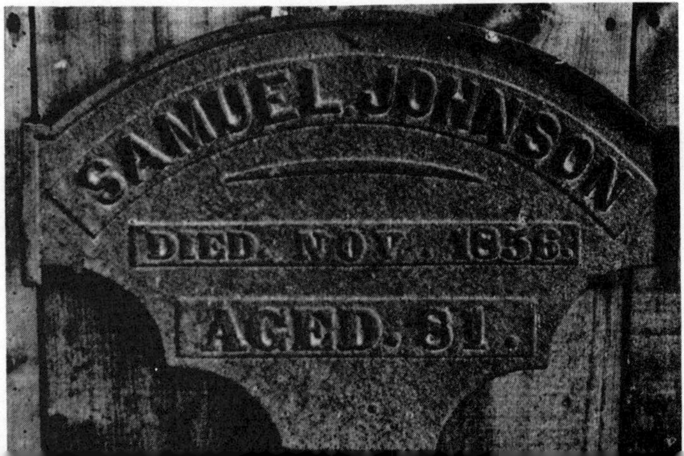

CHAPTER
22
CONCLUSION

It is advisable for the center families in each bishopric, to avoid hiring the world to make household furniture, except for the outer court. And the work concerning hiring the world to work around and among Believers, is it not written in the Holy Laws set forth by the hand of Almighty God, whereby all of Zion's children must be directed. Millenial Laws, 1821. Revised, 1845.

It was an easy matter for the church elders to discourage contact with outside workmen in 1845 when the Shaker population was at its peak. After the Civil War there were fewer and fewer applicants and the Shakers reached a low of one thousand members by the turn of the century. By 1931 there were only two hundred Shakers surviving, and the majority of these were women. It is obvious that many of the trades and products of the Shakers had either to be abandoned or that outside help would have to be hired. In order to keep the lucrative trade in Shaker chairs and boxes, the latter alternative was resorted to.

By a method of trial and error the Shakers had been

able to ascertain which of their many products would support them. They could look back on a long and successful history of having produced an incredible amount and assortment of objects. Besides those mentioned previously, thousands of small notions such as combs, buttons, and other items of bone (made early in their history), numerous tools, an enormous amount of industrial equipment such as an improved washing machine for institutions, a variety of health products as well as food products, beautiful articles in needlework, and magnificent textiles that may never be definitely

TOP: *Early Shakers made pipes and pipe stems of both red and white clay found on their property.* OLD CHATHAM.

BOTTOM LEFT: *The Shakers purchased pottery for kitchen and commercial use. This jug, however, is thought to have been made by Shakers in Alfred, Maine.* OLD CHATHAM.

BOTTOM RIGHT: *Advertising poster for Shaker baskets and other goods.* OLD CHATHAM.

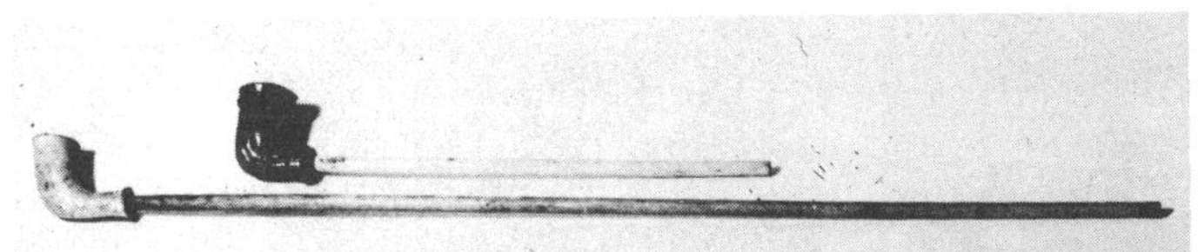

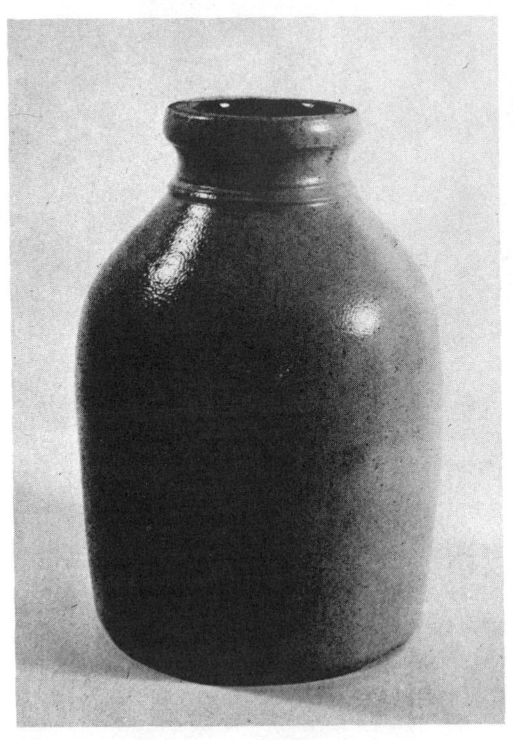

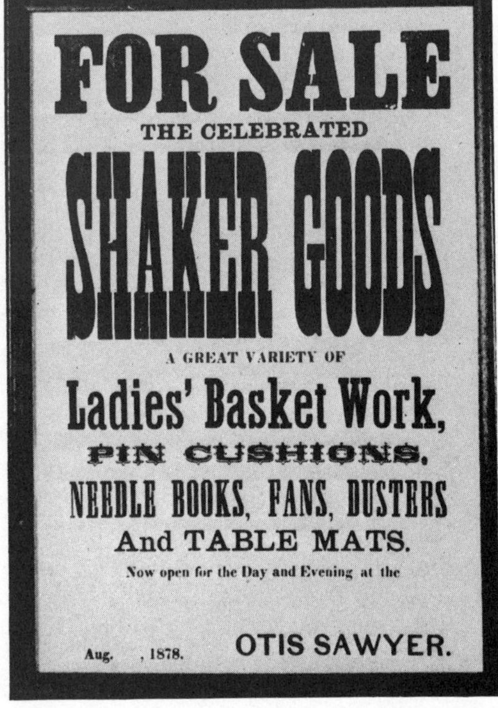

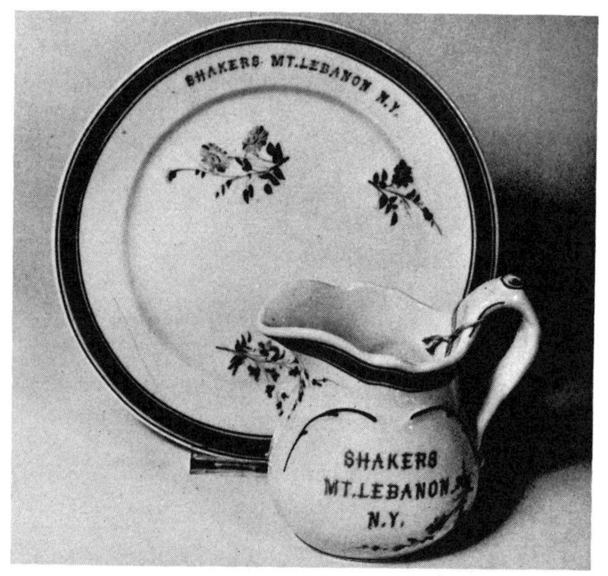

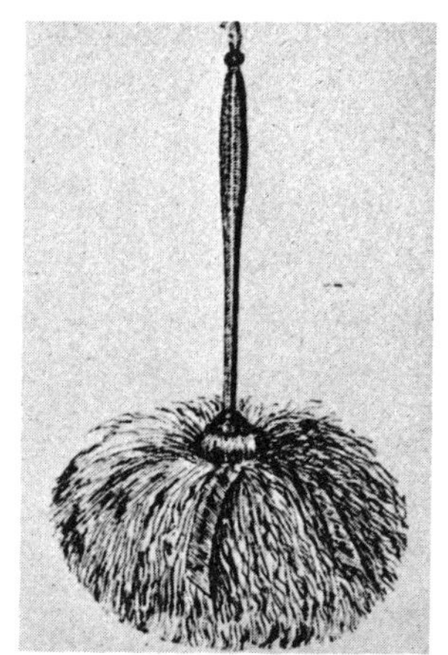

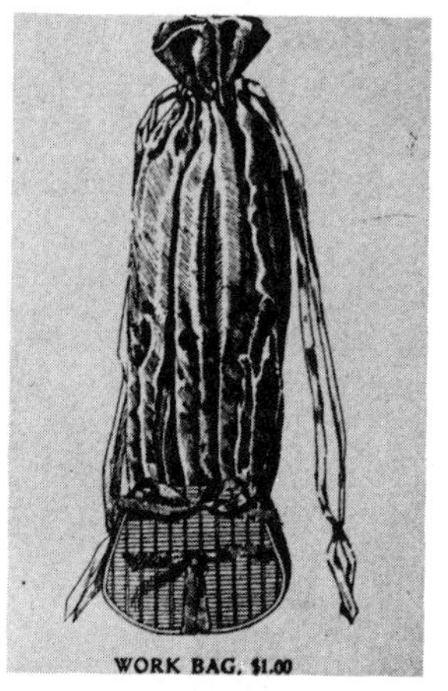

WORK BAG, $1.00

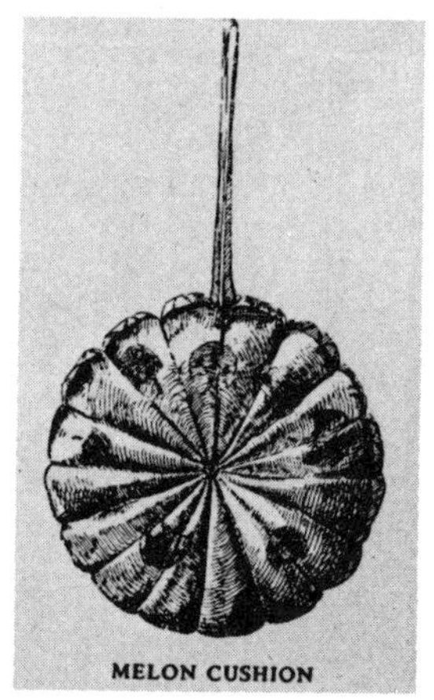

MELON CUSHION

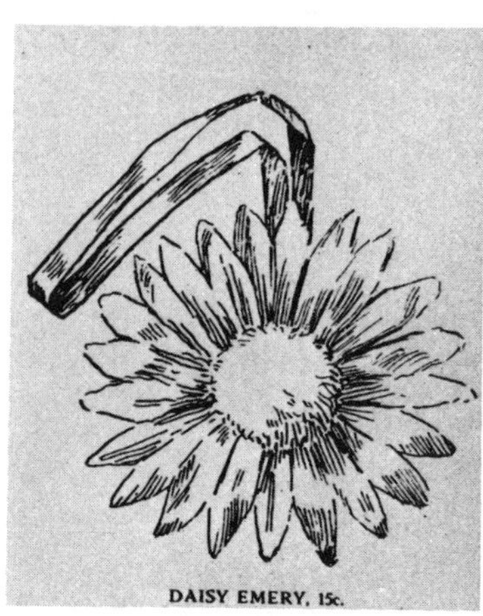

DAISY EMERY, 15c.

TOP LEFT: *As far as is known, the Shakers did not make any ceramic tableware. This hand-painted heavy dinnerware was made to order for Mt. Lebanon Shakers in England in late nineteenth century. Green borders, pink and green flowers.* OLD CHATHAM.

REMAINDER: *At the beginning of this century a wide assortment of "notions" and small gift items were made by the sisters to sell in their shops. These drawings and price list were taken from a catalogue issued by Shakers.* OLD CHATHAM.

Miscellaneous Articles

PRICE LIST

** Shaker doll with bonnet and cloak, 15-inch	$5 00
** Shaker doll with bonnet and cloak, 10-inch	3 00
—* Bureau cushion, No. 1	1 00
—* Bureau cushion, No. 2	75
—* Bureau cushion, No. 3	50
*** Jewel box, square, No. 1	1 25
*** Jewel box, square, No. 2	90
*** Jewel box, square, No. 3	60
*** Jewel box, oblong	75
* Oblong carrier, No. 1	3 50
* Oblong carrier, No. 2	2 50
* Oblong carrier, No. 3	1 00

15

identified as coming from Shaker looms, and many other items are part of Shaker history.

At the beginning of this century, although a painful pattern of selling property and consolidating their members continued, the sisters were able to continue their work of making objects to sell in their shops. They also sold gift items to the summer resorts that had sprung up in the New York and New England areas surrounding their remaining properties. Kitchen products were still made and sold and a few of their more successful medicines were still being manufactured well into this century.

While necessity forced the earlier surviving Shakers to sell their farmlands and buildings, often at disadvantageous prices, it also compelled many Shakers to dispose of their possessions as well. However, the few surviving Shakers, ironically not many more than the first handful of Believers who followed Mother Ann to America, seem to have a strong sense of their sect's own place in history and will make provisions for preserving their remaining possessions, and many Shaker items that are being returned to them, in Shaker museums that have already been established on the two remaining Shaker properties in Canterbury, New Hampshire, and Sabbathday Lake, Maine. Buildings at both settlements are being carefully restored by those who know and understand best the history of Shaker folk art and industries.

However, it was the "world's people" who, at the outset of interest in Shaker history, showed the Shakers the value of their own heritage and their importance in American applied art. The story of the Shaker Village at Hancock, Massachusetts, is an example of interested outsiders banding together to preserve the magnificent architecture and the beautiful farmlands that nurtured the crops that were so important to the success of that community.

As the Hancock Shakers began to dwindle pathetically in number, buildings fell into disrepair and crops were

TOP: *Mold and mallet for making strawberry-shaped emeries that were used in sewing boxes.* BELFIT.

LEFT: *This needlecase from Canterbury is hand sewn and hand painted. Cover is light blue silk (1925).* BELFIT.

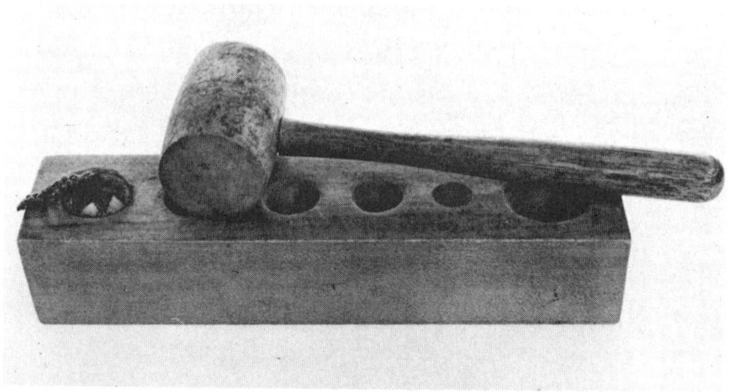

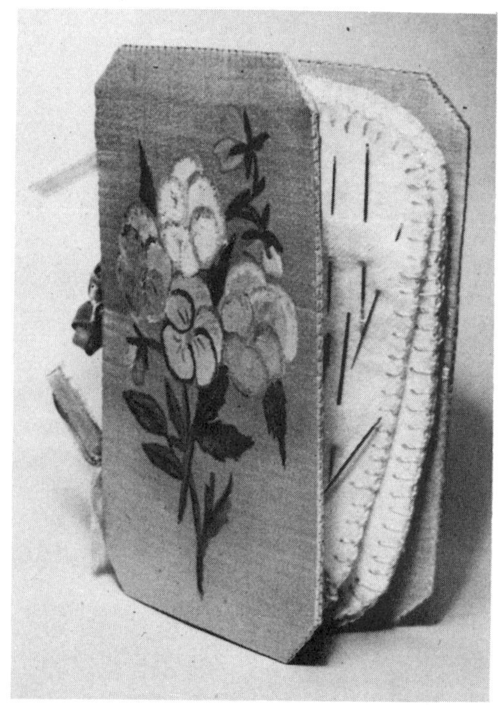

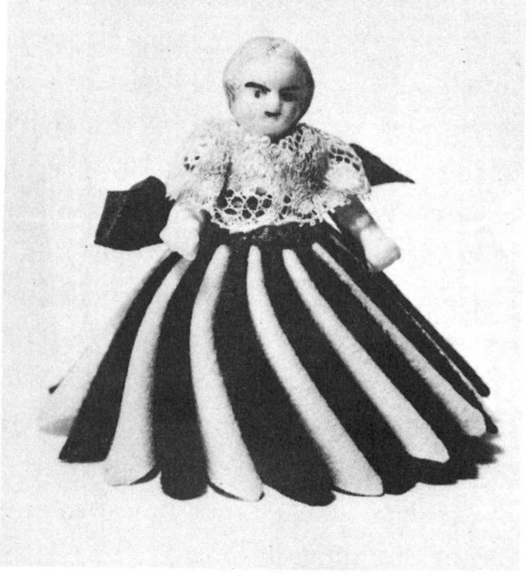

ABOVE: *This small bisque doll was purchased and dressed by the Shakers to be sold as a penwiper. Skirt fabric is scraps left over from cloaks.* BELFIT.

no longer grown. In order to save tax money, the few remaining Shakers who lived at Hancock in the 1930s and 1940s felt they had no alternative but to tear down the buildings that were no longer needed. Pathetically, in the early 1960s only two elderly sisters were living at Hancock in a building designed to house comfortably one hundred brethren and sisters. It had become time to dispose of the property and close Hancock forever. The property could easily have fallen into the hands of developers, and the history of the Hancock Shakers could have been lost forever. However, one foresighted woman was able to convince the Shakers to settle for a price somewhat lower than that they had asked in order to have the community restored and turned into a museum that would be open to the public. The Hancock restoration has been extremely successful. It is unfortunate that by the time the village was sold, most of the original furnishings had also been dispersed. A concerted effort on the part of interested citizens has led to the return of the lost furniture or its replacement with more from other Shaker communities.

The collection of Shaker objects at the Old Chatham Shaker Museum, while not housed on what was formerly Shaker property, is also the effort of one person. Not only the objects themselves, but the machinery used to make them and, in many cases, examples of the stages of manufacture for many of the items and also the advertising used in promoting Shaker products are all part of the collection at Old Chatham. Extensive restoration

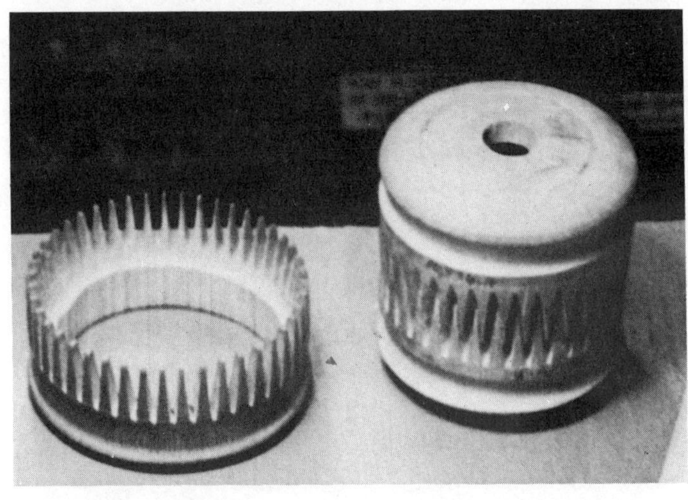

Wooden shampoo combs made by Shakers. OLD CHATHAM.

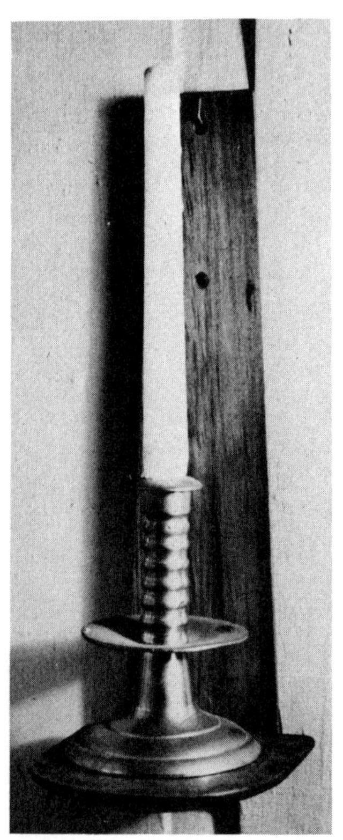

to Shaker machinery and tools is also evident at Old Chatham, and this is extremely important in the preservation of Shaker industrial history.

There are, of course, many other collections of Shaker folk art and industrial products, some private and some public. Shaker furniture has long been recognized as being important in the story of American applied art. However, in telling a complete story of Shaker folk art and industries, an herbal medicine label is as important as the finest Shaker-made trestle table. A simple varnished box or a carefully made woven basket has as important a place in American and Shaker history as any early Shaker chair. A beautifully made wood dipper or a carved wooden scoop is as much an indication of the Shaker's reverence for wood as a clock case or a sewing table.

The Shakers have given their country a legacy of beautifully made handcrafted objects that were designed with honesty and functionalism in mind. The Shakers are also responsible for the invention and manufacture of many conveniences for the home, workshop, and farm. Those to whom they sold their products knew the Shakers for their honesty and fine workmanship. To know something of the products made for the Shakers' own use and for sale to the world is to know something of the success of the way of life for those who followed Ann Lee's teaching. In its own time and place, Shakerism worked for those who chose it and enriched the outside world from which these craftsmen had isolated themselves.

Candle sconce, made by Shakers, is graceful and nicely proportioned. Brass candlestick is not Shaker. BELFIT.

MUSEUMS AND PUBLIC COLLECTIONS OF SHAKER ARTIFACTS

Delaware
Henry Francis DuPont Museum, Winterthur.

District of Columbia
National Museum, Smithsonian Institution

Kentucky
Kentucky Museum, Bowling Green
Shaker Museum, Auburn
Shakertown at Pleasant Hill, Inc., Harrodsburg

Maine
Shaker Museum, Sabbathday Lake Shaker Community

Massachusetts
Boston Museum of Fine Arts, Boston
Fruitlands Museum, Harvard
Hancock Shaker Community, Inc., Hancock

New Hampshire
Canterbury Shaker Museum, East Canterbury

New York
Shaker Museum, Old Chatham

Ohio
Dunham Tavern, Cleveland
Cincinnati Art Museum (American Wing), Eden Park
Glendower (historic house museum), Lebanon
Golden Lamb Hotel, Lebanon
Shaker Historical Society Museum, Shaker Heights, Cleveland
Warren County Historical Society Museum, Lebanon
Western Reserve Historical Society Museum, Cleveland

Pennsylvania
Philadelphia Museum of Art, Philadelphia

Vermont
Shelburne Museum, Shelburne

Wisconsin
Milwaukee Art Centre: Villa Terrace

In addition, Shaker Museums are being planned in Bethlehem, Connecticut, and Enfield, Connecticut.

SELECTED BIBLIOGRAPHY

BOOKS

Andrews, Edward Deming. *The Community Industries of the Shakers.* New York State Museum Handbook 15. Albany: The University of the State of New York, 1933.

———*The New York Shakers and Their Industries.* Circular 2. New York: New York State Museum, 1930.

———*The People Called Shakers.* New York: Oxford University Press, 1953.

———*Shaker Furniture.* New Haven: Yale University Press, 1937.

Andrews, Edward Deming and Faith Andrews. *Shaker Furniture: The Craftsmanship of an American Communal Sect.* New York: Dover Publications, Inc., 1964.

Christensen, Erwin P. *The Index of American Design.* New York: The Macmillan Company, 1950.

Earle, Alice Morse. *Home Life in Colonial Days.* New York: Charles Scribner's Sons, 1898.

Lamson, David R. *Two Years Experience Among the Shakers: Being a description of the manners and customs of that people; the nature and policy of their government, their marvelous intercourse with the spiritual world, the object and uses of confession, their inquisition, in short, a condensed view of Shakerism as it is.* West Boylston: 1848.

Melcher, Marguerite Fellows. *The Shaker Adventure.* Princeton: The Princeton University Press, 1941.

Morse, Flo. *Yankee Communes: Another American Way.* New York: Harcourt, Brace, Jovanovich, Inc., 1972.

Neal, Julia. *By Their Fruits.* Chapel Hill: The University of North Carolina Press, 1947.

Nordhoff, Charles. *The Communistic Societies of The United States.* New York: 1875.

NEWSPAPER and MAGAZINE ARTICLES

Andrews, Edward Deming. "The Shakers in a New World." New York: *Antiques,* October 1957.

Bullard, Sister Marcia. "Shaker Industries." New York: *Good Housekeeping,* July 1906.

Emery, Stewart M. "Shaker Sect Reduced by Its Own Doctrines." New York: *New York Times,* November 28, 1926.

Lynes, Russell. "After Hours: The Shakers." New York: *Harper's Magazine,* December 1966.

Stagg, Anne. "Home of the Hancock Shakers." New York: *House and Garden Magazine,* July 1968.

"Pioneer Functionalists." New York: *Time Magazine,* October 19, 1959.

"Shaker Revival." New York: *Time Magazine,* April 1861.

MUSEUM PUBLICATIONS

The American Shakers. New Lebanon: Shaker Community, Inc., 1961.

Calendar: The Living Art of the Shakers. Shakertown at Pleasant Hill, Kentucky. 1971.

A Guide to Shaker Museums and Libraries, 1971. Old Chatham, New York, 1971.

Industries and Inventions of the Shakers and *Shaker Music.* Sister Bertha Phelps and Sister Lillian. Canterbury, New Hampshire. Published by Canterbury Shakers. Undated.

The Catalog of the Shaker Museum at Old Chatham, New York. 1968. (The Shaker Museum Foundation.)

Paint Colors. Shaker Museum at Old Chatham, New York, 1969.

In addition many Shaker almanacs, journals, catalogs, etc., were consulted. Some of these appear as illustrations. Others are untitled, undated, and unsigned.

INDEX